The American Suburb

DISCARD

The American Suburb

THE BASICS

Jon C. Teaford

Routledge
Taylor & Francis Group
New York   London

Routledge
Taylor & Francis Group
270 Madison Avenue
New York, NY 10016

Routledge
Taylor & Francis Group
2 Park Square
Milton Park, Abingdon
Oxon OX14 4RN

© 2008 by Jon C. Teaford
Routledge is an imprint of Taylor & Francis Group, an Informa business

Printed in the United States of America on acid-free paper
10 9 8 7 6 5 4 3 2 1

International Standard Book Number-13: 978-0-415-95165-4 (Softcover) 978-0-415-95164-7 (Hardcover)

Library of Congress Cataloging-in-Publication Data

Teaford, Jon C.
   The American suburb : the basics / Jon C. Teaford.
      p. cm.
   Includes bibliographical references and index.
   ISBN 978-0-415-95164-7 (hardback) -- ISBN 978-0-415-95165-4 (pbk.)
   1. uburbs--United States. 2. Suburban life--United States. I. Title.

HT352.U6T43 2007
307.74'0973--dc22
                                      2006036677

Visit the Taylor & Francis Web site at
http://www.taylorandfrancis.com

and the Routledge Web site at
http://www.routledge.com

CONTENTS

ILLUSTRATIONS

"The scenes that illustrate this book are all about us," wrote Jane Jacobs in her unillustrated 1961 classic *The Death and Life of Great American Cities*. Jacobs wrote in an era of lingering urban dominance, but the present is an age of suburban hegemony. If the readers of this book seek illustrations, they should look out their windows with eyes free of the blinders of past stereotypes. Contemporary suburbia is all about us.

PREFACE

The United States is a suburban nation. A majority of Americans live in the suburbs, and a large share work, shop, and spend their leisure time there as well. Rural America accounts for a dwindling proportion of the nation's population and business, as do the once preeminent central cities. The cities of Atlanta and Boston are home to only about 10 percent of the people in their respective metropolitan areas, and the figures for St. Louis, Cleveland, and Pittsburgh are not much higher. These are historic hubs, the aging stars around which the sprawling metropolitan regions have long orbited. Yet their centripetal pull has sharply diminished, and in a number of metropolitan regions the satellite communities have escaped their orbit and headed off in a direction independent of the old core municipalities. The central cities are no longer central to the lives of most metropolitan Americans; the amorphous mass beyond the core city limits is the workplace, playground, marketplace, and bedroom of America.

For Americans the notion of city limits has been vital to the concept of suburbia. Unlike in Britain, where the term *suburb* refers to a peripheral area whether inside or beyond a major city's boundaries, in the United States the federal census bureau and most commentators have defined suburbia as that zone within metropolitan areas but beyond central city limits.[1] Because of the strong tradition of local self-rule in the United States, this political distinction between suburb and central city has been vital to discussions of suburban development, lifestyle, and policy. American suburbs are not simply peripheral areas with larger lawns and more trees than districts nearer the historic hub. They are governmentally independent political units that can employ the powers of the state to distinguish themselves from the city. With control over land use planning and independent taxing and regulatory powers, they can individually mold their residential and commercial development. And with separate school governments they can fashion an educational system suitable to the class aspirations of their residents. Any discussion of American suburbs must invariably confront the rivalry and tension between the central cities and outlying jurisdictions. The American suburb is not just a neighborhood; it is a distinct governmental entity with all the coercive power necessary to fashion its own destiny.

Given suburban success in overshadowing the central cities, the term *suburb* has become problematic for contemporary America. In the twenty-first century American suburbia is no longer *sub* to the *urb*. In fact, many scholars and informed observers regard Americans as living in a postsuburban world where the concept of suburb is perhaps obsolete. Commentators have suggested such alternative terms as *edge cities*, *urban villages*, *technoburbs*, and *urban realms*, but the term suburb has survived in American parlance and seems destined to remain part of the nation's vocabulary. Complicating the problem with nomenclature is the reality that the so-called suburbs are a diverse collection of communities, embracing markedly different patterns of settlement. Some are older industrial communities; others are characterized by sleek, glass-encased office towers and glitzy shopping malls; still others are low-density, semirural retreats; and a large number are aging residential towns with single-family, detached houses on small lots. Thus the communities Americans call suburbs are neither subordinate to the historic hub nor outwardly similar to one another in appearance, economic base, or social composition. Despite their increasing independence and manifold diversity, American suburbs do share a common characteristic that distinguishes them from the central cities and enables one to consider them as a distinctive class. From their founding and throughout the history of their development, America's central cities have perceived themselves as regional centers—hubs that dominate their hinterlands and compete with other great cities in the nation and the world. This view of their role was basic to the development of the urban empires of New York, Chicago, and San Francisco in the nineteenth and early twentieth centuries. In addition, it underlay efforts to bolster the centripetal pull of older hubs during the urban renewal era. Even in the twenty-first century it has been evident in the central cities' initiatives to maintain an emotional grip on a large hinterland populace by securing or retaining professional sports teams and building the facilities for these symbols of big-league status. The central cities claim to be the "Hub of the Universe," the "Queen City," the "Big Apple"; their development has been dominated by the notion of their centrality to the lives of a regional population.

The suburbs, however, are those communities whose development has not been dominated by the need or desire to be *the* city, the dominant hub of a region, or one of the great centers of the nation. They acquired the bulk of the nation's offices, retailing, and manufacturing space and the accompanying jobs, and some populous, rapidly expanding communities labeled *boomburbs* grew to be as large as or larger than some of the older, better-known central cities. The suburbs welcomed the resulting tax revenues and did not necessarily discourage population growth or commercial development. Moreover, they grew relatively independent of the older central city, their residents having little concern for or interest in its welfare or problems. But the underlying rationale in their development was not a desire to become one of the nation's great cities. Their leaders were fashioning principalities, not empires. Whether industrial suburbs, upper-middle-class residential havens, boomburbs, or other types of communities, they did not aspire to be central cities, the focus of all metropolitan endeavors, or the rival of London, Paris, New York, or Chicago.

Basically, the suburbs are the product of a different mentality from that underlying the central cities, and that mentality survives to this day. Suburbia's multitudinous communities have rendered the older notion of the city largely obsolete and have created the amorphous metropolitan regions of today where there is no dominant single focus for the lives of residents throughout the area. They are not *sub*ordinate to the urb; but they are *sub*versive to the whole concept of the urb, the commercial and cultural focus of an extensive hinterland, and thus perhaps are deserving of the title *sub*urb after all. Their triumph marks the victory of the amorphous metropolitan mass over the focused metropolis of the past. They have supplanted the concept of the city as a center with the now prevailing notion of the city as a fragment.

In the United States, then, the suburbs are not peripheral complements to the city; instead, they have largely superseded the city, creating a new centerless world where the old, clear-cut boundaries between urban and rural have dissolved and the long-standing centripetal pull of downtown has diminished to a faint tug. Americans have liberated themselves from the city and fashioned a posturban nation with population spread over vast regions and commuters traveling in every direction. The diverse communities beyond the central city limits may have little in common, but together they have reconstituted the settlement patterns and lifestyle of the nation, subverting traditional notions of the city.

This subversion has elicited choruses of complaints, and few concepts have been so roundly damned or assumed such pejorative connotations as that of the suburb. As early as 1949, Pulitzer

Prize–winning poet and suburban housewife Phyllis McGinley observed that "to condemn Suburbia" was "a literary cliché."[2] Fifty years later this observation was equally true. Throughout the intervening decades, few commentators dared to laud the suburbs, but instead the literate classes with a discouraging lack of perception or imagination smeared the area beyond the central city as a bland, homogeneous zone producing dull drones in look-alike houses whose culinary tastes tended toward a Big Mac and who deemed a chrome-plated car high art. Consuming miles of virgin countryside, draining wetlands, leveling forests, displacing endangered flora and fauna, suburbanites were portrayed as shallow bourgeois hordes wreaking havoc with civilization and nature. Critics identified suburban sprawl as a major national problem, a blight threatening the environment and the general welfare of American society. Recognizing the subversive nature of the suburban trend, central city mayors repeatedly blamed their problems on uncaring residents beyond the municipal limits, and generally suburbanites were stereotyped as selfish, materialistic, exclusive, and indifferent to the problems of the nation and the world. In the early twenty-first century, commentators were even attributing the nation's supposed plague of obesity to the auto-borne suburban lifestyle. Though scholars and commentators have occasionally noted the falsehood and superficiality of the stereotypes and myths associated with suburbia, the negative images have survived, instilling in American minds a simplistic portrait of their metropolitan world.

This book will attempt to dispel some of these myths and stereotypes, describing the American suburbs of the early twenty-first century and the problems and issues facing them. Most notably it will emphasize the diversity of suburbia and will reject the superficial notion that suburban America is some homogeneous, featureless blob, stretching on seemingly forever in an undifferentiated sprawl of settlement. In fact, the American suburbs include some of the nation's most densely populated communities as well as areas zoned to accommodate more horses than human beings. Suburbia reflects the ethnic diversity of America more accurately than the central cities, providing homes for Hispanics, Asians, and blacks as well as non-Hispanic whites. It comprises slums as well as mansions, main streets as well as malls, skyscrapers as well as schools. Some suburbs are particularly gay-friendly; others are planned for senior citizens. Some are known for their fine schools; others are examples of educational failure. Traveling through America's suburbs one sees a full range of experience, a diversity of lifestyles, a rich variety of built environments. Comprising a majority of Americans, suburbia is not an undifferentiated enclave, a homogenized haven. It is a vivid mosaic composed of all the varied fragments of American life and society.

Any perceptive observer would already know this, but curiously even those who spend their entire lives in the suburbs seem to believe some of the conventional stereotypes that clash with the reality around them. Moreover, these stereotypes influence the nation's public policy debates. Central city officials continue to exploit traditional conceptions of an essential hub surrounded by parasitical bedroom communities, claiming that their core jurisdictions require the bulk of public aid and concern. Many suburbanites continue to view their turf as refuges, decrying the traffic, commerce, and influx of diverse people who seem to shatter this long-standing and beloved image. Suburbanites cling to a stereotypical suburban-ness long after the stereotypical community of single-family homes with happy families comprising two heterosexual parents and two amiable children has disappeared. Similarly, leaders of the historic hubs attempt to perpetuate a sense of their communities' centrality decades after the department stores have moved to suburban malls and downtown movie palaces have yielded to outlying multiscreen venues. Metropolitan Americans in both the central city and suburbs clutch at dreams that are increasingly incompatible with reality. This book will also examine the efforts of suburbanites to cope with these changing realities. It will discuss economic development in the great metropolitan regions of America as well as the governance of those regions. American business has moved to the suburbs, and the suburban response to commercial development is a significant factor in the nation's recent economic history. The willingness of suburbanites to welcome additional business has markedly influenced commercial decentralization. Suburban business incentives and tax policy can prove a boon to certain businesses deemed desirable whereas other commercial concerns might struggle to find a suburban site. This book will attempt to map the complex maze of suburban government, revealing the multitudinous adaptations of the government structure to suburban needs and desires. Characterized by a strong belief in grassroots rule and government tailored to the citizenry, American suburbia has developed a public sector baffling to many but satisfactory to millions of residents and taxpayers. Suburban government may be difficult to comprehend, but it has worked for many decades and continues to do so.

Other significant issues to be discussed are housing and the barriers to equal access to the suburbs. Though American suburbs house a broad range of people, including both the rich and the impoverished, a major concern of the early twenty-first century is housing affordability and whether the American dream of a single-family suburban home may prove beyond the reach of a growing share of the citizenry. Often criticized for their exclusionary policies, which effectively bar moderate and low-income Americans, many residential suburbs in the twenty-first century may well increasingly become the domain of the fortunate few—or they may become the home of the unfortunate many who have heavily mortgaged their future in a desperate bid to secure a suburban home no matter the cost.

Perhaps preeminent among the suburban issues of the early twenty-first century is sprawl. This book will discuss the antisprawl campaigns and the growing concern for land-use planning in metropolitan America. Can Americans stop metropolitan sprawl or need they even be that concerned about it? Is continuing suburban expansion America's dream or its nightmare? And how are the suburbs responding to these concerns? In the suburban nation of the United States, few issues are as vital to the everyday life of its citizens as the current and future development of the sprawling metropolitan regions. From the traffic jam of morning commuters to the tranquility of suburban evenings, the nature of metropolitan life will depend on the planning of suburbia and decisions about what and how much land should be consumed and how it may be developed.

This book will examine the current and future heart of the American nation. Knowledge of the evolution, development, policies, and plans for suburbia is essential to an understanding of the United States. The amorphous mass of metropolitan population beyond the central city boundaries may appear a motley mess to some observers, but those *slurbs* are the engine of the nation, and the following pages will seek to explain that vital but complex mechanism.

1
CREATING SUBURBIA

For many Americans the word *suburb* conjures up an image of post–World War II single-family tract homes, products of the age of automobiles and superhighways. Yet one basic fact of American suburbia is that it has existed virtually as long as the nation itself. It is not an offspring of the automobile or postwar federal mortgage insurance and freeway programs. Suburbia was created over the past two centuries by millions of Americans who wanted to pursue an economic endeavor or lifestyle incompatible with the policies or development patterns of the central city. The American suburb is a prime example of the nation's tradition of expansive freedom and mobility. Taking advantage of the abundance of peripheral land, entrepreneurs and home seekers in both the nineteenth and twentieth centuries pursued their own particular aspirations in outlying communities. They laid out sprawling factories, estates, residential subdivisions, and shopping malls, creating a way of life not possible within the confines of the central city. Moreover, state lawmakers maximized the opportunity for local self-rule, allowing Americans in all types of outlying communities, whether densely or sparsely populated, industrial or residential, to fashion their destiny exempt from the dictation of central city rulers. Suburbia reflects the desire of Americans over the decades to do it their own way, to create alternative communities in pursuit of a profit or a dream.

Before the Automobile

During the early nineteenth century, the appendages of America's urban centers were already reaching out beyond the city limits. In the borderlands around Boston, New York, and Philadelphia, urban merchants established country seats that served as summer retreats and their principal homes upon retirement. Businesses requiring sprawling sites or engaged in noxious enterprises also lined the roads into cities that could not accommodate them, or would not allow the odors, waste products, or smoke of such establishments. Livestock pens, slaughterhouses, tanneries, brickyards, and glass factories were all among these outcasts. As early as 1799, a Philadelphia newspaper reported that "persons who are disposed to visit the environs of this city... are saluted with a great variety of fetid and disgusting smells, which are exhaled from the dead carcasses of animals, from stagnant waters, and from every species of filth."[1] Outside Boston the Brighton Cattle Market flourished, and Massachusetts's largest slaughterhouse was in East Cambridge, just across the Charles River from Boston. Nearby, soap works profited from the slaughterhouse by-products and brick makers stripped the clay beds on discarded farms to serve the building needs of New England's largest city.[2]

Around New York City the earliest commuter suburbs developed, spawned by the improved and expanding ferry service linking Manhattan with nearby shores. In 1814 the first steam ferry began carrying passengers between New York and the then-independent community of Brooklyn, and the following year a Brooklyn newspaper was already claiming that the nascent Long Island suburb "must necessarily become a favorite residence for gentlemen of taste and fortune, for merchants and shopkeepers of every description, for artists, artisans, merchants, laborers, and persons of every trade in society." In 1823 an advertisement boosting "Lots on Brooklyn Heights" promised that its subdivision was "the nearest country retreat, and easiest of access from the center of business that now remains unoccupied," offering "as a place of residence all the advantages of the country with most of the conveniences of the city." In Brooklyn Heights, "gentlemen whose business or profession require daily attendance into the city" could "secure the health and comfort of their families." Such promises attracted customers. Between 1820 and 1840, Brooklyn's population increased fivefold to 36,000, whereas the population of the central city of New York rose at only half that pace. Meanwhile, ferry service to Brooklyn expanded, and by 1854 the Union Ferry Company offered 1,250 crossings each day, charging only two cents per trip.[3]

During the decades before the Civil War, ferries crossing the Hudson River opened Jersey City to commuters, and in 1838 the Hoboken Land and Improvement Company was created to develop Hoboken, New Jersey. Fourteen years later, one observer found it was "becoming a thickly settled embryo city." By this time, ferries ran every ten to fifteen minutes between New York City and Jersey City at a fare of three cents per person.[4] In 1836 a subdivision of suburban villas in New Brighton on Staten Island offered yet another housing option to ferry-borne commuters seeking to escape crowded Manhattan. Long Island, Staten Island, and New Jersey all were becoming bedrooms of New York where weary Gotham entrepreneurs could retreat at the end of each day.

The railroad, not the steam ferry, however, was the primary progenitor of mid-nineteenth-century commuter suburbs. Offering Americans an unprecedented degree of mobility, the railroad opened the possibility of a semirural lifestyle to those urban toilers who could afford the fare. The result was clusters of suburban homes around outlying depots in urban areas throughout the United States. As early as 1849, fifty-nine commuter trains converged on Boston each day, allowing the city's businessmen to maintain homes in outlying Cambridge, Brookline, or Newton. "Somerville, Medford, and Woburn," advertised one railroad, "present many delightful and healthy locations for residence, not only for the gentleman of leisure, but the man of business in the city, as the cars pass through these towns often during the day and evening, affording excellent facilities for the communication with Boston."[5] During the 1850s, three commuter railroads linked New York City with Westchester County to the north. As a result the population of Yonkers more than doubled during the decade, and the new suburban town of Mount Vernon took root.

Chicago was emerging as the nation's premier rail center, and as such, a leader in the development of railroad suburbs. In 1855 the opening of the Chicago and Milwaukee Railroad along the shore of Lake Michigan led one optimistic observer to enthuse: "The New York and Philadelphia suberbs [sic] will now meet with a rival." The Chicago Tribune proclaimed the lakeshore north of the city "a region which nature has designed as the home of refinement and taste, and soon to be lined with beautiful suburban villages and flourishing cities."[6] Over the next few years, the line did attract commuters and in the words of a local newspaper, afforded "business men an excellent opportunity to avail themselves of the beautiful quiet of a country residence without shortening the number of hours usually devoted to their daily avocations."[7] Railroads were also affording this opportunity to commuters living west and south of the city. By 1873 one account of Chicago's suburbs told of five or six thousand heads of households, "all of whom do business in the city, and form a large per cent of the passenger list of the 100 or more trains that enter and leave the city daily."[8] A year later another author reported that there were "a dozen trains daily, at a fare of ten cents the trip," linking the southern suburb of Hyde Park to Chicago, and hourly trains from the western suburb of Austin conveyed passengers to the city in "only twenty-five minutes" at a commuter rate of "one hundred rides for $7.50." According to this observer, the railroads could expect to carry thousands of additional commuters in the future, for the fact was "thoroughly established that ninety-nine Chicago families in every hundred will go an hour's ride into the country, or toward the country, rather than live under or over another family, as the average New Yorker or Parisian does."[9]

Among the by-products of this rise in commuter traffic were soaring prices for outlying land and widespread speculation in suburban town sites. In 1870 an account of Cincinnati's suburbs reported, "a wonderful advance has taken place in the price of lands" in the suburb of Clifton, "eligible lands in this locality hav[ing] increased about forty-six hundred per cent in twenty-four years."[10] Three years later a speculative boom swept the Flatbush area outside of Brooklyn. "Lots in the best portion of this place, 25 x 150," wrote one commentator, "are held firmly at $3,000 in some instances which could have been bought a few years ago for $600."[11] A Chicago-area booster contended that land in the southern suburb of Woodlawn purchased at $160 per acre in 1866 was bringing $7,000 per acre by 1873. In 1874 this same observer was claiming that in the environs of Chicago "80,000 acres or 125 square miles of territory will be demanded by the ultimate consumers within the next decade." If this proved true, "each of our twelve railroads in the suburban traffic" would be lined with "a continuous belt of village population ... extending for half a mile on each side of the track for ten miles."[12] Already the city's leading real estate journal claimed that development was engulfing territory that "a few years ago was one complete swamp, having no particular use but for hunting and fishing ... If building continues at the same rate, the whole section south of the city limits to Englewood will be one dense mass of houses."[13]

By the early 1870s sprawl and speculation were, therefore, eating up the land around America's largest cities. But profit was not the consuming motive of all mid-nineteenth-century suburban developers. Instead, a number of idealistic suburban pioneers sought to fashion an alternative environment where those forced to work in the city could maintain a home life attuned to the tranquility, beauty, and purity of nature and where families could thrive safely removed from the urban ills threatening the health and morals of youth. Laid out in what became known as the romantic style of planning, these ideal suburbs were characterized by large, irregular lots, naturalistic landscaping, and curving streets that conformed to the natural terrain and contrasted starkly with the sharp right angles, straight thoroughfares, and identical narrow lots of the urban grid. They were not simply extensions of the city, indistinguishable in their layout from the neighborhoods of New York, Philadelphia, or Chicago. They offered a specifically suburban plan reflecting emerging upper-middle-class views of what suburbia should offer its residents.

The earliest example of romantic suburban planning was Llewellyn Park in Orange, New Jersey, only thirteen miles by rail from New York City. Laid out in 1853 by the wealthy merchant Llewellyn Haskell, it was located on a picturesque mountain slope capped by a rugged cliff. Haskell was a member of a religious cult that believed perfection on earth was possible through correct living, and the natural terrain, curving lanes, and three- to ten-acre lots of Llewellyn Park were intended to provide a setting for such a faultless existence. Designed as "a retreat for a man to exercise his own rights and privileges," it was created "with special reference to the wants of citizens doing business in the city of New York, and yet wishing accessible, retired, and healthful homes in the country."[14]

Haskell, however, was not alone in his desire for such a natural retreat. In 1857, Chicago-area Presbyterians laid out Lake

Forest along the shore of Lake Michigan with a maze of curving lanes winding along the site's ravines and bluffs. In 1869 a visitor described the community as "simply a collection of elegant private parks and ornamental forms," but noted, "the design here … is to aid nature by Art and not to bully her."[15] The same could be said of suburban Glendale, north of Cincinnati. Also laid out in the 1850s, it repeated the pattern of curving streets, large lots, and quiet appreciation of nature. Writing of the irregular street pattern, one account observed: "Whichever way the stranger takes, he is constantly impressed with the thought that he has made a mistake, and whatever point he attains is certain to be some one unlooked for." Glendale's residents clearly did not intend to provide easy access to strangers or accommodate those seeking to reach a destination as quickly as possible. Rather in 1870 a visitor described the community as "a collection of beautiful homes, with ample grounds and profuse shrubbery, approached by circuitous avenues, and distinguished for the air of comfort and retirement"; in Glendale "quiet landscapes say to fatigued limbs and wearied minds, 'Here is rest.'"[16]

Perhaps the most famous of these romantic suburbs was Riverside, Illinois, laid out in 1869 based on a plan by the nation's foremost landscape architect, Frederick Law Olmsted. Located on a rail line nine miles west of Chicago and conceived as "a model suburban neighborhood" by its promoters, Riverside included the curving streets, large lots, trees, shrubs, and air of rusticity increasingly deemed desirable by well-to-do Americans in search of an outlying home.[17] In a classic statement of romantic planning precepts, Olmsted recommended to Riverside's developers "the general adoption, in the design of your roads, of gracefully-curved lines, generous spaces, and the absence of sharp corners, the idea being to suggest and imply leisure, contemplativeness and happy tranquility."[18] According to Olmsted, properly planned suburbs offered "the most refined and the most soundly wholesome forms of domestic life, and the best application of the arts of civilization to which mankind has yet attained."[19] Under Olmsted's guidance, Riverside would supposedly provide this ideal life for its well-to-do residents.

By 1870, then, an upper-middle-class suburban ideal had emerged that continued to influence metropolitan development into the twenty-first century. Suburbia was deemed a retreat nurturing happy tranquility and wholesome domesticity, a place conducive to the most desirable family life and combining the advantages of city and country. Nature, home, family, and peace were all components of the ideal upper-middle-class suburb and were to be preserved at all costs. In 1870 many Americans believed that the good life was found in such communities, and 130 years later their descendants did so as well.

Suburbia, however, was not all happy, affluent families, lush landscaping, and natural beauty. In the late nineteenth century, as in earlier years, many business concerns located beyond the central city limits, and with the development of large-scale manufacturing, the open spaces of suburbia proved especially appealing to sprawling industrial giants. Among the most common suburban industries were the nation's stockyards and meatpacking plants. In 1865 Chicago's giant Union Stock Yards were constructed south of the city in the town of Lake, and in the years following, packinghouses relocated to the vicinity of this "great bovine city." These enterprises in turn attracted an army of workers whose cottages spread across the north end of Lake. At the beginning of the 1880s the area was home to about 12,000 people; by 1889 this figure had risen to 37,000.[20] From 1872 on, the stockyards and packing plants of St. Louis clustered across the Mississippi north of East St. Louis, Illinois, and Nebraska's giant Union Stock Yards was located in South Omaha beyond the Omaha city limits. In 1892 the Cudahy Packing Company left Milwaukee for a new home in the specially created suburban community of Cudahy south of the city limits. Between 1890 and 1910, South San Francisco, across the municipal boundary in San Mateo County, attracted the Bay Area's Union Stockyards and packing plants, and in the early twentieth century suburban South St. Paul became the livestock and packing hub of the Twin Cities area.[21] These meatpacking suburbs bore little resemblance to sylvan Glendale or tranquil Riverside. In 1886, South Omaha suburbanites complained of "how we are exposed without any protection against tramps and murderers—having no jail, no church, one school house (and that falling to decay), one saloon for every twenty inhabitants, one gambling house, [and] two houses of ill-fame."[22]

Yet meatpackers were not the only entrepreneurs attracted to a suburban location. In the Pittsburgh area the great steel mills and other sprawling plants were found in outlying communities along the river valleys spreading out from the city. Andrew Carnegie operated state-of-the-art steel mills in Braddock and outside of Homestead, eight miles by rail from the city of Pittsburgh. In 1890 George Westinghouse relocated his electrical manufacturing works from Pittsburgh to a suburban site where he created the town of Wilmerding to house his workers. By 1899, 55 percent of the production workers in the metropolitan district of Pittsburgh were employed in the suburbs; the central city accounted for a minority of the area's manufacturing employment.[23] Ten years later a student of the region observed: "The time is soon coming when all the large industries will be eliminated from the city, and Pittsburgh proper will become simply the commercial and cultural headquarters of its district."[24]

Elsewhere the suburbanization of industry was not so pronounced but still evident. During the first decade of the twentieth century, the once residential suburb of Norwood became a hub of manufacturing in the Cincinnati region as large plants relocated from the crowded Queen City to the green fields of the outskirts. Because largely middle-class Norwood did not have adequate housing for poorly paid wage earners, thousands of workers traveled outward each day from the inner city to the suburb, establishing a pattern of reverse commuting that would become increasingly common throughout the nation in the late twentieth century. Meanwhile, Granite City, Illinois, was developing as one of the industrial centers of the St. Louis area. Founded in 1893 specifically to provide a site for a graniteware factory, the community offered employment to 8,500 workers by the beginning of the twentieth century. An estimated 65 percent of these workers lived in Granite City with 35 percent commuting in from St. Louis. The central city also benefited from Granite City's payrolls with an estimated 70 percent of the money earned in the industrial suburb being spent in St. Louis. Decidedly a working-class community, Granite City and its environs housed one of the largest clusters of Macedonian and Bulgarian immigrants in the United States, most of these newcomers crowded into the squalid slum neighborhood known as Hungary Hollow.[25]

The late-nineteenth-century development of beltline railroads around the nation's major rail centers also encouraged the decentralization of manufacturing. These lines allowed trains to bypass the crowded hubs, and offered desirable outlying industrial sites where the beltline intersected with the trunk lines converging in the central city. Like the outer belt freeways of the late twentieth century, these circumferential railroads were magnets for commerce and drew money and people to the metropolitan rim. For example, in 1891 the Chicago Heights Land Association embarked on a scheme to create a manufacturing suburb south of Chicago at the intersection of the recently completed Elgin, Joliet, and Eastern beltline and the Chicago and Eastern Illinois trunk line. In 1891 and 1892 alone more than fourteen thousand lots were offered for sale in the new town of Chicago Heights, and within a decade the ideal site had attracted major manufacturing plants.[26]

Chicago Heights, Granite City, South Omaha, and South San Francisco all attracted a working-class population to staff their emerging industries. Some working-class suburbs, however, offered little employment but acres of inexpensive housing. A few of these were also ethnic enclaves where residents could escape the heterogeneity of American life. East of St. Louis, Brooklyn, Illinois, developed as a black-dominated community whose working-class residents commuted to the steel mills, slaughterhouses, and railroad shops of nearby industrial suburbs. In 1908 a national magazine described it as "governed solely by negroes... who believe that a higher degree of civilization is attainable for them through isolation from whites."[27] Farther north in Illinois the community of West Hammond hugged the southern boundary of Chicago and the western limits of the meatpacking center of Hammond, Indiana. Though devoid of industry, it attracted working-class Polish families eager to own a home. In 1890 a Chicago real estate journal announced that the syndicate marketing West Hammond's lots intended to sell exclusively to Poles because of "the sentiment on the part of these people to obtain homes at a minimum cost at the same time to cultivate an acquaintance as far as possible among their own race by establishing churches and schools compatible with their own desire."[28] Just as blacks were fashioning their own civilization in Brooklyn, West Hammond was becoming a predominantly Polish suburb where Chicago-area immigrants could purchase modest cottages on streets named for Polish kings and saints.

Enhancing the outward flow of working class and middle class alike was the electrification of streetcar and rail lines in the 1890s. The horse-drawn streetcars of the 1870s and 1880s plodded along at a pace of about five miles an hour, but the new electric-powered lines could carry passengers to the metropolitan outskirts at more than twice that speed. As a result, some bucolic suburbs that had attracted steam railroad commuters in the 1840s and 1850s experienced a new flood of streetcar-borne residents. Between 1885 and 1900, Brookline, Massachusetts, more than doubled in population as Henry Whitney built an electric line into central Boston and sparked the beginning of apartment and townhouse development in the northern half of the suburb.[29] Electric streetcars also facilitated the outward migration of industry. The reverse commute of workers from inner-city Cincinnati to suburban Norwood was only possible because of the web of electric trolley lines.[30]

With larger cars and higher speeds, the interurban electric railroads further encouraged early twentieth-century metropolitan sprawl. For only a five-cent fare, an interurban carried Granite City workers to downtown St. Louis in thirty-five minutes.[31] From 1890 to 1915, such lines developed throughout the United States, but nowhere were they more significant than in the Los Angeles area. By the second decade of the twentieth century, the Pacific Electric Railway system operated along hundreds of miles of track reaching from the San Gabriel Valley in the east to Santa Monica on the west and from the San Fernando Valley in the north to Orange County's Newport Beach in the south.[32] All along the lines residential subdivisions sprouted, establishing the sprawling pattern of settlement for which Southern California became noted. Long before there were freeways, Southern Californians were spreading out along the electric interurban lines realizing the American dream in single-family homes.

Suburban Californians and their ilk elsewhere in the United States were not only building homes, they were also creating governments. During the nineteenth century the states adopted a permissive stance toward municipal incorporation, allowing virtually any community to incorporate as a separate municipality. The result was thousands of independent cities and villages, many clustered near the boundaries of the nation's major central cities. During each decade from 1860 to 1890, Chicago's Cook County witnessed the creation of ten new municipalities; the municipal birthrate soared in the 1890s as twenty-six additional municipalities were organized and then slowed between 1900 and 1910 when the Chicago area produced fourteen incorporations. By 1910, Pittsburgh's Allegheny County included sixty-five independent cities and boroughs, suburban Bergen County, New Jersey, immediately west of New York City, was the site of fifty such governments, and thirty-two cities and towns clustered within a ten-mile radius of downtown Boston. Southern California was not exempt from this madness for new municipalities, with twenty-five separate cities scattered across Los Angeles County in 1910.[33] On the West Coast this rush to incorporate was especially pronounced during the first decade of the twentieth century. In 1905 Los Angeles Countians petitioned to incorporate twelve communities and the following year the figure rose to thirteen.[34]

Americans sought incorporation for a number of reasons, the most common being the desire for municipal services. In 1871 West Cleveland, Ohio, chose to incorporate because of the need for "greater power over roads, public grounds and police than is presently enjoyed." Nineteen years later, proponents of municipal status in the Denver suburb of Elyria emphasized the lack of drinking water, streetlights, drainage, and the "widespread nuisance from the stench of dead animals." In 1892 the inhabitants of Whitefish Bay, north of Milwaukee, opted for municipal government in order to establish a local school; parents disliked "the idea of sending their children 2½ miles through snow and storm" to the existing Milwaukee Township school.[35] Occasionally municipal status preserved the advantages that a community already enjoyed. In Bergen County, New Jersey, incorporation was a means of preserving local schools and warding off consolidation with school districts having weaker tax bases.[36]

Yet incorporation also served to preserve the distinctive moral atmosphere of a community. During the late nineteenth and early twentieth centuries, many Americans deemed liquor an intolerable evil and used newly acquired municipal powers to exclude unwanted saloons and their habitués. In Los Angeles County, antisaloon sentiment was a factor in the incorporation of Pasadena, South Pasadena, Compton, Pomona, and Monrovia.[37] When Monrovia incorporated in 1887, one of the first acts of the southern-born deputy city marshal was to march into the local saloon and announce: "We-all have incorporated and we-all don't want you here."[38] Along the Lake Michigan shore north of Chicago, the suburbs of Evanston, Wilmette, Winnetka, Glencoe, Highland Park, and Lake Forest were all officially dry; when Highland Park incorporated in 1869 the eight saloons within its limits were forced to close. Henceforth the community was a wholesome retreat for Victorian families.[39]

Other communities, however, achieved municipal status in order to promote, rather than eradicate, sin. In 1903, Lucky Baldwin successfully plotted the incorporation of Arcadia, California, so he could operate a racetrack free from the meddling of Los Angeles County authorities. Moralists warned that the new municipality was "to be made a gambling hell and booze pleasure park," and Baldwin publicly admitted that he dreamed of his city becoming the "Monte Carlo of the West."[40] Incorporated in 1874, predominantly German Gross Point, Illinois, immediately west of Wilmette, was an oasis of alcohol in the dry expanse of northern Cook County. A visitor described it as a place "to mingle with the Teutonic revelers and drink lager beer."[41]

Whereas Pasadenans fashioned an enclave of moral purity and Baldwin a haven of sin, some manufacturers created separate cities to protect their economic interests. Fearful of heavy taxes if its Midwestern refinery was annexed to Hammond, Indiana, Standard Oil officials in 1894 incorporated the refinery site, creating the low-tax haven of Whiting. In 1901 the Carnegie Steel Company secured the incorporation of the industrial suburb of Munhall, the site of its giant mill, and thereby ensured a lower tax rate.

Five years later the stockyards and slaughterhouses immediately north of East St. Louis incorporated as National City, henceforth enjoying minimal taxes and exemption from municipal regulation of the odors and filth resulting from meatpacking.[42] Though saloonkeepers, steelmakers, and teetotaling devotees of wholesome family life were carving metropolitan America into municipal fragments, central city leaders as yet were not too concerned about the prospect of a suburban noose choking future expansion. During the late nineteenth century, suburbia was generally regarded as a transition phase between country and city; once suburbs reached a certain stage of development they would supposedly seek union with the central city and boost its census ranking. "It is 'manifest destiny,'" commented one observer in 1873, "that New York and Brooklyn must ... become united as one great city."[43] Similarly, in 1885 a *Chicago Tribune* article pronounced: "It is the history of all American municipalities that they absorb their populous suburbs. The gravitation is resistless."[44]

Contemporary events seemed to support this sense of inevitable amalgamation. Between 1867 and 1873, Boston annexed the independent towns of Roxbury, Dorchester, Brighton, Charlestown, and West Roxbury, and between 1870 and 1910, Cleveland absorbed the separate municipalities of East Cleveland, West Cleveland, Brooklyn, Glenville, South Brooklyn, Corlett, and Collinwood. From 1887 through 1889, Chicago conducted a vigorous annexation campaign, conquering the suburban municipalities of Lake, Hyde Park, and Lake View.[45] The number of square miles within Chicago's city limits more than quadrupled; by 1890 it could boast of the largest area of any American municipality. Threatened by the possibility that Chicago might also become the nation's most populous city, New Yorkers embarked on a consolidation scheme that resulted in 1898 in the merger of New York City with Brooklyn, Queens, Richmond, and what is today the Bronx. By the close of the nineteenth century, New York City had realized its manifest destiny, and Brooklyn had become a mere borough of the larger municipality of greater New York.

A desire for better services doomed many suburbs to extinction. In 1869 a proponent of the annexation of Dorchester to Boston claimed that through union with the central city, "Dorchester would have her streets laid out in a systematic manner and all well lighted …. A vote for annexation was a vote for progress, a vote against annexation was a vote for high taxes in a sleepy town or a one horse city." Three years later a resident of East Cleveland said much the same thing when he judged: "Life in the city, with a fire and police department, schools, etc., better than in a village where these advantages cannot be enjoyed."[46] In 1889 a Chicago-area supporter of annexation reiterated this when he observed: "The people of Lake View are not getting the return on their money which they would get were they annexed to Chicago …. They pay high taxes and get—what? Bad water, poor schools, worse sewerage."[47] In the late nineteenth century, big city services were still far superior to those of most suburbs, and that was argument enough for many suburbanites to abandon independence and become urban residents.

Already, however, metropolitan cooperation was emerging as an alternative to consolidation. Confronted with a persistent problem with sewage disposal and water pollution, the Illinois legislature in 1889 established the Chicago Sanitary District, which comprised Chicago and its nearest suburbs. Without sacrificing their independent status, the suburbs joined with Chicago in common cause to protect the water supply of the metropolitan region. In 1895 the Massachusetts legislature took similar action when it created the Metropolitan Water District charged with supplying a much-needed pure water supply to Boston and eighteen nearby suburban towns. By the close of the nineteenth century, it was becoming clear that suburbanites did not need to choose simply between union and independence. There was a middle path of regional governance that would prove of increasing significance in the coming century.

By the early twentieth century, then, many of the foundation stones of America's suburbs were in place. Fragmentation of governmental authority mitigated by pioneering regional cooperation already characterized metropolitan America. Development of new modes of transportation had induced a diverse pattern of sprawl. Some suburbs were upper-middle-class bucolic refuges where affluent Americans could maintain a model family life free from the evils of alcohol. Other suburbs were manufacturing hubs where industrialists could build expansive mills along outlying rail lines in the open spaces of the metropolitan fringe and establish municipal governments to ensure low tax rates. Still other fringe communities were ethnic villages where residents could celebrate Polish holidays and drink German beer. And the outward migration of many Americans had spurred widespread land speculation and subdivision, phenomena that would characterize metropolitan development in future decades as well. At the beginning of the twentieth century the American suburban prototype was established.

The Advent of the Automobile

Though steam railroads, electric streetcars, and interurbans had already facilitated the commute from America's central cities to burgeoning suburbs, between 1910 and 1940 the advent of the automobile accelerated the pace of outward migration. In 1910 there were only about 458,500 automobiles nationwide; by 1920 this figure was up to 8.2 million and by 1930 the number reached 23.2 million or about one automobile for every five Americans.[48] Millions of Americans still relied on streetcars and trains for transportation to work or shopping, but now they also had the alternative of travel by private passenger cars. Motor vehicles filled the thoroughfares, freeing Americans from dependence on rails, and allowing them to settle suburban tracts farther removed from commuter stations. In 1910, 24 percent of the residents of the metropolitan districts containing the nation's twenty most populous cities lived in the suburbs; by 1940 this rose to 37 percent.[49] During the prosperous decade of the 1920s suburban expansion was especially pronounced as population growth in the territory beyond the central city limits outpaced that within the hub. Whereas the population of the city of Cleveland rose only 11.8 percent between 1920 and 1930, the rate of growth for the Cleveland metropolitan district as a whole was 27.7 percent. The respective rates for St. Louis and its metropolitan district were 6.3 percent and 20.7 percent and for Boston were 4.4 percent and 14.9 percent. Suburbia was booming.[50]

In the Detroit metropolitan area the rise of the automobile very directly spurred the growth of suburbia. Giant auto plants sprawled outside the Detroit city limits, giving birth to a whole new crop of industrial suburbs. In 1909 Henry Ford began mass production of his Model T in a sprawling plant on an eighty-acre site along a beltline railroad in the suburb of Highland Park. During the following decade the Dodge brothers opened their plant in the adjacent suburb of Hamtramck. Between 1910 and 1920 the population of Highland Park soared from 4,120 to 46,499, and that of Hamtramck rose from 3,559 to 48,615. By the early 1920s Ford was shifting the base of his operations to the western suburb of Dearborn, igniting breakneck growth in that community; between 1920 and 1930, Dearborn's population increased twentyfold from 2,470 to 50,358. One of General Motors' manufacturing hubs was Pontiac, the booming seat of Oakland County immediately north of Detroit.

The impact of manufacturing growth in Highland Park, Hamtramck, Dearborn, and Pontiac was felt in many nearby communities. Workers commuted from Ford's Highland Park plant to emerging settlements along the southern limits of Oakland County, spurring an epidemic of suburban subdividing. From 1910 to 1919 developers platted almost 8,000 acres in Royal Oak Township, 3,000 acres in 1916 alone, more than twice the acreage subdivided in all of Oakland County prior to 1910. Between 1918 and the end of 1924, the population of suburban Ferndale rose from 2,000 to 13,000. Ford workers likewise settled on inexpensive lots along unpaved streets in nearby Berkley and Clawson, where they erected makeshift housing and pioneered the suburban fringe without benefit of piped water or sewers.[51] Meanwhile, south of Detroit the suburbs of Ecorse and River Rouge offered low-cost residences for both black and white workers in Ford's Dearborn plants.[52]

Detroit was not the only metropolitan district witnessing the fast-paced development of industrial suburbs. Between 1910 and 1940 the Los Angeles area was industrializing, and a major share of the new plants was in the suburbs. Southern California leaders advocated the dispersion of industry throughout the metropolitan area, hoping to create an uncongested region of workshops in the sun in marked contrast to the crowded, sooty manufacturing hubs of the East. In 1924, one business booster pronounced that "industries must be scattered throughout the whole metropolitan district ... such decentralization will make for better living conditions and better citizenship, as well as for cheaper overhead costs."[53] The same year a prominent business leader described "The Los Angeles of Tomorrow: From Inglewood to Capistrano, and from Redondo to San Bernardino, industrial communities and centers will be scattered over this southland, each with its bungalows in which will live contented workmen with happy families, and gardens and flowers and lawns."[54]

By the mid-1920s this dispersion was already evident in sprawling Southern California. In 1911 a New York entrepreneur announced his intention to develop the community of Torrance, a planned industrial city southwest of Los Angeles. Frederick Law

Olmsted, Jr., the son of the planner of Riverside, Illinois, was hired to design the carefully conceived community. More significant was the development of industry in the suburbs southeast of Los Angeles. The municipality of Vernon developed as an industrial haven, a low-tax community with few residents but designed to serve the interests of manufacturers. Nearby, the working-class suburbs of Maywood, Huntington Park, and Bell housed the industrial workers employed in Vernon; Bell was described as "an island of homes in a sea of industry." East of Los Angeles the subdivisions of Belvedere were home to Mexican workers. The movie industry also located in the suburbs with Metro-Goldwyn-Mayer and United Artists building studios in Culver City and Warner Brothers moving to Burbank.[55]

Further contributing to the dispersed pattern of Southern California settlement was the development of communities adjacent to the region's scattered oil fields and refineries. With the advent of gasoline-fueled automobiles, petroleum consumption soared and the Los Angeles basin cashed in on the heightened demand. In 1911, Standard Oil founded El Segundo along Santa Monica Bay, west of Los Angeles, as a refinery site. Brea was another refinery town, and nearby La Habra was the California headquarters of Standard Oil.[56] In 1924, Signal Hill incorporated as a municipality to keep its oil fields from being annexed to neighboring Long Beach. By 1930 the Signal Hill field had sprouted about 1,200 derricks operated by 130 companies. The city clerk admitted that Signal Hill was created to serve the special needs of the petroleum industry. "Because of the impossibility of conforming such a gigantic industry to the restrictions and ordinances of the average metropolitan city," he observed, "it was deemed wise by those most interested to incorporate Signal Hill as a separate municipality."[57] Most of the oil field communities were a far cry from the sylvan tranquility of a Lake Forest or Riverside. "Suburbs of this sort present many of the aspects of the frontier mining-camp," reported sociologist Harlan Douglass in 1925. "Their sordidness [was] redeemed only by the outdoor climate and the somewhat esthetic tradition of the California bungalow."[58]

All across the nation, working-class Americans were fashioning suburban communities that the more affluent might deem sordid. Along the metropolitan fringe, subdividers offered cheap lots to workers who built makeshift structures and raised chickens and vegetables in their backyards. South Gate, southeast of Los Angeles, was one such community; one of its principal subdivisions was promoted as "a town of, by and for workingmen," a place "where the working man is welcomed and given an even break." In 1924 South Gate lots sold for $20 down and $10 per month, and thousands of eager working families took advantage of the price and became suburbanites.[59] Rather than hiring professional contractors, many opted for do-it-yourself construction, building their own houses with scrap lumber and adding new rooms when they had the time and money. Nearby Bell Gardens offered similar opportunities. As one Bell Gardens resident explained, "You can almost always scrape together ten dollars a month as long as you can have a place to live. We've built our house a little at a time as we could pay for it." The result was not a community of elegant homes. A sociologist studying Bell Gardens in the 1930s described the consequences: "Here is a perfectly cubical building about half the size of a one-car garage and covered with tar paper. It is not a chicken coop or a rabbit pen but the home of a family."[60]

Such self-built suburban communities were not confined to Southern California. In the 1920s, foreign-born workers employed in Chicago's west-side factories bought cheap lots in the DuPage County community of Westmont, where they could have a home of their own and some land for a garden and livestock. In 1923 the local priest reported: "Nearly all of my flock are about one month's wages ahead of poverty."[61] Outside of Detroit, a real estate firm developed Garden City as a community for autoworkers seeking to buy "farmlets," which were 147 feet wide and 135 feet deep. "It offers the means of a great saving in your grocery bill," the firm advertised, "or the opportunity to live much better for less cash outlay." As in other self-built suburbs, there were no curbs, pavement, or sewers, and many of the early homes were simply frame structures built on wooden posts sunk into the ground. Some residents lived in their garages until they scraped together enough to build an actual house.[62]

Though racial restrictive covenants excluded non-Caucasians from such communities as South Gate, African Americans did create some of their own makeshift suburbs. In 1924, Cleveland's black newspaper advertised a subdivision that offered "a chance to raise chickens and garden truck, and still be close enough to the city of Cleveland so that residents could come and go from their work within 30 minutes time." For only $10 per month, African Americans could buy a lot in "the garden spot of this county."[63] Nearby was another garden spot for blacks, Chagrin Falls Park. Here chicken coops, vegetable gardens, and self-built houses dotted the landscape. One resident reminisced about the building of her family's home: "The neighbors dug the basement by hand, and my father and another man that lived down the street built the house .... We paid for the stuff as we went along." Explaining why these black suburbanites invested their sweat and money in the community, a local woman stated simply: "Everybody at that time wanted a little place of their own."[64]

With the advent of prohibition in 1920, a good many Americans went in search of a place of their own where they could satisfy their thirst free from government meddling. Thousands of pleasure seekers found that place in the suburbs. During the automobile age, suburbia was well suited to defiance of the prohibition laws and other moral codes as well. Its scores of autonomous municipalities were beyond the authority of big-city police, and the mayors and police chiefs of the poorer suburbs were easily bribed. Moreover, the automobile provided ready access to municipal enclaves of sin along the metropolitan fringe. Red light districts offering sex, gambling, and drink had once clustered near the central city downtowns, but in the automobile age suburban roadhouses became the new emporiums of pleasure. Along outlying highways in permissive suburban municipalities, violators of the moral codes escaped puritanical America.

No one recognized the advantages of suburbia so well as the Chicago mobster Johnny Torrio and his henchman Al Capone. They operated a string of suburban roadhouses complete with prostitutes, gambling, and liquor, and a number of suburban officials were on their payroll. The small suburb of Burnham, south of Chicago, was home to some of the earliest of the mobsters' establishments, but the crown jewel of the Torrio-Capone suburban empire was working-class Cicero. After reformers began cracking down on prohibition violators in the city of Chicago, Torrio and Capone moved the center of their operations to the compliant suburb. Wide-open Cicero was home to 161 gambling establishments and 123 saloons, and gangland gunplay further marred its moral reputation.[65] One wit commented: "If you smell gunpowder, you're in Cicero."[66] The nearby village of Forest View became known as Caponeville and was home to the Torrio–Capone gang's largest brothel, the Stockade, with a staff of sixty prostitutes. The suburban municipality's founder lamented that Forest View's streets were "now little more than thoroughfares for the automobiles of gunmen, booze runners, and disorderly women."[67]

Cicero's Detroit-area counterpart was the heavily Polish suburb of Hamtramck. During the 1920s and 1930s it won a reputation as "the wild west of the middle west" and as "a cancer spot and crying disgrace."[68] Hamtramck police convoyed liquor through the city's streets, mayors regularly landed in the penitentiary, and public officials profited from payoffs from brothel keepers. A gambling establishment operated a few feet from the police commissioner's place of business, and Detroit newspapers reveled in the reports of sin and scandal emanating from the benighted municipality. Like Burnham, Cicero, and Forest View, Hamtramck represented a municipal enclave of sin, cashing in on the governmental fragmentation of metropolitan America.

Between 1910 and 1940 suburbia, however, was not simply a refuge for Al Capone, Standard Oil, Henry Ford, and factory workers seeking to raise chickens; it also embodied the dreams of many middle-class and upper-middle-class Americans who sought wholesome havens of family life and upscale retreats where they could enjoy nature free from the proletarian masses and gun-toting hooligans. In "The Defense of Suburbia," an article appearing in a national magazine in 1928, one contented suburbanite expressed this viewpoint: "We moved so the children might be near the grass and the trees …. With the suburb as a base we have rediscovered the out-of-doors." Responding to a questionnaire distributed to commuters in Westchester County north of New York City in the early 1930s, an accountant likewise summed up the feelings of many business and professional men when he listed among the advantages of suburban life that it enabled him "to bring up [his] daughter in [a] healthy and clean atmosphere, without undesirable associations and contacts."[69] Real estate advertisements repeatedly emphasized the natural and social advantages of suburbia. "Nestled among the estates and rolling hills, beautiful trees and natural beauty unmarred by city invasion, there is afforded every home owner the restful and healthful license of a country atmosphere," claimed one 1928 advertisement for a suburban development in Oakland County, Michigan. The promoter of Great Neck Gardens in suburban Long Island told prospective buyers "the people that you want for neighbors are here," people who could "appreciate" and "afford to enjoy" the beauty of this subdivision.[70] The vision expressed in nineteenth-century Lake Forest and Riverside was still very much alive. Suburbia could be a bucolic utopia for those able to afford it.

One of the most famous upper-middle-class retreats of the era was Scarsdale, New York, twenty miles north of midtown Manhattan. Threatened with annexation by adjacent White Plains, in 1915 Scarsdale residents mobilized and incorporated as a separate village. Defending the community's independent identity, one opponent of annexation observed that Scarsdale was "exclusively a residential community. Its plan of development has been unique and high class."[71] And during the following quarter century the community pursued a policy to keep Scarsdale exclusively residential and high class. New subdivisions in the 1920s imposed stringent deed restrictions. For example, the Berkley subdivision required that any dwellings erected on the lots cost at least $25,000 at a time when the average bungalow for a middle-income family cost $5,500. Significantly, the deeds also prohibited the keeping of chickens, cows, and other barnyard livestock.[72] Though the residents of plebeian South Gate and patrician Scarsdale both sought fresh air and land of their own, they clearly intended to use their land for different purposes. No shacks or chicken coops marred the landscape of the upscale New York suburb; gardens in Scarsdale grew roses not rutabagas.

To reinforce the high-class residential character of their community, Scarsdale residents adopted stringent zoning ordinances. In the early 1920s America's cities and villages were still experimenting with zoning ordinances, and not until 1926 did the United States Supreme Court uphold the constitutionality of municipal measures to determine land use. But upper-middle-class suburbs were eager to use this new power to protect their status. Arguing for zoning to exclude commercial establishments, one Scarsdale resident claimed that he and his neighbors moved to the community "knowing there were no stores and preferring just the kind of community which we now have." Yet if future land use was not severely restricted, "instead of stepping off the trains at once into the peaceful country, we should have to pass by the same kind of life which we gladly leave behind us in New York." This sentiment triumphed, and 97 percent of Scarsdale land was zoned for single-family residences.[73] Like a growing number of upper-middle-class suburban havens, Scarsdale was using the force of law to maintain its exclusive lifestyle.

To perpetuate privilege from one generation to the next, Scarsdale residents were also investing in a first-rate public school system. Upper-middle-class suburbanites wanted a school system that would prepare their children for the finest colleges, and they were willing to pay for superior facilities and faculty. A study from the 1930s reported that Scarsdale and the nearby and equally affluent suburb of Bronxville spent more per pupil than any of the other villages in New York, and together with the well-to-do Long Island suburb of Garden City, ranked highest in academic achievement. From the Scarsdale High School class of 1928, four graduates each went to Cornell and Dartmouth and two each to Colgate, Columbia, Mount Holyoke, Vassar, and Wellesley.[74] Scarsdale's investment in education was clearly paying off.

Local versions of Scarsdale graced the outskirts of metropolitan areas across America. In the Cleveland area, Shaker Heights was the preferred upper-middle-class retreat, its population soaring from 1,600 in 1920 to almost 17,800 ten years later. Shaker Heights' developers Oris and Mantis Van Sweringen envisioned a residential community of the highest quality and required prospective home builders to hire "a graduate architect" or a person with comparable credentials because "without the guidance of a competent architect, imagination may easily run to the freakish in residences." Not only would the community have a tasteful outward appearance, it was intended to provide an ideal environment for raising the children of the affluent. "All that conserves home-spirit is cultivated," the Van Sweringens promised; "that which is inimical is barred."[75] The village of Shorewood, north of Milwaukee, made much the same claims. According to a publication from the 1930s, Shorewood gave "an impression of shade and affluence" and "every foot of land was restricted, either by deed stipulation or village ordinance." Moreover, the local school system was "one of the most elaborate in the country for a village of Shorewood's size."[76] To the south in the St. Louis area, Ladue was a mecca for the affluent with zoning restrictions ensuring low-density development. In 1938 its zoning commissioners boasted: "Ours is one of the few communities in St. Louis County that are unspoiled by uses generally objectionable to desirable residential sections."[77] Meanwhile, in Miami the elite were moving to suburban Coral Gables, in Dallas the high-class suburb was Highland Park, and in the Los Angeles area, Beverly Hills was winning a worldwide reputation for wealth and privilege.

Other suburbs were developing as refuges for families that could not afford Scarsdale or Shaker Heights but still sought a home and yard of their own outside the city and in subdivisions with higher standards than those of South Gate, Bell Gardens, or Westmont. Thousands of freshly minted Dutch Colonials arose along the streets of middle-income suburbs, and mid-priced bungalows seemed to sprout everywhere along the metropolitan rim during the 1920s. In the late 1920s Mills and Sons Company built the bungalow community of Westwood in the suburb of Elmwood Park west of Chicago. Advertised as "The World's Largest Bungalow Development," by 1929 Westwood housed more than one thousand families in modest homes selling for $8,750.[78] In New York, Illinois, and California the story was the same. Suburbia was becoming home to everyone from chicken-raising factory workers to bungalow-dwelling office workers and Scarsdale-bound executives.

As the population of suburbia soared, so did the number of suburban municipalities. The multiplication of governmental units so evident in the nineteenth century continued during the period between 1910 and 1940. By the latter date there were 289 incorporated places in the New York metropolitan district, 137 in metropolitan Pittsburgh, 118 in the Chicago area, and 56 in metropolitan Los Angeles.[79] The increase was especially pronounced in some suburban counties. In Long Island's Nassau County immediately east of New York City, the number of municipalities rose from twenty in 1920 to sixty-five in 1940; the increase in St. Louis County, Missouri, was from fifteen to forty-one.[80] During the 1920s, twenty-two additional suburbs secured municipal status in the Detroit area and twenty-nine in metropolitan Cleveland.[81] Moreover, there was a proliferation of special districts dedicated to providing a single service, such as water, street lighting, or fire protection. In Nassau County the number of special districts rose from 87 in 1920 to 173 in 1933. With a complex overlay of municipalities, townships, school districts, and special districts, the pattern of local government in suburbia was becoming unintelligible. "There are so many local jurisdictions that it was not possible to prepare a map of the county or even of one town showing local unit boundaries," reported one survey of Nassau County's government.[82]

The prospects for meaningful consolidation of this hodgepodge of units also seemed to be diminishing. From 1910 to 1940 the largest American cities found it increasingly difficult, if not impossible, to annex new territory and absorb the suburbs into one imperial city. Using the lure of its water supply, the city of Los Angeles was able to annex 356 square miles of thirsty territory between 1910 and 1927, but no other major hub was so successful in forcing consolidation.[83] Chicago suffered repeated rebuffs from suburbs dedicated to preserving their independence. Between 1909 and 1914, Evanston voters defeated a consolidation proposal, residents of Oak Park twice rejected annexation to Chicago, and Cicero did so in four separate elections. In 1926 voters in suburban St. Louis County defeated by a two-to-one margin a proposal to

unite with the city of St. Louis and form one giant municipality; eight years later suburbanites in Milwaukee County likewise
overwhelmingly rejected a scheme for consolidation with the city
of Milwaukee.[84] Even the city of Los Angeles did not always triumph. In 1923 a corps of movie stars united in a successful battle
to defeat annexation of Beverly Hills, and in both 1917 and 1924,
residents of Santa Monica decisively defeated proposals for union
with Los Angeles. Similarly, in 1920 and 1925 Burbank rejected
merger with Los Angeles, and in 1926 Alhambra's electorate did
so by a better than two-to-one margin.[85]

As public services improved in the suburbs, outlying residents
no longer had reason to join with the central city. The schools
of Shorewood and Shaker Heights were superior to those of Milwaukee and Cleveland, and paved streets, sewers, and piped water
were standard features of all but the poorest and least developed
suburban municipalities. In 1910 and 1922, Cleveland attempted to
absorb the middle-class suburb of Lakewood, but satisfied suburbanites vetoed the big city's plans to grow even bigger. "Lakewood
now provides ample school facilities, police, fire, city planning,
zoning, and sanitary protection to its inhabitants and uniformly
good street paving and improvements," argued suburban foes of
consolidation, and Lakewood "is ready, able and willing to enlarge
these facilities as population increases, according to a standard of
excellence which Cleveland cannot afford." Similarly, a newspaper in suburban West Allis, Wisconsin, warned, "Milwaukee ... is
faced with financial difficulties," and "with eyes of greed they look
upon West Allis and other suburbs to pay their obligations and in
return receive less service at a greater cost." An editor in the St.
Louis suburb of Webster Groves claimed his community "would
stand to gain absolutely nothing from" consolidation but only suffer an invasion of "saloons, soft drink parlors, pool rooms, dance
halls and this type of undesirable so-called amusements."[86] The
best suburbs offered exemplary services and a wholesome family

life; they saw no benefits from union with the cash-strapped, morally tainted central city.

By 1940, then, Americans were aware that suburbia was no longer a provisional stage that would eventually yield to absorption into the big city. The suburbs were here to stay, for the advantages of separation far outweighed the benefits of union. In suburbia each independent community could protect and preserve its own way of life without having to compromise with other fragments of metropolitan society. Scarsdale and Shaker Heights could fashion a perfect upper-middle-class lifestyle without interference from New York City and Cleveland. Cicero and Hamtramck were enclaves of an alternative morality that would suffer if subject to the raids of Chicago or Detroit police. South Gate and Bell Gardens residents could raise chickens and erect shacks, pursuing a lifestyle forbidden in Beverly Hills. And manufacturers in nearby Vernon enjoyed municipal rule tailored to their needs. In the automobile age as in earlier decades, American suburbia offered a rich diversity of landscapes and lifestyles. To preserve this diversity and protect the peculiar needs of each fragment, suburbanites were uniting to hold the central city at bay.

Post–World War II Suburbs

At the close of World War II, the United States embarked on a period of accelerated suburbanization, leading to the eventual dominance of suburbia in American life. In the postwar era, the Federal Housing Administration insured low-interest, long-term mortgages for millions of veterans, enabling an increasing number of Americans to buy a new house on the metropolitan fringe. Each year from 1947 through the 1950s the number of new housing starts remained above 1.2 million, peaking in 1950 at 1,952,000, more than twice the prewar high mark set in 1925. As housing construction boomed, the suburban population soared. The metropolitan population living outside central cities more than doubled from 35 million in 1950 to almost 76 million in 1970. In 1950, 41.5 percent of Americans living in metropolitan areas resided outside a central city. The United States was a predominantly urban nation. By 1960 this figure had risen to 48.6 percent, and in 1970 it was up to 54.2 percent. From the mid-1960s on, the majority of metropolitan Americans lived in the suburbs.

Meanwhile, the construction of limited access, multilaned freeways enhanced the mobility of auto-borne Americans, allowing them to commute farther from work and travel greater distances to shopping and entertainment. The Federal-Aid Highway Act of 1956 created the interstate highway system and provided federal funding for thousands of miles of outer belt expressways, which gradually became the main streets of metropolitan America. As people migrated outward so did businesses, clinging to the freeways and their interchanges like iron filings to a magnet.

The best-known symbol of postwar suburbanization was the Levittowns, giant housing subdivisions in New York, New Jersey, and Pennsylvania created by Levitt and Sons in the late 1940s and the 1950s. The first was the Long Island Levittown, a community of 17,447 mass-produced houses built between 1947 and 1951. Describing the breakneck pace of construction, *Time* magazine reported: "New houses rose faster than Jack ever built them; a new one was finished every 15 minutes." The result was rows of look-alike, four-room houses on 60-by-100-foot lots that sold originally for $6,990. Even after Levitt and Sons raised the price to $7,990, veterans could purchase a Levittown home for less than it cost to rent an apartment; the price of home ownership was only $58 a month with no down payment. "No longer must young married couples plan to start living in an apartment, saving for the distant day when they can buy a house," *Time* commented. "Now they can do it more easily than they can buy a $2,000 car on the installment plan."[87]

But Levittown was not open to all young married couples. Instead, Levitt and Sons restricted sales in the Long Island community to Caucasians only, fearing that racial integration would offend white customers. "We can solve a housing problem, or we can try to solve a racial problem," William Levitt argued, "but we cannot combine the two."[88] In 1957 the African American Myers family discovered the racial limits to the American dream when they moved into Levittown, Pennsylvania. Hundreds of people congregated outside their house, some of them throwing stones, and automobiles blowing their horns and playing their radios loudly drove by the Myers home in the middle of the night. State troopers had to be called in to disperse the crowds and protect the family.[89]

Though the Levittowns were the most famous postwar subdivisions, there were large-scale projects throughout the nation. South of Chicago, American Community Builders erected Park Forest, a development of 31,000 people living in garden apartments and single-family homes that sold for $12,500 to $14,000. Southern California's version of Levittown was Lakewood, located between Los Angeles and Long Beach. In early 1952 an Associated Press article described the new community: "Almost 8,000 homes have been completed by assembly-line methods [and] beans and sugar beets have been replaced by broad boulevards and quiet side streets, green lawns and frame homes."[90] Thousands of additional two- and three-bedroom, moderately priced houses rose in the bean fields, and by 1960 the city of Lakewood had more than 67,000 residents and covered seven square miles.

In one metropolitan area after another, suburban growth was transforming the countryside. North of Detroit the population of Oak Park increased sevenfold from 5,267 to 36,632 between 1950 and 1960; according to a Detroit newspaper, "Almost overnight thousands of new homes grew like mushrooms after a warm summer rain."[91] Nearby Livonia was home to 17,534 people in 1950 and 66,702 in 1960; in the mid-1950s its chamber of commerce labeled it "The Hottest Spot in America."[92] Compared with the Detroit suburb of Warren, however, Livonia appeared lukewarm. Warren recorded a rise in population from 727 in 1950 to 89,246 in 1960. Northwest of Chicago, subdivider Kimball Hill in the early 1950s laid out Rolling Meadows, a community of two- or three-bedroom ranch houses for working-class whites. Though dismissed by more affluent observers as "Meadow Ghetto," "Rolling Mudholes," and "Plywood City," Rolling Meadows realized the suburban dreams of many migrants from inner-city Chicago. "I can remember sitting out waiting to see the first touch of green that would be our front lawn; and until you've done that—you just haven't lived!" recalled one early resident.[93] Meanwhile in Southern California, Anaheim claimed to be "the fastest growing city in the fastest growing county in the nation," its population doubling from 1950 to January 1955, and then doubling again between January 1955 and December 1956.[94] In 1950 Anaheim was a small town of 14,556 residents; ten years later it was a city of 104,184 inhabitants.

Though the media focused on the giant subdivisions of moderately priced look-alike houses, growth was also pronounced in many of the older enclaves of upper-middle-class privilege. During the 1950s the population of elite Ladue soared 76 percent, in Chicago's north shore suburbs of Glencoe and Wilmette the rise was 50 percent and 56 percent, respectively, and the number of residents admitted to the posh confines of Scarsdale increased almost 37 percent. The great postwar wave of suburbanization was engulfing upper-crust retreats as well as mass-produced subdivisions, spawning thousands of custom-built manses and millions of look-alike boxes.

The popularity of postwar suburbia, however, was not universal. Even before World War II, intellectual elitists cast aspersions on the centrifugal migration, deeming it a threat to civilized life. As early as 1921 the urban commentator Lewis Mumford wrote of "The Wilderness of Suburbia," describing the commuter as "a spectacle much more humiliating than a man without a country; he is a man without a city—in short a barbarian."[95] But in the 1950s criticism rose to a shriller pitch. In his 1956 diatribe *The Crack in the Picture Window*, John Keats proclaimed, "whole square miles of identical boxes are spreading like gangrene"; these suburban subdivisions were "conceived in error, nurtured by greed, corroding everything they touch," and "breeding swarms of neuter drones."[96] Meanwhile, University of Chicago professor David Riesman emphasized the "homogenizing modes of thought and feeling" of suburban life and its "aimlessness, a pervasive low-keyed unpleasure."[97] In 1955 a clergyman deemed suburbia the judgment of a vengeful God: "Suburban domination may well be God's word of judgment upon us his church. For our trespasses and complacency we have been delivered to Babylon."[98] One of the constants of American life in the second half of the twentieth century was the disdain heaped upon suburbia by all manner of commentators who deplored its supposed homogeneity, dullness, and threat to nature and society. Yet at the same time millions of Americans were investing billions of dollars in suburban homes and finding happiness along the metropolitan fringe. Americans loved suburbia, but in the minds of many observers it was an illicit love that had produced a bastard culture.

This new suburban world not only included miles of homes, but was also the site of increasingly large shopping centers. Before World War II the central cities had dominated retailing, and downtown department stores were unequaled purveyors of a wide range of merchandise, but especially clothing and accessories. Suburbanites bought groceries in their residential communities and patronized the drug store closest to home, but prewar suburban shopping districts never rivaled the central city downtown. During the postwar decades, however, this rapidly changed as an increasing number of suburban shoppers abandoned downtown and satisfied their retailing needs along the metropolitan fringe. This change became apparent in the mid-1950s when a number of pioneering retail behemoths opened for business. Financed by Detroit's premier department store J. L. Hudson Company, the 100-store Northland Center opened in 1954 in the Detroit suburb of Southfield. It offered parking for 9,500 automobiles, and its three-story Hudson's anchor store sold a variety and quality of merchandise previously found only downtown. One observer described Northland as "a regional shopping center that transplant[ed] downtown to the suburbs," and in 1959 Southfield's enthusiastic city manager boasted that it had "more shopping area than downtown Flint, and more parking space than downtown Grand Rapids."[99]

Northland was just one among a multitude of shopping centers built during the 1950s and 1960s. The year 1956 proved especially fertile for suburban retail developers; real estate expert Homer Hoyt estimated that the months of September and October 1956 witnessed the opening of more shopping center space than the entire period from 1948 to September 1956.[100] Among the new centers produced that year was Roosevelt Field in Nassau County, an easy drive from the Long Island Levittown. It included a Macy's department store as well as 77 other retailers and 11,000 parking spaces. But the most innovative of the 1956 shopping centers was Southdale in Edina, Minnesota, a Minneapolis suburb. Whereas Northland and Roosevelt Field were open-air centers where shoppers had to brave the elements as they scurried between stores, Southdale was the first enclosed suburban mall, a climate-controlled retail refuge in frigid Minnesota. The mall's hub was a three-story garden court with fountains, tropical foliage, a twenty-one-foot cage containing eighty canaries, and a sidewalk café. In early 1957 a national magazine reported: "The strikingly handsome and colorful center is constantly crowded, and the builders' estimate of 20,000 customers a day already has been surpassed."[101]

The best of the shopping centers, however, were intended to be more than places to shop; they were to be new foci for a suburban America. Victor Gruen, the architect who designed both Northland and Southdale, envisioned his malls as "affording opportunities for social life and recreation in a protected pedestrian environment"; they could "provide the needed place and opportunity for participation in modern community life that the ancient Greek *Agora*, the Medieval Market Place and our own Town Squares provided in the past."[102] In coming decades the malls did become the place for teenagers to hang out, for senior citizens to walk for exercise, for youngsters to visit Santa Claus, and for everyone to pause over coffee and a snack in the food courts. For millions of Americans they supplanted the old downtowns as centers of buying and mingling.

Meanwhile, suburbia was also becoming a more attractive site for industry. After World War II a growing number of manufacturers sought to build sprawling single-floor plants that could accommodate assembly line production. Moreover, they needed plenty of parking for employees plus ample loading space and ready access to interstate highways for the trucks that carried an increasing share of their supplies and output. All this added up to a site in the wide-open spaces of the metropolitan fringe. Land in the crowded urban core was too expensive and too difficult to assemble for most postwar manufacturers. A cornfield on the edge of suburbia fit the bill, and that was where industry was moving.

At the same time, many residential suburbs were growing more receptive to manufacturing. With millions of children crowding suburban schools and armies of new residents demanding police and fire services, outlying communities needed additional tax revenues, but homeowners who struggled with mortgage payments sought to avoid any hike in tax rates. The solution was tax-rich industries. In 1956 the development plan for a Detroit suburb summed up the argument when it noted that new industry offered "the best prospect of increased tax base. More industry will help achieve a high level of municipal services without a proportionate increase in tax burden for the residential owner. Its benefit will be felt by every taxpayer."[103] Sugar-coating this remedy was the advent of industrial parks. As the name implied, these were tastefully landscaped tracts of light manufacturing that masked industry behind shrubbery and threatened residential property values as little as possible. In 1957 a Long Island publication claimed, "the industrial park ... promises to be a vital contributor in terms of greater employment opportunities and a more equitable sharing of local taxes. One of its chief attractions is that it need not clash aesthetically or otherwise with the existing suburban nature of Long Island's two Eastern Counties."[104] Through the development of industrial parks, suburbia could reap ample tax revenues without sacrificing the sylvan, low-density atmosphere so desired by many residents.

Not only was suburbia welcoming landscaped industrial parks but also sprawling corporate campuses. In the 1950s and 1960s, a growing number of corporations were opting for new headquarters in the suburbs, and many chose to locate in parklike campuses where the lawns, trees, and ample parking contrasted markedly with the abandoned headquarters in the congested central cities. In 1954 General Foods moved from Manhattan to a 46-acre estate in suburban Westchester County, thereby escaping the crowds, filth, and noise of the city. At the opening of the suburban headquarters the company's president informed employees: "We shall ... find ourselves working in a parklike setting and a more peaceful atmosphere with reduced nerve strain on everyone."[105] In succeeding years, others followed General Food's example, fleeing Manhattan for the suburbs. By 1967, for example, Pepsico was drafting plans for a headquarters on the former site of Blind Brook Polo Club, also in suburban Westchester, whereas American Can was negotiating a relocation to 228 acres in the wealthy suburb of Greenwich,

Connecticut.[106] Corporate executives favored suburban locations convenient to their homes, but major corporations also moved to suburbia to tap into the supply of educated middle-class women who could staff their offices. Suburban headquarters promised a shorter commute, a better labor pool, and supposedly a cleaner, less stressful environment.

By the 1960s corporate campuses were not the only signs of an outward migration of office employment. The central city downtown had traditionally been the unchallenged hub of the office sector; that was where executives, lawyers, accountants, and secretaries congregated each workday. But across America, the position of the downtown area was slipping. In suburban Clayton, Missouri, immediately west of St. Louis, high-rise office buildings rose during the 1960s creating a downtown skyline previously alien to suburbia. In 1968 a study by two urban geographers proclaimed Clayton "a new metropolitan focus in the St. Louis area" and "an urban sub-capital."[107] Meanwhile, in the Detroit metropolitan area, Southfield attracted the regional headquarters of major corporations and office towers appeared along the fringes of the booming Northland Shopping Center. By 1970 more people commuted from central city Detroit to work in Southfield than made the traditional commute from suburban Southfield to Detroit. In metropolitan Chicago, suburban Oak Brook was also gaining fame not only for its popular shopping mall, but also as a center for office employment. By the early 1970s it housed the world headquarters of the McDonald's fast-food chain and like Southfield, accommodated many regional corporate offices.

Throughout the United States suburbia was emerging as a 24-hour center of life and as a place where Americans worked and shopped as well as slept. Before World War II, industrial suburbs had provided jobs for millions of Americans, but during the postwar decades, suburbia's role as a hub of business was expanding. Already in 1972 the suburbs accounted for 55 percent of the retail sales in metropolitan New York, 60 percent in the Los Angeles area, and 74 percent in the Detroit region. For the fifteen largest metropolitan areas in the United States, suburbia's share of retail sales averaged 64 percent. That same year suburbia's share of manufacturing employment in these fifteen areas averaged 60 percent, with the metropolitan fringe accounting for over two-thirds of the factory jobs in metropolitan Boston, Pittsburgh, Baltimore, and Detroit. By 1978 the headquarters of 170 of the Fortune 500 corporations were in the suburbs, up from only 47 in 1965, and as of 1979 there were more head offices of large corporations in New York City's suburbs than in the city itself.[108]

Moreover, this outward migration of business and employment appeared to be accelerating, for the 1980s witnessed an unprecedented expansion of suburban office space and commercial development in general. In 1984 construction began on a 28-story office tower and 33-story apartment building in booming Southfield. By the close of the 1980s, Southfield had surpassed downtown Detroit as southeastern Michigan's premier office district. "As the hub of southeastern Michigan and the heart of the metropolitan area," the city's mayor boasted, "Southfield has it all."[109] Meanwhile, the Cumberland business node around the I-285 and I-75 interchange outside of Atlanta was becoming one of the major office centers of the South, rivaled by suburban Perimeter Center north of Atlanta. In 1988 a 31-story office high-rise opened in Perimeter Center and was soon joined by a twin tower of equal height. DuPage County, west of Chicago, was not impressed, for it boasted the newly built Oakbrook Terrace Tower, another 31-story monument to the suburban office sector. In suburban St. Louis County, office space more than doubled from 18 million square feet in 1980 to 45 million square feet in 1992. By the early 1990s the suburban county had almost 70 percent more occupied rentable office space than did the city of St. Louis's central business district. Although the county's population remained constant during the 1980s, the number of people employed within this suburban area soared 46 percent.[110]

Suburbia was even moving toward cultural independence. In 1986 the $73-million Orange County Performing Arts Center opened in suburban Costa Mesa, California, giving heavily populated, fast-growing Orange County its own cultural hub. "In population, commerce, education, and technological creativity, Orange County shed its role as a suburb of Los Angeles years ago," observed the *Los Angeles Times*. With the opening, however, Orange had "shed its role as a cultural suburb as well."[111] The *New York Times* architecture critic agreed when he pronounced the building of the performing arts center as "a kind of coming of age for far-flung American suburbs."[112]

By the close of the twentieth century, then, America's suburbs accounted for the bulk of metropolitan population and business, and were expanding into the realm of high culture. Southfield's mayor was only exaggerating slightly when he said his community had it all. The historic central cities were no longer central to the lives of millions of Americans, and one could live, shop, and work in Southfield and never cross the boundary into Detroit. More than a century and a half of migration had resulted in the triumph of suburbia and the creation of a suburban nation. Whereas in the nineteenth century railroads enabled middle-class residents and noxious or expansive industries to migrate outward, in the twentieth century, motor vehicles facilitated an accelerated centrifugal movement resulting in truck-dependent suburban plants, auto-oriented shopping malls, and rows of houses with projecting two- or three-car garages.

During both centuries the suburban landscape was diverse with mansions, shacks, and steel mills, as well as elegant estates. Given the opportunity, a broad range of Americans moved outward, investing their lives and money along the metropolitan fringe. Though the Federal Housing Administration and interstate highway system eased the outward flow, the dispersion of population and business predated these federal programs. Millions of Americans wanted their own homes with shrubbery and lawns in wholesome independent municipalities away from the central city. Others sought to raise chickens and vegetables on farmlets that were an easy commute from their factory jobs. And still others wanted to take advantage of suburban independence to build roadhouses replete with sinful pleasures or factories polluting the air and water but paying minimal taxes. There was no single suburban way of life. Instead, the green fields of suburbia offered diverse ways of life away from the restrictive authority of big-city assessors, health authorities, and police, and removed from the corruption, congestion, and stressful hubbub of the central city. The metropolitan frontier beckoned to millions of Americans who wished to stake out their own spheres. These suburban pioneers opted out of the big city, preferring the governmentally fragmented and socially dispersed pattern of life known as suburbia.

2
DIVERSE SUBURBIA

In his seminal 1925 study of suburbia, Harlan Douglass reported: "Suburbs so manifestly differ from one another that even the most generalized account of their character ... could not ignore the fact."[1] In the early twenty-first century Douglass's observation remains equally true. Suburbia was not a uniform, homogeneous realm in the 1920s, nor is it today. American suburbs of the twenty-first century include a wide range of communities, the poorest as well as the richest, the overwhelmingly white and the exclusively black. Some are old with most of their housing dating from before World War II; others are new, having sprouted thousands of freshly minted homes during the past two decades. They accommodate all manner of lifestyles, gay and straight, senior citizens as well as fertile families abundant with children. And they come in all sizes. Some suburban municipalities have a few hundred residents; others have a few hundred thousand. American suburbia is a varied expanse of habitation, a richly contrasting mosaic that corresponds to the diversity of contemporary American life.

First-Tier Suburbs

Prominent among the varied suburbs are the first-tier suburbs, older, inner-ring communities that largely developed before World War II or in the decade and a half immediately after, and which are built out with no further room for growth. During the late 1990s and first decade of the twenty-first century, this inner ring of suburbia attracted a good deal of attention from commentators who reported on its existing or anticipated decline and decay. In 1999 the federal Department of Housing and Urban Development (HUD) announced that "nearly 400 suburban jurisdictions in 24 states meet HUD's criteria of distress" because of population losses and high rates of poverty.[2] That same year the Fannie Mae Foundation commissioned a survey of urban specialists asking them to rank "the top 10 most likely influences on the American metropolis for the next 50 years"; among the ten most cited was "deterioration of the 'first-ring' post-1945 suburbs." "Many of these suburbs have aged badly," concluded the foundation's report, and were "too close to the central city and its problems."[3] In 2000, University of Virginia professors William Lucy and David Phillips published *Confronting Suburban Decline*, in which they identified "the period since 1980 as the era of suburban decline because of ... widespread deterioration."[4] And in 2002, Myron Orfield claimed that 40 percent of the residents of America's twenty-five largest metropolitan regions lived in "at-risk suburbs" that were "often more fragile than the [central city] communities they surround." Among these were 391 "at-risk older communities" characterized "by slow population growth (or decline), relatively meager local resources, and struggling commercial districts."[5] One after another the experts were diagnosing many of America's suburbs as seriously ill, and the social malady seemed to be spreading outward at an accelerating pace.

Faced with this purported onslaught of decline, some first-tier suburbs organized coalitions to further their interests. In 1996 the

First Suburbs Consortium of Northeast Ohio formed, dedicated to advancing the cause of sixteen inner suburbs of Cleveland. "What brings us together," explained the vice mayor of Cleveland Heights, "is the recognition that the older, established communities are not getting a fair deal. The state and federal governments subsidize the development of farmland at the edges, and that puts us in a very uncompetitive position."[6] Other older Ohio suburbs felt likewise, and the Cleveland group spawned a coalition of five inner suburbs of Columbus and another consortium of seventeen suburbs of Cincinnati. To the north the Michigan Suburbs Alliance composed of twenty-four cities was spreading a similar message. "We [try to stop] the cycle of build-and-abandon, and encourage rebuilding these older communities," the executive director of the alliance reported.[7] Meanwhile, in the Kansas City area, the First Suburbs Coalition organized, uniting communities that were "experiencing some of the same challenges that have plagued core cities, including businesses moving out and declining retail sales, increases in rental housing, stagnant or declining housing values, and issues related to maintaining their infrastructure."[8] These first suburbs were winning the attention of some politicians; in May 2005 Senator Hillary Clinton of New York introduced in Congress the Suburban Core Opportunity Restoration and Enhancement (SCORE) Act, which proposed a $250 million fund to aid older suburbs. "These communities face a number of challenges including minimal population growth, relatively large elderly populations, shrinking household incomes, and increasing rates and concentrations of poverty," announced Senator Clinton.[9]

Yet this wave of concern about troubled inner suburbs veils the fact that the first-tier communities are not all alike. Instead, the inner ring is a diverse zone encompassing the nation's social and economic extremes. Inner suburbs are not necessarily fragile; many are extraordinarily durable. In America's suburbs, age and proximity to the central city do not equate with decline. There is no consensus among Americans that older suburbs are obsolete, out-of-fashion, and best discarded. Some inner suburbs are troubled, exhibiting all the symptoms of social disaster. Others remain affluent and highly desirable, suffering from an embarrassment of riches. In his study of first-tier suburbs, William Hudnut correctly concluded, "possibly the most important generalization that can be made about them is that no generalization can be made about them."[10] A survey of contemporary first-tier suburbs reveals scores of distressed communities as well as an equal number of suburbs that are holding up well.

One prime example of a poor and often troubled inner suburb is Chelsea, Massachusetts. Located immediately north of Boston, Chelsea was basically built out as early as 1930 when its population reached nearly 46,000. By 2000 its 35,000 residents were tightly packed within the city's 1.8 square miles, producing a population density of 19,400 people per square mile, more than 50 percent greater than Boston's density of 12,200 per square mile. Approximately half of Chelsea's population was Hispanic, and 39 percent of its residents were born outside the United States. These newcomers crowded into rental units; the 2000 census found that 20 percent of all Chelsea renters lived in overcrowded units (one or more persons per room), and the city's community development plan of 2004 reported that some cost-conscious immigrants lived ten to twelve people per apartment.[11] In 1999 the city's median household income was only $30,200 compared to the Massachusetts median of $50,500, and 20.6 percent of Chelsea families lived below the poverty line, three times the Massachusetts figure of 6.7 percent. Chelsea had, therefore, the demographics of an urban slum: It was poor, crowded, and disproportionately foreign born.

Moreover, Chelsea's recent past has earned it notoriety as a troubled community. In 1991 the city became the first Massachusetts municipality since the 1930s to be placed in receivership. Basically, the state took control of the bankrupt community. Exercising near-dictatorial powers, the state-appointed receiver was responsible to the governor not to the local electorate. In effect, Massachusetts suspended Chelsea's local rule.[12] Earlier in 1989 the Chelsea School Committee had also admitted defeat when it asked Boston University to assume management of the community's schools. In a unique arrangement, the failed public officials invited a private university to take charge of the troubled and poorly performing public school system. Chelsea was an extraordinary example of the collapse of all aspects of local government.

By the first decade of the twenty-first century, Chelsea's fortunes were improving. It emerged from receivership in 1995, and Boston University's oversight seemed to produce positive results in the public schools.[13] Yet Chelsea's experience was a vivid reminder that older suburbs could suffer the most humiliating fate.

Chelsea certainly is not an anomaly among early twenty-first-century American suburbs. In the Pittsburgh region the old industrial suburbs have lost their manufacturing base and seem doomed to irreversible decay. By 2004 eight of the suburbs in Pittsburgh's Allegheny County were officially designated by the state of Pennsylvania as fiscally distressed and thus requiring special aid. Owing to deindustrialization, Rankin, Duquesne, Clairton, East Pittsburgh, McKeesport, Neville Island, and Braddock had all lost 50 percent of their property tax base since 1980. In the early twentieth century Rankin, a hub of tax-rich industry in the eastern suburbs of Pittsburgh, claimed to be the wealthiest municipality in the United States; by the early twenty-first century it was among the poorest, having already spent more than ten years on the distressed list.[14] Its manufacturing based decimated, Rankin had to rely more heavily on residential property for revenues, but in 2000 the median value of its owner-occupied housing was only $25,700 as compared to a median of $119,600 for the nation as a whole. In 1999 its median household income was $13,382, less than one-third of the national median; 40.2 percent of the families lived below the poverty line. Because of its poor tax base and continuing service demands, Rankin's tax burden was heavy. In 2004 the combined municipal and school district millage in Rankin was the second highest of 128 municipalities in Allegheny County.

In nearby communities the situation was almost as bad, with municipal authorities skimping on services to save money. "Right now, the police department is at an all-time low," a Homestead homeowner complained in 2004. "I would like to see drug enforcement better. The drug dealing is out of hand." "Can you imagine the city of McKeesport with no police department?" asked McKeesport's mayor. "We are dangerously close to having that happen."[15] In 2004 the only Allegheny County municipality with a millage rate higher than Rankin's was Wilkinsburg, an aging inner suburb of 19,000 residents that displayed all the symptoms of terminal decline. "At any given time," reported the mayor, "there's about 500 abandoned houses in Wilkinsburg." Many of the remaining occupied dwellings had fallen on hard times. "We had more homeowners in the sixties than now," the city council vice president observed. "Those houses have been broken up into apartments by slumlords who don't keep properties up."[16]

Equally dismal examples of first-tier suburban distress blight the Cleveland and Detroit metropolitan areas. Predominantly poor and black, the suburban municipality of East Cleveland resembles a stereotypical ghetto rather than the middle-class suburb of popular mythology. In 2000, 32 percent of its population fell below the poverty line, and it had the highest rate of residents on public assistance of any community in Cleveland's Cuyahoga County, including the much-distressed city of Cleveland itself. East Cleveland's rate of birth to teenagers was twice that of the county as a whole, as was its rate of infant mortality. Though in 2000 East Cleveland accounted for only 3 percent of Cuyahoga County's suburban population, in 1999 it was the site of 27 percent of all the county's suburban violent crimes.[17] In the 2003–2004 school year, the East Cleveland school district met only five of the state's eighteen indicators of adequate academic achievement and recorded a graduation rate of 54 percent as compared to the state average of 84 percent.[18]

Surrounded by the city of Detroit, the municipality of Highland Park is unchallenged as the most troubled inner suburb in Michigan. As the site of Henry Ford's first mass production plant, Highland Park boomed as an industrial suburb between 1910 and 1930, but its population plummeted from a high of 53,000 in 1930 to 16,700 in 2000. Exacerbating problems was the concurrent decline in its tax base. In 1995 the Chrysler Corporation closed its plant in Highland Park, transferring operations to the outer suburb of Auburn Hills. With Chrysler went Highland Park's source of revenue. Between 1990 and 2000 the taxable value of property in Highland Park dropped a staggering 58 percent (Auburn Hills's taxable value soared 209 percent), and at the beginning of the twenty-first century the once-great industrial suburb had the lowest taxable value per capita of any community in southeast Michigan.[19] Destitute, in 2001 Highland Park became a ward of the state under the control of a state-appointed emergency financial manager. According to a report to Michigan's governor, "During the first year under the Emergency Financial Manager, painful steps were taken to stem the financial hemorrhage. City services were slashed, payless paydays occurred and numerous previously unidentified debts, liabilities and other financial problems were uncovered."[20] The birthplace of mass production was suffering the worst pangs of deindustrialization.

To the west the St. Louis area also has its share of suburban disasters. Dropping in population from 82,295 in 1950 to 31,542 in 2000, East St. Louis, Illinois, grew increasingly poor and black during the last half of the twentieth century. In the process it attracted inordinate scholarly attention as a classic example of decay. Despite the introduction of casino gambling intended to boost the local economy, in the first decade of the twenty-first century its vacant lots and abandoned housing remained grim monuments to the decline of the industrial Midwest. On the Missouri side of the Mississippi River, the smaller inner suburb of Wellston attracted less nationwide notoriety but was equally blighted. Between 1950 and 2000 it lost three-quarters of its population, a fall from 9,396 to 2,460. At the beginning of the twenty-first century, more than one-third of its remaining families lived in poverty, and charitable house building by Habitat for Humanity seemed to be the community's leading enterprise.

Even in sunny Southern California prognosticators of inner suburban decline can find ample evidence to support their dreary views. Poverty is especially common in the Gateway Cities region south of Los Angeles, a suburban expanse comprising twenty-seven cities and 1.7 million residents. Yet abandonment and desertion are not characteristic of the Gateway Cities. Instead, the region's poorest suburbs are crowded with immigrants from Latin America. In 2001, a region leader observed: "In many ways the Gateway Cities Region is the social laboratory of the United States encompassing as it does many of the urban challenges such as a large immigrant population, poorly performing schools, decaying urban centers and the flight of skilled and knowledgeable people."[21] One of the Gateway Cities is the working-class bedroom community of Maywood. With 28,000 people crammed into its 1.2 square miles, it is the most densely populated city in California with a population density twice that of Chicago, Philadelphia, and Boston; among major American cities, only New York City is more densely populated, but not by much. According to the 2000 census, it was 96 percent Hispanic and 92 percent of the population spoke a language other than English at home. Moreover, its per capita income was less than half the median for the United States as a whole. Maywood is not a discarded industrial suburb like Rankin or Highland Park.

Rather it is a way station for low-income immigrants with large families seeking a better life in Southern California.

From Massachusetts to California, then, America's inner suburbs have not been spared the problems of deindustrialization, immigration, and general social decay. The list of troubled suburbs is long, and many of the first-tier communities unquestionably deviate from suburban stereotypes. They are not middle-class realizations of the American dream. Highland Park and East St. Louis are American nightmares, but their story is not a tale of riches to rags, of mansions to tenements. In their heyday the most distressed communities had not been wealthy residential enclaves or retreats for the upper middle class. Wellston, East St. Louis, Highland Park, Rankin, and Chelsea developed as working-class communities, but had slipped toward the welfare class by the beginning of the twenty-first century. Among the not-so-affluent Gateway Cities are South Gate and Bell Gardens, suburbs that before World War II accommodated refugees from the Great Plains Dust Bowl in self-built shacks. In the early twenty-first century their bungalows are home to a new round of migrants, Latin Americans seeking to improve their economic condition. Many suburbs are troubled, but there have always been troubles in suburbia.

Yet the distressed first-tier suburbs tell only half the story. For every poor inner suburb there is a golden enclave from the past that survives and demonstrates remarkable durability. Some of America's oldest suburbs are among its wealthiest, and they still attract successful strivers willing to pay top dollar for a home in a prestigious suburb.

This is evident in Massachusetts where Brookline boasts of being the nation's oldest suburb yet is also home to many of the region's elite. Four miles west of downtown Boston and bordered on three sides by the central city, Brookline was already a commuter destination prior to the Civil War and was a mature suburb by the close of World War II. Its population peaked at 59,000 in

1970, but despite a slight drop in the number of residents it remains a strong and viable municipality. Its ten-year plan adopted in 2005 described Brookline's "tax base and financial management [as] among the strongest in the state." It was "one of only 12 Massachusetts communities with a bond rating of Aaa from Moody's, the highest rating possible," and it boasted the fifth-highest total property value of any municipality in the state. According to the confident plan, "Affluent, 'revenue-rich' Brookline can afford high-quality services."[22] Though a majority of the population lives in apartment buildings, there are many costly homes. In 2004, Brookline ranked second in median single-family home price among the 161 municipalities in the Boston metropolitan region, its median figure being an impressive $975,000.[23] The ten-year plan observed: "Brookline's location close to Boston, its excellent public schools, and its overall high quality of life make it one of the country's most expensive communities." Regretfully, it added, "it has become a truism that many of Brookline's current residents could not afford today to purchase their own homes."[24]

Bordering both Brookline and Boston, the city of Newton is another example of a community that has gained in value as it aged. In 2000, 56 percent of its housing stock was over 60 years old; 81 percent had been standing over 40 years. Yet it too was an expensive community with a median single-family home price in 2004 of $691,400. Moreover, its estimated median household income for that year was almost three times that of Chelsea.[25] In 2001 a planning report concluded that Newton offered "few housing opportunities for any other than comfortably affluent households." In marked contrast to the crowded immigrant communities of Chelsea and Maywood it was "a city of mostly large homes serving mostly small households." Also unlike less fortunate inner suburbs, it maintained "an exemplary standard of education" that was "a central component of the City's attractiveness as a place in which to live."[26]

Even among the politically mobilized first suburbs of Ohio many communities hardly qualify as distressed. Leading the central Ohio consortium are the affluent suburbs of Bexley and Upper Arlington, both built out, but also both among the most prestigious addresses in the Columbus metropolitan region. Though joined in combat with East Cleveland for more resources from the state and federal governments, Bexley and Upper Arlington in 1999 enjoyed median household incomes more than three times that of the benighted Cleveland suburb. Whereas in the 2003–2004 school year East Cleveland schools met only five of the eighteen indicators specified by the state department of education, equally aged Bexley's exemplary schools satisfied all eighteen criteria, outperforming even central Ohio's elite outer suburb of Dublin.[27] Similarly, among the members of the southwest Ohio consortium are well-to-do Wyoming and Montgomery, and the mid-nineteenth-century retreat of Glendale. After more than a century and a half, hardy Glendale is still holding its own. In 1999 its median household income was also more than three times that of East Cleveland and nearly 70 percent higher than the national median, and the median value of its homes was almost double the national figure. Further west one of the mobilized Kansas City first-tier suburbs is elite Mission Hills; in 1999 it had a median household income more than four times the national figure and a median home value nearly five times that of the nation. In 2005 the community's proud mayor referred to the average Mission Hills home as worth $800,000, and the city's website proclaimed, "a place as beautiful as Mission Hills is hard to leave."[28] Anyone born on the wrong side of the tracks in Columbus or Kansas City would likely turn a deaf ear to the plaints of Bexley, Upper Arlington, and Mission Hills. By the standards of most Americans they are not suffering.

Elsewhere in the country other durable first-tier suburbs are aging gracefully and in many cases very profitably. Chicago's north shore suburbs of Winnetka, Wilmette, and Glencoe peaked in population in 1970, but during the succeeding four decades they have grown increasingly elite. In 2004 the *Chicago Tribune* reported that home prices in these suburbs had "more than doubled in the last 10 years, easily outstripping the growth of housing costs in the wider Chicago area .... The towns, which historically housed those with middle and upper incomes, are becoming affordable only to the wealthy."[29] Like Wellston only three miles to the north, Clayton, Missouri, hugs the western perimeter of the city of St. Louis and was built out by the beginning of World War II. There the similarities end. With seven million square feet of first-class office space and some of the wealthiest residents and most expensive homes in the St. Louis area, Clayton is a twenty-first-century success, socially and economically a world apart from its depressed northern neighbor. On the west coast the municipality of Beverly Hills surrounded by the central city of Los Angeles, was largely developed by 1950. Yet in the twenty-first century it is as much a symbol of opulence and riches as it was in the 1930s and 1940s. In September 2005 sixteen homes in the Beverly Hills zip code of 90210 sold at a median price of $2,334,000.[30]

A prime example of an old durable suburb that has survived in a highly fragile metropolitan environment is Grosse Pointe, Michigan. Located about seven miles from both downtown Detroit and distressed Highland Park, Grosse Pointe has survived unscathed amid the ruins of Motor City deindustrialization. Though a majority of its housing dates from before 1940, it is the residence of families with six-figure incomes and homes to match. In 1999 its median household income was more than four times that of Highland Park, and its median housing value was more than five times the Highland Park figure. The Grosse Pointe Master Plan for 2003 noted, "the community has undergone relatively minor changes" since the previous master plan was adopted in 1976.[31] The same could not be said of neighboring Detroit or Highland Park. During a quarter century of marked decline in the industrial hubs of southeast Michigan, Grosse Pointe remained a serene enclave of stability. The serenity of some older first-tier suburbs has been disturbed, however, by too much economic success. Rather than being undesirable cast-offs, these communities have become too desirable, attracting wealthy purchasers who clear older homes and replace them with larger, more up-to-date and ostentatious dwellings. This teardown phenomenon swept through many inner suburbs in the 1990s and is continuing at a seemingly accelerated pace in the twenty-first century. An address in these first-tier suburbs is so sought after, that buyers with deep pockets are willing to purchase an expensive house just to obtain the lot, and then pay for clearance of the valuable land for the construction of an even more expensive structure. Neighbors complain about the bulky mansions arising next door making their homes look small and destroying the architectural harmony of the neighborhood. But the teardown trend is the ultimate indicator of the desirability of inner suburbs to those with the most money.

The Boston area has seen its share of teardowns. Each year during the early 1990s the Historical Commission of Newton reviewed about twenty to thirty requests to demolish structures. In the early twenty-first century it has faced more than one hundred demolition requests per year.[32] Elite Wellesley to the west of Newton witnessed 201 demolitions between 1999 and 2004 and the construction of 189 replacement houses. These new dwellings were on average 2.5 to 3 times larger than the houses they replaced. In 2001 the average new home in the United States was 2,265 square feet; the average replacement house in Wellesley was 4,978 square feet. This *mansionization* of Wellesley has stirred animosity among existing residents who fear that they might be priced out of the community and resent the outsized structures overshadowing their homes and destroying green space by covering too large a share of the lot. A 2004 survey conducted for the 2005 to 2015 update of Wellesley's comprehensive plan found that the second-highest priority of town residents was to "enact restrictions on single-family home size to maintain neighborhood character."[33]

In the Midwest, the Chicago area leads in the number of teardowns as many of the older suburbs are scenes of real estate bonanzas. The western suburb of Hinsdale is the teardown capital; between 1986 and 2004 there were 1,300 teardowns in the community, and by the latter year more than one-fourth of Hinsdale's single-family housing stock was replacement structures. "Five years ago homes were at the $1 million level," one Hinsdale real estate agent commented in 2004. "Today most seem to be at $2 million." Moreover, she noted, "whereas in the past, homes valued at $200,000 to $500,000 were considered teardowns, lately $1 million homes are coming down."[34] In the process, much of the community's history seemed to be disappearing. Commenting in 2002 on the destruction in Hinsdale, the National Trust for Historic Preservation claimed: "Approximately half of the homes torn down were historic, including 19th-century Victorians, Sears 'kit houses,' Prairie-style bungalows and Tudor Revival homes designed by local architects."[35] Along the north shore, teardowns are also commonplace. For example, in 2003 fifty-nine houses in Wilmette were destroyed.[36] A planner in neighboring Winnetka complained: "A certain amount of change is inevitable, I know, but you get too many teardowns and you start losing the character of your community."[37]

Just as dramatic is the teardown trend in Dallas's upscale inner suburbs of Highland Park and University Park. Developed as upper-middle-class havens in the early twentieth century and surrounded by the city of Dallas, the two Park Cities have survived as elite enclaves that have progressed from rich to richer. Highland Park especially has been synonymous with wealth and power in the Dallas area. Equally aged and equally close to their central city downtowns, the Texas and Michigan Highland Parks stand at opposite ends of the economic and social spectrum, exemplars of the diversity of America's suburban first tier. Attracted by the snob appeal and quality environment of the Park Cities, wealthy Texans have torn down older mansions and replaced them with newer and larger mansions. From 1989 through 2003, 420 teardowns were approved in Highland Park, a community of 2,600 homes, and from 1994 through 2003 there were 970 teardowns in University Park, equal to one-fifth of that suburb's houses.[38] In 2002 the *Dallas Morning News* architecture critic reported that "the Park Cities streets are rapidly filling up with bloated, Big Hair houses that are too big for their lots but not, unfortunately, for an overheated real estate market."[39] The following year an official of the National Trust for Historic Preservation observed: "What is happening in the Park Cities is truly alarming. From what we know, that area has the most intensive tear-down activity of anywhere we've seen in the country."[40] Created in 2000, Preservation Park Cities was organized to halt the bulldozers, builders, and purportedly tasteless homeowners. But in 2001, University Park's building and zoning administrator expressed the economic realities facing the communities. "People have to pay such a premium for the lot, they have to maximize the house they put on it to justify the cost."[41]

Wealthy communities have grappled with teardowns, passing restrictions on the bulk and height of replacement houses and adopting demolition delay ordinances to give officials time to determine if threatened structures have historical or architectural significance and can be saved. Organizations like Preservation Park Cities have mobilized to save the physical fabric of inner suburbs. Possibly they will succeed and the teardown trend may prove a transitory phenomenon in suburban history. It is, however, a revealing trend that illuminates the divergent fates of inner suburbs. Both Highland Park, Texas, and Highland Park, Michigan, have suffered destruction of their early-twentieth-century built environment. In the case of the Texas city, excessive demand has led to destruction; in Michigan an absence of demand has doomed the city's abandoned buildings. In the early twenty-first century a first-tier suburb may be palatial or a pariah. It may be a magnet for wealth or a near vacuum accommodating impoverished remnants. As William Hudnut has recognized, no generalizations apply.

The Ethnic Diversity of Suburbia

Ethnic generalizations also do not apply. According to the long-standing stereotype, suburbia is an all-white, Anglo community where everyone looks alike and prefers to keep it that way. Yet this has never been an accurate picture, and in the twenty-first century it contrasts sharply with reality. Between 1990 and 2000 the minority share of America's suburban population rose from 18 percent to 25 percent, with the black suburban population rising 38 percent, the number of Hispanic suburbanites soaring 72 percent, and suburban Asians up 82 percent. The zone beyond the central city limits houses a rich ethnic mix, often more diverse than many disproportionately black central cities. Just as suburbia includes the rich and poor, it also accommodates every shade of skin, religious predilection, and immigrant culture.

African Americans are well represented among the new suburbanites. By 2000 39 percent of all blacks living in metropolitan areas with populations exceeding 500,000 resided in suburbia.[42] Many of these live in relatively impoverished older suburbs, black enclaves of poor and working-class residents who have inherited the well-worn, discarded communities of whites. The first-tier suburbs of East Cleveland, Ohio, Highland Park, Michigan, East St. Louis, Illinois, and Wellston, Missouri, are all poor and over 90 percent African American. Such suburbs as Mount Vernon, New York; East Orange and Irvington, New Jersey; and Lauderdale Lakes and Opa-locka, Florida, are also examples of predominantly black reservations accommodating the poor and those one step above poverty. Throughout the United States suburban ghettos perpetuate the American traditions of racial segregation and economic want.

Suburban blacks, however, are not confined to African American enclaves or scattered pockets of poverty. In some metropolitan areas, African Americans occupy large swaths of suburbia that include both decaying impoverished neighborhoods and freshly minted subdivisions marketed to the affluent. The nation's largest predominantly black suburban realm is Prince George's County, Maryland, north and east of Washington, DC, with a population of 826,000 in 2004, of whom two-thirds or 542,000 were African Americans. Hugging the border of the District of Columbia, many older Prince George's neighborhoods are little more than extensions of the capital's ghetto, with many problems and few opportunities. But beyond the Capital Beltway, the outer county is the home of more successful African Americans who can afford new four-bedroom, three-bath manses and who demand first-rate schools. Reporting on this mecca for the black upper middle class, the *New York Times* has described the county's Woodmore subdivision as "a predominantly black gated community ... with private security, town houses, sprawling estates and a golf course." Other nearby golf communities and subdivisions with curving lanes and well-sodded lawns also accommodate black suburbanites buying into the American dream. Prince George's, in fact, has been viewed as the fulfillment of black aspirations. "For black people, we are talking about the last frontier—political and economic power," the African American county executive has proudly proclaimed. For him, Prince George's County is the "jewel in the crown of the American post-civil rights era."[43] In suburbia, African Americans have finally triumphed.

Another black-majority suburban county is Clayton County, Georgia, on the south side of the Atlanta metropolitan area. Sixty percent of its 2004 estimated population of 268,000 was African

American. Though on the average less affluent than Prince George's, Clayton still offers many moderate and middle-income blacks a stereotypical suburban lifestyle in post–World War II detached dwellings with yards and space to raise children. And it offers political power with blacks constituting a majority of the board of county commissioners during the first decade of the twenty-first century.

To the south the city of Miami Gardens, Florida, is further evidence that African American suburbia no longer consists simply of small, anomalous pockets of black life. Incorporated in 2003, Miami Gardens is a municipality of 105,000 residents, about one-third the size of the central city of Miami. In 2004, 79 percent of its residents were African American as well as its mayor and all of its city council members. With an African American population equal to that of the central city, Miami Gardens can justifiably boast of being "the heart of Black Miami."[44] African Americans in Miami-Dade County have long chafed under the dominance of whites of Cuban birth or ancestry. With the creation of Miami Gardens, however, African Americans declared their independence from Cuban rule, claiming a major segment of the county's turf as their domain. Incorporation as a black-majority suburban municipality ensured that South Florida's African American heart would be ruled by blacks. Yet Miami Gardens is not an off-the-beaten-track enclave that few whites ever enter. It is the site of the Miami Dolphins professional football stadium, where the 2003 World Series champion Florida Marlins baseball team also plays. As such, Miami Gardens is a destination for hundreds of thousands of sports fans from throughout the region. Populous, independent, and a destination for people of all ethnic backgrounds, the new city of Miami Gardens clearly testifies to the major presence of African Americans on the South Florida suburban scene.

Suburban blacks have not only congregated in predominantly African American jurisdictions. Some suburban communities have accommodated both blacks and whites for a number of years without suffering massive white flight or rapid racial turnover. As early as the mid-1950s, black families began moving into the upper-middle-class Cleveland suburb of Shaker Heights, and by 1970 African Americans constituted nearly 15 percent of the community's residents. Yet local community associations and city authorities endeavored to ensure that Shaker Heights neighborhoods remained attractive to whites as well as blacks. Thus the racial balance has shifted only gradually with the black share approaching 25 percent in 1980 and reaching 34 percent in 2000. To the north, the suburb of Cleveland Heights has also promoted integrated living, experiencing incremental increases in the black population but no wholesale racial turnover. In 1980, 25 percent of the residents were black; by 2000 this was up to 42 percent. But from 1990 to 2000, the suburb's African American population actually inched upward a mere 4 percent. This contrasted markedly with adjacent East Cleveland, which during the 1960s and 1970s turned quickly from a white lower-middle-class suburb to an overwhelmingly black community deemed by whites as an irredeemable slum. Both Shaker Heights and Cleveland Heights have forestalled such a transformation, achieving a level of ethnic diversity and relative stability in defiance of the American tradition of racial separation.

Oak Park, Illinois, however, is the preeminent example of a suburb dedicated to maintaining diversity. Just beyond the western limits of Chicago, the middle-class suburb developed during the late nineteenth and early twentieth centuries and claimed among its distinctions the home, and many of the creations, of famed architect Frank Lloyd Wright, as well as the boyhood residence of novelist Ernest Hemingway. Yet by 1970, Oak Park was clearly in the path of outward black migration. Already Chicago's west side was a black ghetto, and Oak Parkers did not wish a similar fate for their community. Consequently, they embarked on a policy of welcoming African American newcomers while also seeking to retain white residents. To deter white flight, the suburb banned the blockbusting and panic peddling techniques of real estate agents, and forbid "for sale" signs, which in large numbers might cause a selling stampede by white homeowners. Moreover, in 1978 the municipal government created the Equity Assurance Program "to insure the single-family residences in the village of Oak Park against the possibility of economic loss, and thereby help to eliminate irrational fears of racial change."[45] If after five years their homes sold at a lower price than originally valued, homeowners who participated in the program were guaranteed a reimbursement of 80 percent of their loss. In other words, the village insured against loss owing to racial transition, thus assuaging fears that black neighbors would depress property values.

The Oak Park Housing Center also steered blacks away from neighborhoods that seemed in danger of becoming all black, and encouraged them to disperse throughout the suburb. The housing center's work was widely publicized, and in 2005 its newsletter boasted, "we are viewed as a model by other communities seeking to maintain racial diversity."[46] And its efforts seem to have succeeded. "Now," remarked one Oak Parker at the beginning of the twenty-first century, "there are no racially identifiable areas in the village, no pockets that are all black or all white."[47]

Reinforcing this commitment to ethnic mixing is the Diversity Statement adopted by the Oak Park village president and board of trustees in 2003. "We reject the notion of race as a barrier dividing us and we reject prejudicial behavior towards any group of people," the statement reads. "We believe residency in this Village should be open to anyone interested in sharing our benefits and responsibilities."[48] Census data testify to this commitment; Oak Park's black population has increased gradually from 11 percent of the village total in 1980 to 22 percent in 2000. Thus, as African Americans have moved in, whites have not packed their bags and left town en masse. Oak Park has progressed successfully toward its carefully regulated goal of suburban diversity.

Shaker Heights, Cleveland Heights, and Oak Park are all old, first-tier suburbs, developed before World War II and adjacent to the central city. Yet some of the nation's newer, booming suburban areas also include thousands of African American residents. Gwinnett County, Georgia, east of Atlanta, is a preeminent example of seemingly unrelenting suburban sprawl, having soared from 32,000 residents in 1950 to 700,000 in 2004. It ranked as one of America's fastest growing counties during the 1990s, doubling in population between 1990 and 2004. It is a land of giant shopping malls and myriad housing subdivisions, but in 2004 it was also the home of more than 120,000 African Americans who constituted nearly 18 percent of the county's population. During the 2005–2006 school year, 25 percent of its public school students were black, whereas 42 percent were non-Hispanic white.

Another suburban giant is Aurora, Colorado, a community whose population soared from 11,000 in 1950 to 292,000 in 2004. A 1999 University of Michigan study designated Aurora as "the most integrated city in the United States, beating out 106 other big cities." In 2001 blacks constituted 14 percent of Aurora's population and the figure was slowly rising. Its mayor boasted, "We are trying to make diversity a source of strength …. Ours is a nationally recognized effort." One Aurora resident observed: "I feel sorry for people who live in all-black or all-white neighborhoods because they don't know what they're missing."[49]

Moreno Valley, California, east of Los Angeles in booming Riverside County, also proclaims its diversity. Twenty years after its 1984 incorporation, this young community had a population of 165,000, with African Americans accounting for 19 percent of the residents. Its Community and Economic Development Department describes Moreno Valley as "a solidly, middle class, growing community populated by a diverse population of young families who are living in an environment that is becoming increasingly safe and prosperous."[50] Moreno Valley claims, then, to be the suburban dream, safely and securely accommodating black families as well as Hispanics who constitute 38 percent of the population, and white Anglos making up 32 percent of the Moreno Valley ethnic mix.

Aggregate figures for suburban jurisdictions, however, can be misleading. Though thousands of blacks are living in diverse suburbs, not all of them are living next door to whites. For example, University City, Missouri, is an older middle-class, first-tier suburb of St. Louis that has maintained a relatively stable racial composition, with blacks constituting 43 percent of the population in 1980, 48 percent in 1990, and 45 percent in 2000. The presence of large numbers of African Americans has not triggered a mass white exodus from the community, as it did in adjacent Wellston. For decades it has been a biracial community, but it is also largely segregated in its housing patterns. Its *Comprehensive Plan* for 1999 reported that in 1980, 75.7 percent of the residents north of Olive Boulevard were African American, and by 1998 this was up to 89.0 percent whereas 3.2 percent of those south of Delmar Boulevard were black in 1980 and 6.5 percent in 1998.[51] In other words, the north side of University City was black and the south side was white, and during the last decades of the twentieth century this pattern did not change. University City as a whole was racially diverse, but many of its neighborhoods were not.

Moreover, University City is not an anomaly. Throughout the United States many suburban blacks live in majority-black neighborhoods. In 2000 in the Newark and Miami metropolitan areas, 60 percent of suburban blacks lived in majority-black neighborhoods; in the Atlanta and Cleveland metropolitan areas the figure was 56 percent, and in the St. Louis area it was 55 percent.[52] In American suburbia, racial diversity does not necessarily imply integrated living.

American suburbia is not simply black and white. Since the 1960s a marked influx of immigrants from Latin America and Asia has enriched the ethnic mix of the nation as a whole and the suburbs in particular. A study issued in 2003 reported that for the first time since the mid-nineteenth century, more immigrants lived in outlying metropolitan Chicago than in the central city itself. Moreover, in twelve of the nation's twenty largest metropolitan areas, more immigrants were locating in the suburbs than in the central city.[53] By the beginning of the twenty-first century, 50 percent of Hispanics living in metropolitan areas with populations exceeding 500,000 resided in the suburbs. The figure for Asians was 55 percent.[54] Unlike the immigrants of the past, they were not huddled in inner-city tenements. Instead, some of the poorest were crowded into converted suburban garages, whereas the more successful were purchasing suburban homes equal to those of long-established Anglos.

Nowhere in the nation did suburbia have such a Latin flavor as in the Miami metropolitan area where in 2000, Hispanics accounted for 56 percent of the suburban population.[55] In 2000 Miami-Dade County's second largest city, Hialeah, with 226,000 residents was 90 percent Hispanic and 72 percent foreign born; 93 percent of Hialeah residents spoke a language other than English at home. Nearby Hialeah Gardens was equally Hispanic with 96 percent of its residents speaking a language other than English. Hialeah Gardens has, however, bought into the American suburban stereotype; its 2005 newsletter advertises in both English and Spanish that the community is "an ideal place to raise a family." As evidence of this, the city sponsored a Halloween Haunted House and Great Easter Egg Hunt where children could get their picture taken with the Easter Bunny.[56] Both Hialeah and Hialeah Gardens are working or lower-middle-class communities, but South Florida's upwardly mobile Cubans also found homes in posh suburbs. In elegant Coral Gables, where the per capita income was more than double the national figure, 47 percent of the residents in 2000 were Hispanic and 57 percent spoke a language other than English at home.

The suburbs of Los Angeles are almost equally Hispanic; in 2000, 45 percent of Los Angeles area suburbanites were Latino.[57] Hispanics inhabit virtually every suburban area in Southern California but some communities are almost wholly Latin. The Gateway Cities region is majority Hispanic, and not only is Maywood more than 90 percent Latino but so are the nearby communities of Bell, Bell Gardens, Cudahy, Huntington Park, and South Gate. Poor and crowded, these suburbs are the first stop for many Latino newcomers striving for a higher standard of living. "There is a lot more room for the kids to play back home in Guadalajara, but there is no work," explained one member of a nine-person family sharing a two-bedroom apartment in Maywood. "We are better off here. We have enough to eat." Maywood's planning director explained: "It is futile to try to enforce laws against overcrowding. When we go to a house and see six adults living in one room, they say, 'We are just visiting.'"[58]

Southern California Hispanics are not, however, trapped in this low-income Latino ghetto south and east of Los Angeles. Many have spread out across the metropolitan area, moving into what urbanist Robert Lang and *USA Today* have called the "new Brooklyns." One example is Anaheim, California, the home of Disneyland, where according to *USA Today*, "whites are steadily giving way to large, poor, hard-working immigrant families— much like the ones who settled in Brooklyn a century ago and helped to make it famously diverse and vibrant."[59] Yet the comparison is a bit misleading. Twenty-first-century Hispanics move to Anaheim and suburban communities in general for much the same reason young World War II veterans left Brooklyn and opted for Levittown in the late 1940s—to escape the noise, crime, and dirt of the central city and to buy a home of their own with a small yard for their growing family. Despite the high cost of real estate in Southern California, an increasing number of Latinos are buying homes. One study found that in 2003 almost one-fourth of California homebuyers were Hispanic, and among Latinos the homeownership rate rose from 43 percent in 2000 to 46 percent in 2003, the largest increase for any major ethnic group in California.[60]

To escape prohibitive housing prices, a growing number of Hispanics have turned to the Inland Empire of San Bernardino and Riverside counties where real estate is cheaper than in the coastal counties of Ventura, Los Angeles, and Orange. One of the fastest growing regions in the nation, in 2003 the Inland Empire had a population of 3.5 million; an estimated 41 percent of these residents were Latino.[61] With seemingly endless subdivisions of new homes rising in communities like Moreno Valley, the Inland Empire is a suburban frontier beckoning hundreds of thousands of Hispanics.

In Southern California, Hispanics have not only replaced Anglos in communities like Anaheim, they have also moved into black suburbs and threatened African American hegemony. Compton, south of Los Angeles, attracted black migrants in the 1950s and 1960s, and by 1970 African Americans were in control of the city's government. Yet after 1980 the number of Latino residents increased markedly. By 2000 Hispanics constituted 57 percent of the population, and the once-majority blacks accounted for only 41 percent. When the emergent Latinos sought city jobs and school district policies more favorable to Spanish-speaking students, they found the entrenched blacks resistant to change, sparking years of conflict in the late 1980s and the 1990s. One Latino resident of Compton expressed the sentiment of many local Hispanics when he complained: "I found it very painful to know that blacks in power can be just as insensitive to minorities as whites have traditionally been toward their race."[62]

The growing Hispanic presence in suburbia, however, has not been confined to California or Florida. It is evident throughout the nation. By the middle of the first decade of the twenty-first century Gwinnett County, Georgia, was 15 percent Hispanic, and diverse Aurora, Colorado, was 25 percent Latino. Chicago's suburbs have also become increasingly Latin; by 2000, 11 percent of the suburban population was Hispanic. Once a bastion of central and eastern Europeans, Cicero was 77 percent Hispanic and the figure for nearby Berwyn was 38 percent. Cicero's Lithuanian parish of St. Anthony of Padua has become largely Mexican; according to a 2001 survey, five of its seven weekend masses are in Spanish. The suburb of Melrose Park is majority Hispanic and the site of an annual HispanoFest. Even the Hispanic dead have found a home in suburbia. The Forest Home Cemetery in the western suburb of Forest Park advertises a new Our Lady of Guadalupe section for customers seeking eternal rest in a burial ground named for the revered Mexican icon.[63]

Though not as numerous as Hispanics, Asian immigrants have also become a formidable suburban presence, especially in California. Probably the most notable concentration of Asian suburbanites is in the San Gabriel Valley east of Los Angeles, where the communities of Alhambra, Arcadia, Diamond Bar, Rosemead, and San Gabriel were all more than 40 percent Asian in 2000. The Asian capital of what has been called the San Gabriel ethnoburb is Monterey Park, where 62 percent of the 60,000 residents are Asian. Known as Little Taipei after the capital of Taiwan, Monterey Park is the home of Chinese supermarkets, restaurants, and minimalls as well as Chinese-language newspapers. Along the city's main business street, Atlantic Boulevard, the many signs with Chinese characters make English speakers feel decidedly out of place, but many of the community's residents prefer it that way. "Want to know why I moved here?" asked one Asian resident. "Let me tell you something: I usually have a morning walk along Monterey Park's streets. You know what? All I see are Chinese, there are no foreigners at all!"[64] Monterey Park is largely middle class, but for the most affluent Asians, nearby San Marino is a mecca. One of the wealthiest suburbs in Southern California, it was 49 percent Asian in 2000.

Yet Asian Americans are not confined to the San Gabriel Valley, nor do Chinese necessarily prevail in Asian suburbs. Because of its many Vietnamese residents and businesses, a section of suburban Westminster in California's Orange County has earned the title of Little Saigon. More than 3,500 Vietnamese American businesses occupy this three-square-mile zone, which the Westminster Chamber of Commerce describes as "a major tourist attraction representing the largest concentration of shopping and Vietnamese cultural amenities in the world outside of Vietnam."[65] Meanwhile, the San Francisco suburb of Daly City has won the title of Little Manila because of its many Filipinos. Combining the advantages of suburban America with an Asian flavor, Daly City is a welcoming ambience for newcomers from the Philippines. In 2001 its Filipino American vice mayor described the community as allowing "new immigrants to have a sense of living and working in America while enjoying the comforts of the motherland."[66]

Though less numerous than in California, Asians are also finding homes in Chicago suburbs. By 2000 suburban Skokie was 21 percent Asian, the figure for Glendale Heights was 20 percent, and for Hoffman Estates 15 percent. Recognizing this, in 2000 the Korean-language *Korean Central Daily News* moved its offices from the city of Chicago to the northwest suburb of Elk Grove Village. "We need to be close to where Korean-Americans live," explained the managing editor. "Many Korean-Americans are moving to the north and northwest suburbs, and we're following the trend."[67] In 2003 an Indian immigrant to suburban Naperville explained the appeal of his new home in terms that any newcomer to postwar Levittown would have readily understood. "It's very kid-friendly and pretty open," he remarked. "You can have a great family life, and it's clean."[68]

Indians in the New York City area concurred with this view. New York has been the chief port of entry for immigrants from India, but as soon as possible they have opted for homes in the suburbs. Indians constitute the largest Asian group in suburban Long Island, where they jam the Nassau County Coliseum to see personal appearances by the most popular movie stars from India. One Indian teenager from Old Westbury gushed: "It's the whole huge Coliseum filled with Indians. It's just like a concert by Britney Spears."[69] New Jersey is an even more popular destination for upwardly mobile Indians. In Edison, New Jersey, 20 percent of the population in 2000 was Indian, and Oak Tree Road in Edison and adjacent Woodbridge is the retail center for south Asians, offering everything from saris to Bollywood videos. Labeled Little India, Little Calcutta, and Bombay Boulevard, this suburban shopping strip is visual proof of suburbia's rich ethnic mix. A student of New Jersey's South Asians observed that Indians moved to the Edison area because it "offered good schools, a low crime rate, and a commute to New York City of less than one hour. Quite simply, immigrants wanted what most people moving to the suburbs want."[70]

The new immigrants, then, do not pose any threat to the prevailing suburbanization of America. Indians, Chinese, Mexicans, and Cubans all accept the long-standing American notion that suburbia is a safer, more secure and desirable environment, a better place to raise and educate children. The result has been a large-scale suburban migration among the nation's newcomers. Americans can experience a little bit of India in suburban New Jersey, visit the largest concentration of Vietnamese life outside of Vietnam in suburban Orange County, and survive without uttering a word of English in the Spanish-speaking communities of suburban Miami-Dade County. In the late 1980s, two urban geographers sought to identify "the most ethnically diverse urban places in the United States," and discovered that the upper-middle-class Los Angeles suburb of Cerritos ranked highest in diversity with a mix of different Asian and Hispanic nationalities as well as a white Anglo and an African American population. In fact, California suburbs dominated the ranks of the most diverse communities.[71] In the early twenty-first century, an even broader range of suburbs won honors for diversity. American suburbia is not the refuge of a homogeneous few; it is the home of the multihued majority.

Lifestyle Suburbs

Indicative of the diversity of contemporary American suburbia are the many communities tailored to the needs and preferences of specific lifestyles. The heterogeneous mass of suburban America includes havens catering to homosexuals, refuges for the elderly, and semirural oases for those seeking the country life. Exempt from the homogenizing tyranny of a single metropolitan authority, Americans have exploited the governmental fragmentation of suburbia to carve niches for the lifestyle of their choice. American suburbia thus offers a broad range of people the option of being different, of joining with like-minded devotees of alternative lifestyles to pursue their version of the American dream.

Among those who have fashioned an alternative society in suburbia is the gay population. Defying the traditional stereotype of family-friendly suburbs devoted to middle-class morality, homosexuals have created communities where they can pursue their sexual preferences openly and sometimes outrageously. The most notable gay suburb is West Hollywood, California. Surrounded by Los Angeles on three sides and bordering Beverly Hills to the west, until 1984 West Hollywood was an unincorporated enclave of Los Angeles County. The threat of soaring housing costs once the county deregulated rents, and the possibility of fashioning a gay-friendly government led to a successful campaign for incorporation as Los Angeles County's eighty-fourth municipality. The *New York Times* soon dubbed it "Gay Camelot," *Newsweek* labeled it "the new Gay City on the Hill," and *The Nation* acclaimed West Hollywood as "journey's end for a wave of refugees from sexual tyranny as practiced in most parts of middle America."[72]

West Hollywood's first mayor and a majority of the original city council were homosexuals, and during the first twenty years of its history the municipality has maintained its reputation as the very opposite of stereotypical suburbia. Its 36,000 residents are jammed into 1.9 square miles, resulting in a population density greater than any major American city other than New York City. Seventy-eight percent of its residents are renters, living primarily in apartments, and only 6 percent are children. Gay or bisexual men, in contrast, constitute 41 percent of the city's population and dominate the community life.[73] West Hollywood's gay web-site boasts that it is "the hip and happening center of gay and lesbian life in Los Angeles" and describes the city's San Vicente Inn/Resort as "an exclusive all-gay property with private, clothing optional, tropical surroundings."[74] Gay- and lesbian-oriented bars line West Hollywood's Santa Monica Boulevard, which also serves as the site of the Gay, Lesbian, Bisexual and Transsexual Parade and Festival, attracting more than 250,000 people each year. Over 350,000 attend the annual West Hollywood Halloween Costume Carnaval, advertised as "the largest Halloween street party in the United States" with "some of the most outrageous, unique Halloween costumes anywhere."[75]

The East Coast counterpart of West Hollywood is the gay suburb of Wilton Manors, Florida, immediately north of Fort Lauderdale. A middle-class bedroom community of 13,000 residents with housing dating from the mid-twentieth century, Wilton Manors underwent a transformation from straight to gay in the 1990s. By the first decade of the twenty-first century, it was being proclaimed "the new Gay Mecca" and "The Gayest Place in the World," the second city after West Hollywood to have a gay-majority government.[76] According to a gay business website, the city boasted the Better Bodies Gym, "where hot-bodied boys get pumped up before a night on the town" and Costello's Restaurant "where the waiters, like little eye appetizers, are often as yummy as the food."[77] Moreover, in 2004 the sales office opened for the new 272-unit Wilton Station condominium development, the first gated community to target homosexual buyers. Meanwhile, the number of children has declined. Commenting on the absence of trick-or-treaters, in 2004 one longtime resident lamented, "On Halloween I don't even bother buying candy anymore." That same year a migrant from Cleveland, Ohio, summed up the attitude of many of the newcomers to the gay suburb when he explained: "I wanted to be in a place where gayness was a more comfortable aspect of life."[78]

Though West Hollywood and Wilton Manors are the preeminent gay suburbs, certain other communities have also gained a reputation as gay friendly, though not gay dominated. Expanding beyond the boundaries of little Wilton Manors, homosexuals are moving to the adjacent suburb of Oakland Park. To the south, the village of Miami Shores is a hub of gay life, and in the Atlanta metropolitan area, Decatur ranks high in the proportion of same-sex couples. Fashioning comfortable communities of their own, homosexuals are recreating certain suburbs where juvenile trick-or-treaters are giving way to Halloween street parties catering to gay adults. Yet in other suburbs, homosexuals live without feeling the need to transform their community into a gay enclave. They are simply a relatively unobtrusive part of the demographic mix in suburbs throughout the nation.[79]

Just as homosexuals have staked out suburban havens, senior citizens have flocked to age-restricted suburban communities tailored to their lifestyle preferences. The most famous of these is the Phoenix suburb of Sun City, Arizona, founded in 1960 by developer Del Webb. To buy a home in Sun City, at least one household member had to be fifty years old or above, and no children were permitted to reside in the community. Despite the lack of youth, the emphasis was, and has remained, on activity. Sun City was for those seeking an active retirement, and who thus demanded golf courses, shuffleboard courts, tennis courts, and swimming pools as well as a full range of clubs to suit every hobbyist. The community grew rapidly, housing about 44,000 people at build out in 1978. Inspired by this success, in 1978 Webb began development of a second community, Sun City West, two miles to the west of the original development. Completed in 1997 with 31,000 residents, Sun City West boasts nine golf courses, six swimming pools, and thirty-two tennis courts, as well as a busy hospital for residents whose active days are numbered.

Now restricted to those over fifty-five, both the original community and its western adjunct are worlds apart where seniors can enjoy their active retirement lifestyle free from noisy, disrespectful, troublesome youth. Making clear their desire to shed the responsibilities of the larger world and isolate themselves from the burdens of the surrounding metropolis, in 1974 Sun City residents seceded from the local school district, becoming "an unorganized school territory," and thus under Arizona law exempt from local school taxes. In 1997 Sun City West tried to do likewise, but school district residents outside of the age-restricted community vetoed the prospect of losing the property tax revenues generated by the seniors' homes.[80] The secession battles, however, simply emphasize the insular nature of the communities. They are lifestyle fragments that do not wish to shoulder the cost of subsidizing the more youthful lifestyle of their metropolitan neighbors.

The California counterpart of Del Webb was community developer Ross Cortese. During the 1960s Cortese began construction of a number of age-restricted Leisure World communities, including one at Walnut Creek near San Francisco and two in Orange County south of Los Angeles. In 1999 one of these Southern California Leisure Worlds incorporated as the municipality of

Laguna Woods, declaring its independence from the unresponsive Orange County authorities. With a median age of 78, the 18,000-person community has the oldest population of any American city; 86 percent of its residents are sixty-five or above. One-third are classed as disabled, and the municipal government kindly accommodates electric wheelchairs by constructing wide sidewalks.[81] A gated community for senior citizens, Laguna Woods Leisure World is off limits to the young; the security gates ensure a protected lifestyle.

In recent years other suburban areas have also been more than willing to accommodate age-restricted communities. During the first years of the twenty-first century, Massachusetts experienced a boom in age-restricted housing, though the individual retirement projects were on a much smaller scale than Sun City or Laguna Woods. In 2005 a study identified more than 150 age-restricted developments existing or under construction in 93 Massachusetts towns, providing more than 10,000 dwelling units, and an additional 172 projects with 14,000 units in the planning stage in 109 towns. Most of these developments were in suburban towns in the eastern half of the state. Whereas Massachusetts towns proved reluctant to permit construction of family housing that would accommodate school-age children, and thus increase the fiscal burden on the schools, they welcomed senior communities that would not boost educational expenditures. Towns readily adopted zoning measures facilitating the construction of age-restricted dwellings. According to the study, "The belief that age restricted housing will be revenue positive, or at least revenue neutral, is the principal reason such development is accorded preferential treatment."[82]

Meanwhile, New York and New Jersey have also experienced a surge in the construction of senior housing. Between 1999 and 2004, the number of age-restricted dwelling units in Long Island's Nassau and Suffolk counties soared nearly 50 percent from 20,890 to 31,012. Moreover, in the latter year about $300 million of additional senior housing was proposed or under construction in the suburban Long Island counties. "I have a waiting list of over 25,000 people for my buildings," explained a Long Island broker specializing in age-restricted housing.[83] Similarly in New Jersey between 1999 and 2004, developers submitted applications to build 120 age-restricted communities. In 2004 in New Jersey's Monroe Township half of the 14,000 residents lived in senior developments, and 3,400 additional age-restricted homes were under construction. Extolling the active recreational lifestyle, one New Jersey resident of a retirement community proclaimed, "It's like we're in summer camp all the time."[84] But it was a summer camp without fiscally burdensome children, a fact that budget-conscious local authorities greatly appreciated.

Yet another lifestyle niche is the semirural suburb complete with equestrian facilities, bridle paths, ample acreage, winding country lanes, and unspoiled wetlands. To accommodate self-styled devotees of country living, scores of low-density suburbs dot the map of America, dedicated to preserving bucolic oases in the metropolitan mass. In the Chicago area, for example, the upscale suburb of Barrington Hills caters to the horsey set. The *Chicago Tribune* has described it as "mansions hidden from view behind trees and hills, horses grazing on their owners' estates and large swaths of 5-acre minimum zoning."[85] Only 4,000 residents inhabit the 28-square-mile community, and 97 percent of its area is zoned either as equestrian residential (lots of five or more acres) or as open space. Moreover, residents have chosen not to create the public water and sewerage infrastructure necessary for denser development, relying instead on private wells and septic tanks. According to a 2005 draft of the community's comprehensive plan, "Living with nature and adjusting to a relatively low level of accessibility and municipal services are conscious choices for those who reside in Barrington Hills. Residents have selected a more remote countryside life as an alternative to a more intense urban life." The result "is an equestrian, intentionally open coun-tryside oasis within a more chaotic urban metropolitan area." "Living with nature" in Barrington Hills, however, does not mean roughing it. The fifteen new homes constructed from January through June 2005 cost an average of $1,185,707.[86]

In the Sunbelt, equestrian suburbs also cater to those seeking a more natural environment. Faced with the threat of annexation to rapidly developing Pembroke Pines, in 1996 residents of South-west Ranches, Florida, west of Fort Lauderdale, launched a cam-paign for incorporation as a separate municipality dedicated to preserving a rural lifestyle and promoting equestrian activities. In 2000 they achieved this goal, and the new municipality has care-fully nurtured its low-density way of life. As its name indicates, the Florida community's self-image is one of ranches rather than estates, its preferred lifestyle being a bit scruffier than that of Bar-rington Hills. According to its website, "Our Town was formed to stop encroaching development, and all our Council Members have pledged to 'preserve our rural lifestyle,' which includes don-keys braying, roosters crowing, and no sidewalks."[87] It does not have a water or sewer system or streetlights, but it does have an equestrian park and miles of bridle trails. It is rural and proud of it. In order to preserve its bucolic isolation, Southwest Ranches has fought to close roads leading into the community and allow no more than one way into the town and one way out. In 2005 one town council member admitted: "The word going throughout the State is that Southwest Ranches does not care about anyone else and wants to be an island."[88]

This insular character is even more pronounced in Southern California's wealthiest equestrian community, the city of Rolling Hills. Located twenty miles south of Los Angeles, Rolling Hills accommodates fewer than 2,000 residents within its three square miles, and is dedicated to maintaining "a ranch style/equestrian environment with an enduring respect for native wildlife and natural surroundings."[89] Ranked by *Worth Magazine* as number fifteen on its list of the 250 richest towns in America, Rolling Hills is accessible only through three security gates guarded twenty-four hours a day. With twenty-three miles of equestrian trails and panoramic ocean views, it is an idyllic retreat that carefully protects the natural environment as well as the lifestyle of a privileged elite.

All across the United States well-to-do Americans have reserved ample green space for themselves. With only 18,000 residents in 39 square miles, the town of Bedford in suburban Westchester County north of New York City offers large expanses of open countryside to suit the tastes of its plutocratic residents. It boasts of one of the most extensive equestrian trail networks in the northeast, with more than 100 miles of trails in Bedford and the adjacent community of Pound Ridge. It not only nurtures its natural beauty but also the remnants of its rural past. "Much of Bedford's beauty derives from its history," explains the community's *Comprehensive Plan* of 2002, "its hamlets that anchor rural outlying areas, its dirt roads and stone walls, and its acclaimed historic structures and more modest reminders of a farming past."[90] North of Detroit the village of Franklin refers to itself as "The town that time forgot"; a village citizens' committee has described it as "an island of rural serenity in the middle of urban sprawl and fast paced living[,] … a sanctuary for nature and man."[91] It also houses some of the most affluent residents of the Detroit area, those in search of a simple village life and homes worth more than $1 million. To the west, in the wealthy Phoenix suburb of Paradise Valley, Arizona, the community's mission, according to a local history, is "to maintain a residential community in a quiet and country-like setting."[92] Reminiscent of Southwest Ranches, a statement of Paradise Valley's vision and values notes, "The Town promotes the development of a roadway network that serves the community's residents … without facilitating through travel that neither originates in nor is destined for the Town."[93] The gates of

Arizona's paradise are not intended to admit every passing plebeian; the idyllic valley is for those wealthy enough to afford its
mountain views and quiet life. From Paradise Valley to Laguna Woods to Wilton Manors,
American suburbs thus accommodate a wide range of lifestyles.
American suburbia is not an undifferentiated sprawl of population
with one look-alike community succeeding another in a seemingly endless progression. It is a rich composite including starkly
contrasting fragments of metropolitan life. Among Southern California's suburbs are homosexual West Hollywood, elderly Laguna
Woods, and equestrian Rolling Hills, as well as wealthy, first-tier
Beverly Hills, poor, Hispanic, first-tier Maywood, Chinese Monterey Park, multiethnic Cerritos, and contested Compton. In South
Florida the gay mecca of Wilton Manors is a short drive from the
rural island of Southwest Ranches and the Cuban metropolis of
Hialeah. Suburbia offers a smorgasbord of lifestyle choices, and
millions of Americans have taken advantage of the opportunity to
sample the diverse selection.

Boomburbs

The largest among the many diverse species of American suburbs
is the *boomburb*. Robert Lang and Patrick Simmons coined this
term after examining the 2000 census and distinguishing a distinct class of giant suburbs whose size and rapid growth set them
apart. According to Lang and Simmons, boomburbs are "places
with more than 100,000 residents that are *not* the largest cities in
their respective metropolitan areas and that have maintained dou-
ble-digit rates of population growth in recent decades." In 2003
they identified fifty-three such boomburbs in the United States,
including four with populations of more than 300,000, eight with
populations of 200,000 to 300,000, and forty-one in the 100,000
to 200,000 category. Lang and Simmons claim, "boomburbs do

not resemble traditional central cities" and "are not typically patterned in traditional urban form," almost always lacking "a dense business core," but instead have a "loosely configured, low-density spatial structure."[94] These suburbs on steroids are the size of a big city but most often retain an appearance and mentality traditionally associated with suburbia.

The largest boomburb is Mesa, Arizona, east of Phoenix; with a 2004 population of 432,000 it was larger than such better-known urban centers as Atlanta, Minneapolis, and Miami. In 1950 it had been a small town of only 17,000 inhabitants. Second among the boomburbs is Arlington, Texas, midway between Dallas and Fort Worth with 355,000 residents, surpassing in population such superstars of the past as St. Louis, Pittsburgh, and Cincinnati. Whereas mid-twentieth-century St. Louis's population exceeded 800,000, in 1950 Arlington was home to fewer than 8,000 people. Most of the boomburbs are found in the fast-growing Southwest with the Los Angeles, Phoenix, and Dallas metropolitan areas alone accounting for thirty-two of the giant communities. With eighteen boomburbs in 2000, the Los Angeles area clearly led the nation in this new phenomenon. In the Southeast, South Florida was the preeminent boomburb region with three examples, but in the slow-growing Northeast and Midwest, only Naperville, Illinois, west of Chicago, merited boomburb status.

In 2005 Lang identified eighty-six "Baby Boomburbs," communities in the 50,000 to 100,000 population category, which like the larger boomburbs had experienced phenomenal growth during the previous half century.[95] Some of these would never achieve full boomburb status, as were approaching build out, but other of Lang's babies were clearly the boomburbs of the near future. For example, McKinney, Texas, north of Dallas, had a population of 54,000 in 2000, but in 2005 its annual report claimed that McKinney, "one of the fastest growing cities in America," would that year welcome its 100,000th resident, raising it to full boomburb status.[96] Other potential boomburbs were still in the fetal stage in 2000, but during the first decade of the twenty-first century were rapidly passing from babyhood toward recognition as full-scale boomburbs. McKinney's neighbor Frisco, Texas, had 34,000 residents in 2000, an estimated 66,000 in 2004, and was projected to reach 140,000 in 2013.[97] Likewise, the Phoenix suburb of Surprise, Arizona, was home to 39,000 people in 2000, but was expecting a population of 165,000 in 2010, and according to the leading Phoenix newspaper would house 640,500 by 2040.[98] Even more phenomenal was the expected growth of nearby Buckeye, Arizona. With an estimated population of only 7,000, Buckeye in 2003 approved the development of Arizona's largest master-planned community, 35,000-acre Douglas Ranch, proposed to have 83,000 homes, thirty-seven schools, and twenty-two golf courses. Altogether Buckeye's plans included more than 240,000 homes and an anticipated population of 464,000 by 2020 and 600,000 in 2040.[99] "Everybody's talking about Buckeye[,] the little town that was just a gas stop for California- and Mexico-bound travelers," boasted the local chamber of commerce. With an ambition appropriate to a future boomburb, the chamber claimed that the community "could someday be home to more than 1,000,000 residents."[100]

Though proud of their growth, most boomburbs and potential boomburbs eschewed a big-city image, claiming to offer a hometown atmosphere compatible with the traditional suburban stereotype. While predicting an onslaught of hundreds of thousands of newcomers, Buckeye contended that "as Arizona's biggest 'small town,' we still enjoy the great feeling of a small community."[101] The McKinney city council's vision for the community in 2020 describes the town as "a natural beauty" where "people are friendly neighbors."[102] A major city with an estimated population of 234,000 in 2004 and an expected 502,000 residents by 2035, Henderson, Nevada, south of Las Vegas, adopted as its slogan "a place to call home." According to Henderson's assistant city manager, this reflected its "commitment to community, services, small-town family values, and a high quality of life."[103] The Phoenix suburb of Gilbert, Arizona, with 145,000 in 2003, was the nation's fastest growing boomburb in the early twenty-first century, increasing in population by 32 percent from 2000 to 2003, but it chose to remain a "town" under Arizona law rather than a city. "I don't think there are ten people in Gilbert that want to have it called a city," explained the mayor in 2004. Instead, the community's goal is "to be the only 300,000-person small town in America."[104]

In many of the boomburbs, homeowners associations in master-planned and often gated developments shoulder many of the duties of government and make residents feel that they are actually part of a smaller community relatively immune from the meddling of a remote city hall bureaucracy. Responsibility for their streets, recreation facilities, trash collection, and security force is in the hands of a homeowners board of neighbors, thus perpetuating the small-town feel and minimal government presence some of these giant municipalities value. "Homeowners associations enable places to govern lighter," contends Robert Lang. "They can have cities of 200,000 with tiny governments."[105] Walled communities, with gates admitting only friends and neighbors and governed by owners associations, impart a sense of home and security widely associated with village life. These private islands of relative autonomy mean that one can live in a boomburb but still feel like part of a smaller community. Ideally a municipality of myriad homeowners associations can become a 300,000-person small town.

Although many boomburbs attempt to perpetuate small-town advantages, they are not homogenous Anglo retreats where old-stock whites can escape the nation's newcomers. Instead, these large suburban municipalities accommodate millions of Hispanics, Asians, and African Americans, reflecting the ethnic heterogeneity of the South and West. In 2000 Hialeah, Florida, a city of

226,000 people, was 90 percent Hispanic; the boomburb of Santa Ana, California, with 338,000 residents was 76 percent Latino; 50 percent of the 174,000 inhabitants in the San Diego boomburb of Chula Vista were Hispanic; and the figure for Anaheim was 47 percent. "It's not just white people," Chula Vista's city manager said of the flood of new residents that had pushed that boomburb's population to more than 200,000 by 2004. "The diversity factor in the new area is phenomenal. It's a collage of races that have moved in here." According to the city manager, "The racial breakdowns are spread citywide—there is no enclave."[106]

The most integrated city in the nation, Aurora, Colorado, was another boomburb as was diverse Bellevue, Washington, a community of 110,000 east of Seattle. The largest suburb on the metropolitan area's affluent east side, Bellevue was almost one-quarter foreign born in 2000 with Asians constituting 18 percent of the population. It had a higher percentage foreign born than the city of Seattle and the metropolitan region as a whole. At the mini city hall in Bellevue's diverse Crossroads neighborhood, the city provides interpreters in Armenian, Chinese, Korean, Russian, Spanish, Tagalog, Bengali, Hindi, and Urdu for the 12 percent of the residents who are not fluent in English, and the satellite library conducts multilingual story hours. "I absolutely love walking through Crossroads on a Friday night," a city councilwoman remarked in 2005. "You will see families with kids, seniors, disabled people and people of every ethnicity you can imagine."[107]

Though distinguished for their rapid growth, some of these large diverse boomburbs have achieved build out, having no more virgin land for development, or are fast approaching this stage. For these communities, the days of booming expansion are ending, necessitating a shift in perspective as their adolescent spurt gives way to maturity and preferably not stagnation. For example, the Denver suburb of Lakewood, Colorado, was not even incorporated until 1969, yet by 2000 it had 144,000 residents while still claiming to retain "much of its small-town flavor and open space." This open space, however, was for recreation not construction; only a small area of the city remained available for new development, and there was no prospect of annexing additional territory. Consequently, the city predicted a rate of population growth of only 2.8 percent between 2000 and 2010, with 148,000 anticipated residents in the latter year and 152,000 in 2020.[108] In a 2004 interview with Robert Lang, Mayor Steve Burkholder, however, was not discouraged by this prospect. Instead, he looked forward to higher density, mixed-use redevelopment of property near the light rail stations along the Denver FasTrack system planned to link Lakewood to Denver.[109] Lakewood might be passing from the ranks of the boomburbs to the mature status of *bigburb*, but its leaders believe a stable population does not imply decay or decline. They believe that Lakewood can grow both older and better, creating a vibrant mix of commercial space and multifamily housing near the new transit line.

To the south the boomburb of Tempe, Arizona, has become a model for other communities running out of undeveloped land. Surrounded by other Phoenix suburbs, Tempe will not be able to expand beyond 45 square miles and expects to increase slowly in population from 176,000 to 189,000 between 2010 and 2020. But Tempe intends to ensure optimal redevelopment of the land it has. Its *General Plan 2030* states proudly that "Tempe looks forward to preserving and revitalizing itself" and notes that the city "has taken an aggressive position with redevelopment activities because it is land-locked."[110] Reflecting this aggressive stance, in November 2005 the Tempe city council approved the construction of three, thirty-story condominium towers. Intended to provide urban-style apartment living in the landlocked boomburb, the council's action made clear that Tempe was not about to stagnate. Along Tempe Town Lake the community was also projecting a vertical lifestyle with high-rise office and retail space as well as condominiums. Tempe's enthusiastic mayor proclaimed, "The sky is the limit there."[111]

Adjacent Scottsdale, Arizona, is not yet built out, but expects to be within the next few decades. A 2003 report by an Arizona public policy institute announced ominously "for the first time ever, Scottsdale is beginning to run out of land" and questioned whether the perennially successful boomburb might "'sit on its lead' and begin to lag in excellence and innovation." "With 'build-out' only 20 years away, and with its 'jewels' aging," the report asked, "how can Scottsdale re-position itself?"[112] Though one of the wealthiest and most prestigious communities in the nation, Scottsdale cannot escape the anxiety of approaching maturity. As in many other giant suburbs, the boomburb days are passing and Scottsdale as well as neighboring Tempe must adjust accordingly.

Thus the boomburbs include mature communities like Lakewood and Tempe, which are passing to bigburb status; cities like Scottsdale, which need to face a post-boomburb future during the next two decades; babyburbs such as McKinney, Frisco, and Surprise, which are moving into boomburb ranks; and Buckeye, which is poised to progress from embryo to adulthood at a breakneck pace. And the diverse boomburbs are just one type among the many varied categories of American suburbs. Poor, first-tier East Cleveland, rich first-tier Winnetka, gay Wilton Manors, aged Laguna Woods, equestrian Barrington Hills, black Prince George's, Hispanic Hialeah, and Asian Monterey Park are all part of American suburbia. From Chelsea in Massachusetts to Chula Vista on the Mexican border, America's suburbs encompass the variety of the nation. Rather than bland burbs, they are as rich in diversity and as multihued as America itself.

3
COMMERCIAL SUBURBIA

Basic to an understanding of American suburbs is the fact that suburbia is the preeminent zone for business in the United States. In the late nineteenth and early twentieth centuries, manufacturing was already moving to the suburbs, and during the three decades following World War II retailing migrated outward, creating the landscape of parking lots and malls familiar to all Americans. Finally during the last quarter of the twentieth century, a mass migration of office space confirmed the commercial supremacy of the suburbs. Glass-encased high rises sprouted at freeway interchanges, corporate campuses became commonplace suburban landmarks, and research and development facilities sprawled across nearby expanses. The leading hotel chains opened three-hundred-room towers to serve corporate business travelers drawn to the metropolitan fringe, adding one more element to the commercial mix of the American suburb. By the dawn of the twenty-first century, the heart of American business was in the suburbs. They contained the majority of American manufacturing, retailing, and office space. In the amorphous mass of outlying communities, Americans earned and spent most of their cash. American business was suburban.

During the first decade of the twenty-first century there have been no signs of a shift away from this preeminence. Scholars and journalists argue about the exact pattern of suburban business, retailers and developers attempt to discover and satisfy the shopping and spending desires of suburban consumers, and local government officials seek to maximize their tax revenues from this commercial bounty. All of them, however, recognize that the business future of the nation is in the suburbs. That is where the money is to be made.

Edge and Edgeless Cities

In 1991 journalist Joel Garreau announced the advent of a new metropolitan phenomenon, the *edge city*. During the previous two decades urban scholars and metropolitan observers had noted the development of significant commercial nodes along America's metropolitan fringe, proposing various labels for the emerging centers of business. Technoburb, urban village, outer city, and new downtown were all suggested as names for the strange new world developing in American suburbia. Garreau's *Edge City: Life on the New Frontier* (1991), however, reached a broader audience and finally forced most educated Americans to recognize the obvious. Moreover, his edge city label, though unsatisfactory to some, moved into first place in the contest to name the phenomenon of suburban business hubs. "Americans are creating the biggest change in a hundred years in how we build cities," Garreau proclaimed. "Every single American city that *is* growing, is growing in the fashion of Los Angeles, with multiple urban cores." According to Garreau, these multiple cores were the "new hearths of our civilization ... in which the majority of metropolitan Americans now work and around which we live," and they were "not at all like our old downtowns." In Garreau's edge cities, "buildings rarely rise shoulder to shoulder, as in Chicago's Loop. Instead, their broad, low outlines dot the landscape like mushrooms, separated by greensward and parking lots."[1]

So his readers would know exactly what he was examining, Garreau carefully defined what constituted an edge city. An edge city had at least five million square feet of leasable office space, "more than downtown Memphis," had at least 600,000 square feet of leasable retail space, "the equivalent of a fair-sized mall," had "more jobs than bedrooms," was locally perceived as a destination offering employment, retailing, and entertainment, and "was nothing like 'city' as recently as thirty years ago … just bedrooms, if not cow pastures."[2] The edge city was, then, a spanking new place of shopping and office employment that was as significant commercially as the major city downtowns of the past. Garreau helped his readers recognize this new metropolitan species by listing 119 full-fledged edge cities in the United States as well as 73 additional emerging edge cities—hubs that had not quite met Garreau's criteria but seemed well on their way to joining the flock.[3] Throughout the nation from Boston, New York, and Philadelphia in the Northeast, to Atlanta, Memphis, and Miami in the South, to Detroit and Chicago in the Midwest, and Phoenix, Los Angeles, and San Francisco in the West, Garreau discovered examples of his edge city phenomenon, providing ample evidence of the revolutionary change that had engulfed metropolitan America.

In 2003, however, urban scholar Robert Lang challenged Garreau's prognostications, claiming that the edge city did not represent the wave of the metropolitan future. Lang instead argued that the trend was not toward multiple business hubs, but toward a pattern devoid of any commercial cores—a centerless sprawl with businesses scattered throughout suburbia. For Lang the present and future belonged not to the edge city but to the edgeless city. *Edgeless cities* were "a form of sprawling office development" without "the density or cohesiveness of edge cities," and they accounted for the bulk of suburban office space.[4] Suburbia may have been spawning some new downtowns along the metropolitan edge, but commercial coalescence was not the prevailing pattern. Rather, dispersion and spread remained preeminent, with office buildings rising here and there along suburban highways amid an expanse of strip shopping centers and fast-food restaurants.

Examining the distribution of office space in thirteen of the nation's largest metropolitan areas, Lang found that in 1999 the edgeless city accounted for 37 percent of the total and edge cities for only 20 percent. The pattern differed across the nation, though only in New York City and Chicago was the traditional central city downtown the home of a majority of the metropolitan area's office space. Moreover, in the Dallas area Lang found that edge cities actually surpassed the edgeless expanse in office development. In contrast, he identified the Miami area as "the most centerless large region in the nation"; it was "the edgeless metropolis incarnate" with 66 percent of its office space in Lang's edgeless city. In a reexamination of the phenomenon based on 2005 data, Lang found much the same pattern with the edgeless city having risen to a 40 percent share of office space in the thirteen metropolitan areas.[5]

According to Lang, the edgeless city was not simply a remnant of a sprawling past that would soon be supplanted by Garreau's edge cities. Instead, edgeless cities were adding more new office space than the edge cities, leading Lang to claim that Garreau's hubs were "losing their edge." As suburban homeowners rebelled against density, new development, and traffic congestion, the scattered small-scale office buildings of the edgeless city aroused less ire than the gargantuan edge city hubs. They were according to Lang "the ultimate stealth cities" capable of surviving and spreading undetected by the radar of irate homeowner groups dedicated to preserving bucolic suburbia.[6] Smaller and less objectionable than Garreau's five-million-square-foot office behemoths, edgeless city office structures were less likely to suffer mortal wounds from suburban assaults on growth and development.

Any observer of twenty-first-century American suburbia will find ample evidence to support both Garreau and Lang. At busy freeway interchanges office towers soar around gargantuan shopping malls, yet these nodes do not have a monopoly on commercial development. Office parks and low-rise business structures are scattered throughout suburbia, springing up in relative isolation from competing office space. Both sprawl and concentration are readily evident. Moreover, despite his precise definition of the edge city, Garreau's "hubs" of commerce often appear barely distinguishable from Lang's edgeless city. Garreau admits that "a few Edge Cities listed ... are so dispersed across the geography as to challenge the definition," citing as an example the intersection of Route 128 and the Massachusetts Turnpike.[7] In fact, many of his edge cities lack much cohesion; they sprawl rather than coalesce. Minnesota's Bloomington-Edina I-494 edge city runs eight miles along the interstate highway, and the Beaver-Tigard-Tualatin edge city in Oregon spreads through a string of suburbs in a line eight miles long. The central Orange County node identified by Garreau appears to encompass about 80 square miles of Santa Ana, Anaheim, and Garden Grove, and the Illinois Research and Development Corridor extends the entire width of DuPage County, Illinois, stretching along 20 miles of highway. At times, Garreau seems to believe that all suburbia is an edge city, as when he claims, "two thirds of all American office facilities are in Edge Cities."[8] Two-thirds may be outside of traditional central-city downtowns, but if one takes Garreau's edge city definition seriously, this two-thirds figure is wildly inflated.

Actually the line between edge city and edgeless city seems difficult to define. For the very notion of tightly bound hubs is alien to American suburbia. Though some zones may have more office space than others, few suburban areas resemble the central-city downtowns of the past. There may be some concentration, but there is also a great deal of sprawl. A relatively edgeless, amorphous pattern prevails; mapping commercial boundaries is a daunting task and spread is more common than cohesion. Both Garreau and Lang agreed, however, that the United States at the turn of the twenty-first century was confronted by a strange, new commercial geography. The edge was more significant than the core. Notions of a single business hub surrounded by a residential fringe were woefully obsolete, and claims that older central cities were in fact central to American business were increasingly hollow.

Nowhere was the commercial preeminence of suburbia more evident than in Fairfax County, Virginia. Southwest of Washington, DC, and home to one million residents, in 2006 Fairfax was the site of six Fortune 500 corporate headquarters as well as the headquarters of nearly 300 trade associations and professional societies. Its business community was also ethnically diverse. Six Fairfax companies won a place on *Black Enterprise* magazine's listing of the 100 largest black-owned businesses, and eleven were included among *Hispanic Business* magazine's 500 largest Hispanic-owned concerns. Moreover, Fairfax was in the forefront of technological development with more than 4,900 technology firms. Fairfax boasted 103.5 million square feet of office space, making it the largest commercial office market in the Washington metropolitan area and in the state of Virginia.[9] The supply of office space increased more than 50 percent between 1990 and 2005.[10] In 2006 there were a total of 534,000 jobs in the booming county.[11]

Fairfax leaders were eager to attract even more employers. It was the only county in the United States with five marketing offices overseas, maintaining representatives in Britain, Germany, Israel, India, and South Korea. Fairfax leaders realized that their county was part of a global economy competing with metropolitan centers throughout the world. It was a major player on the world business scene and not a bedroom appendage of Washington, DC. "Every discussion around the country has been that our competitors are not St. Louis and Seattle. Our competitors are all over the world: Shanghai, Delhi, Mumbai," commented a member of the county's governing board. "We need to recognize that. Otherwise we are going to be left behind."[12] In its 2006 promotional literature, the county economic development authority claimed it was definitely not lagging. It boasted, "the county has added more than 10,000 new business establishments and 250,000 jobs since 1990."[13]

Among Fairfax's commercial centers was one of the nation's most notable edge cities, Tysons Corner. In the early 1960s, Gerald Halpin purchased empty fields at the intersection of the Capital Beltway, then under construction, and routes 123 and 7 for eight cents per square foot and built a low-rise office structure for a mere $56,000. "We started out with two-story buildings, then we tore them down to make way for 15-story buildings," Halpin reminisced in 2003. "Eventually, those will give way to 30-story buildings. It's all evolution."[14] Aiding this evolution was the construction of the single-level enclosed Tysons Corner Shopping Center in 1968. In the mid-1980s the mall doubled in size when it added a second level. In 2005 it expanded an additional 362,000 square feet, bringing its total to 2.3 million square feet and making it the fifth or sixth largest shopping mall in the nation.[15] It boasted more than 290 stores including such prestigious anchors as Bloomingdale's, Lord & Taylor, and Nordstrom. Nearby Tyson's Galleria opened in 1988 as an 800,000-square-foot "high fashion mall," and in 2005 included among its anchors upscale Saks Fifth Avenue and Neiman Marcus.[16] Moreover, as of 2003 Tysons Corner claimed an awesome 25.6 million square feet of office space as well as Hilton, Sheraton, Marriott, and Ritz Carlton hotels.[17] About 100,000 people were employed in the edge city.

Yet in the first decade of the twenty-first century, Fairfax officials and developers were planning an even grander future for

Tysons Corner. In 2011, a MetroRail line is scheduled to reach the edge city providing rail service to the auto-oriented hub. Anticipating this new mode of transport, planners and builders proposed an increase in the density of the edge city with a marked rise in office, retailing, and high-rise residential space. Moreover, they hoped to transform Tysons Corner into a pedestrian-friendly environment where one could walk between the office complexes and shopping malls rather than having to rely almost exclusively on automobiles. They envisioned recreating Chicago's Loop or Midtown Manhattan in Fairfax; the new Tysons Corner would become a dense, 24-hour, multifunction hub for the county where one could arrive by rail and leave the automobile at home. "Right now, Tysons Corner is the world's most successful office park," observed the president of the county Chamber of Commerce in 2005. "What we want is a downtown."[18]

These proposals, however, did not escape the suburban radar of nearby homeowners; their reaction exemplified the obstacles in the path of edge city expansion. "I think that vision of Tysons as being the Manhattan of Fairfax County is flawed," commented an active member of the citizens association of nearby McLean. "I think our politicians and our planners have a view of a much more urban Fairfax County than our residents wish to have."[19] The association president agreed, "What's going to happen to the surrounding communities when 10,000 new condominiums are built there? Our roads are already absolutely jampacked."[20] "Oh, my god!" cried a McLean activist. "We'd like to be able to drive [the six miles] from McLean to Vienna in less than a day."[21] In Fairfax as elsewhere in the nation, the edge city was not always a welcome neighbor. Traffic and congestion were not part of the suburban dream, but they seemed to be the unintended consequences of the nightmare of excessive development.

Fairfax, moreover, could boast more than one edge city. Eight miles west of Tysons Corner was Reston, a carefully planned new town founded in the 1960s, which by the beginning of the twenty-first century had developed into a major node of business enterprise. With 17.8 million square feet of office space and 1.7 million square feet of retailing at the end of 2003, Reston was catching up to Tysons. And it had what Tysons Corner lacked, a pedestrian-friendly, mixed-use urban center with office buildings, cafes, theaters, stores, and a Hyatt hotel lining a main street and public plaza where shoppers and workers could stroll or simply sit and watch the passing throng. Though surrounded by ample parking facilities, Reston Town Center conformed to the early twenty-first-century planning predilection for compact, pedestrian-oriented developments. Between its opening in 1990 and 2004, it won twenty-three regional and national awards for design, construction, and operation; among them was the American Institute of Architects Award for Excellence in Urban Design.[22] Imitating the ambience of a traditional downtown, it seemed to inject an element of urbanity into the sprawling suburbs. Promotional literature described Reston Town Center as "a lively mix of retail, dining, entertainment, hotel and office space in a European-style town setting."[23] Whereas Tysons Corner exemplified the edge city run amuck, an untamed product of developers' desire to profit, Reston demonstrated that edge cities could conform to planners' visions of a civilized world.

Though Fairfax County provided evidence of Garreau's edge cities, it was also an exemplar of the edgeless city. During the first decade of the twenty-first century, Tysons Corner and Reston combined accounted for only about 42 percent of the county's office space. A majority of the office inventory was scattered across Fairfax, the economic development authority identifying seventeen office submarkets in the county.[24] Moreover, the lesser submarkets were expanding, with Chantilly and Centreville experiencing the most office construction in 2005 and Annandale leading in office condominium sales.[25] Northern Virginia's first biotechnology incubator, Bio-Accelerator, was located in Springfield, as was Springfield Mall with more than 250 stores. The 180 shops of Fair Oaks Mall also challenged Tysons' retailing supremacy.[26] The Chantilly-Dulles-Fairfax Center area of Western Fairfax actually boasted more retail and hotel space than the Tysons Corner district.[27]

Tysons Corner was not truly *the* downtown of Fairfax County, the one hub around which the remainder of the county rotated. It was just a single business district in a commercial expanse of what Garreau might deem multiple edge cities and Lang regard as edgeless cities. Commercial coalescence in a compact node was not the prevailing trend in Fairfax. Real estate experts knew that in Fairfax, as in much of suburbia, what counted was access to the highway, not a location in a traditional downtown cluster. Writing of the office market in Western Fairfax at the beginning of 2006, real estate experts noted the importance of "Toll Road visibility" to developers. "Building sites that are visible from the Toll Road are the commercial real estate equivalent of beachfront residential sites," they explained. "They are more sought after and achieve higher rental rates."[28] The commercial pattern of Fairfax, suburbia, and the nation in general appeared to be one of linear sprawl. Business would expand in edgeless metropolises as far as the superhighway extended.

The commercial decentralization of Fairfax County is replicated throughout the nation. In the Chicago area, for example, the leading edge city is the northwest suburb of Schaumburg, a municipality that incorporated in 1956 with only 130 residents. Like Tysons Corner, however, Schaumburg developed quickly at the convergence of major highways, the Northwest Tollway and Interstate 90, and owed much of its commercial eminence to a giant shopping center, Woodfield Mall. Opened in 1971, Woodfield by the early twenty-first century had 2.7 million square feet of retail space, claimed to be the nation's second-largest mall, and boasted of being the leading tourist attraction in Illinois with 27 million visitors per year and hundreds of bus tours.[29] Given its advantageous location on heavily traveled highways only eight miles from O'Hare International Airport, Schaumburg proved to be fertile ground for office development, producing a bumper crop of structures in the 1980s. At the beginning of the twenty-first century it had 11.6 million square feet of office space, including the headquarters of the Motorola Corporation. Altogether 78,000 people were employed in Schaumburg, though the resident population of the city was only 75,000. Promotional publications proudly proclaimed, "There are more businesses in the Schaumburg area than in downtown Philadelphia, Washington, D.C., Dallas, or Portland."[30]

Yet Schaumburg's story is not one of limitless expansion. It is not, nor will it be, the boomtown it once was. Excessive development in the 1980s led to a glut of office space in the following decade. Not until the late 1990s did office construction resume, though at a reduced pace; between 1999 and 2004 the city approved the construction of an additional 1.5 million square feet of office space.[31] In 2002 the community was planning for a total of anywhere from 13.5 to 18 million square feet of office space by 2020.[32] At most, the office inventory was expected to expand by 60 percent in two decades. In other words, Schaumburg's leaders anticipated continued growth, but at a more moderate pace than the breakneck rate of the 1970s and 1980s. As Schaumburg approached build out, commercial development was expanding westward along the Northwest Tollway, just as it was sprawling along the fringes of Fairfax County's superhighways. Though still prosperous and significant as a commercial node, Schaumburg was losing some of its edge as the commercial decentralization of northeastern Illinois proceeded without interruption.

On the West Coast, Bellevue, Washington offers another example of the uneven fortunes of edge cities. Incorporated as a municipality in 1953 with only 5,950 residents, Bellevue developed as an upscale residential suburb of Seattle, with a population of nearly 74,000 largely upper-middle-class inhabitants by 1980. In the 1980s and 1990s, however, it grew rapidly as a commercial powerhouse with towering office structures rising in the downtown area around the city's giant retail magnet, Bellevue Square Mall. With Microsoft's corporate headquarters located in the adjacent suburb of Redmond, Bellevue was a prime beneficiary of the dot-com boom of the late 1990s, and emerged as a major center of computer-related businesses. Whereas the city's population rose about 50 percent between 1980 and 2000, reaching 110,000 in the latter year, the number of jobs in the boomtown soared more than 200 percent to 130,000 in 2000.[33]

Garreau categorized Bellevue as an edge city, the premier example of that phenomenon in the Northwest. Yet actually there were four job centers of varying density in the city, making it perhaps more of a hybrid edge-edgeless city. In 2000 only about 30 percent of the employment was in the downtown area where glass-encased office towers and the upscale mall created a stereotypical edge-city landscape. Nearly 40 percent of the jobs, however, were in the State Route 520/Bel-Red Corridor, which sprawled eastward toward Microsoft's headquarters, and two other linear zones shared most of the remaining employment.[34] During the first decade of the twenty-first century planners sought to curb this sprawl by concentrating commerce as well as apartment buildings in the downtown area, and creating a more lively, dense, mixed-use hub where suburbanites would walk to destinations rather than drive. Designated in local and regional plans as one of the Seattle area's "Urban Centers," downtown Bellevue was intended to accommodate the bulk of the city's commercial development during the period 2000 to 2020.[35]

During the first years of the twenty-first century, however, these dreams of a vital urban center had to be put on hold as the dot-com bust and nationwide recession ravaged Bellevue's economy. Office vacancy rates in downtown Bellevue soared from 1.6 percent in 2000 to 26.4 percent in 2002, and remained above 20 percent in the second quarter of 2004.[36] Construction halted on the 20-story Bellevue Technology Tower, leaving a 70-foot-deep hole and partially finished underground parking garage in the city's center. An aborted condominium project won the nickname of "shrink-wrap building" after it was mothballed in a plastic covering.[37] By the middle of the decade, Bellevue's economic mood was again upbeat, with new offices, hotels, and condominiums on the drawing board. In November 2005, the first stage of the Lincoln Square project opened, a 42-story tower housing a Westin hotel as well as luxury residential condominiums and 310,000 square feet of retail space. A 27-story office building was planned to follow. Developers were gradually coming back to the Bellevue market, announcing ambitious plans and predicting a new boom.

Despite the commitment of planners and developers to a vitalized urban center, some observers still felt downtown Bellevue fell short. Referring to Bellevue Square Mall as "Blah-vue Square," one shopper complained, "It's like every other place in America." The sales manager of one of the mall stores expressed much the same sentiment: "Bellevue is a weird place. There is not really a downtown here—you have to go to the mall."[38] Describing Bellevue as a "wealthy, developer-driven city that has a tradition of orderliness," a Seattle journalist criticized the city center as "squeaky clean, obviously prosperous, vastly more ambitious than any of the other Eastside downtowns—and perfectly forgettable."[39] But a leading developer excused downtown Bellevue's flaws: "It is an adolescent awkwardness, and now you are starting to see some things come together."[40]

During the early twenty-first century, the edge and edgeless cities are, then, works in progress. Both Tysons Corner and Bellevue are dedicated to becoming more "urban," though planners seem to mean more like Reston Town Center rather than more like the grime of Chicago or the empty sidewalks of downtown Detroit. Problems persist, and there is a history of false steps. Critics deplore the traffic of Tysons and the blandness of Bellevue, and the overdevelopment in Schaumburg and overreliance on high-tech computer-related business in Bellevue have affected the fortunes of these edge cities. In Fairfax, the northwest suburbs of Chicago, and the eastside suburbs of Seattle, the line between edge and edgeless city has remained blurry. Varying degrees of sprawl and concentration coexist, but nowhere is there a true urban center reminiscent of Chicago's pre–World War II Loop or downtown Seattle of the same era. There are nodes, corridors, and scatter-site developments; there is not one metropolitan center, a common downtown for the region. Everywhere the suburbanization of business is apparent.

Whether edge city or edgeless, this commercial decentralization is not a patternless sprawl, without reason or rationale. Since World War II, business has moved outward from the historic hubs following the centrifugal path of highways, wealth, and talent. Throughout the United States, highway visibility is to commercial property what an ocean view is for residential properties. Land visible from the highways is the most highly prized location because the chief mode of metropolitan transport is the automobile. Customers, clients, and employees, are all auto-borne, and maximum access to the auto-borne means greater business and higher profits. In Virginia, in Illinois, and along the West Coast this has induced commercial sprawl. So long as people drive, the linear extension of business along expressways and the development of commercial nodes at highway intersections will continue.

Commercial development, however, is not evenly distributed along the highways and around the intersections of America's suburbs. Both retailing and office development seek out well-to-do suburban areas and shun less affluent zones. Mall developers want to locate near consumers with money; corporate executives want to locate their offices an easy commute from their homes. Consequently, well-to-do Fairfax County has attracted considerably more office space and retail business than less affluent and predominantly black Prince George's County, Maryland, across the Potomac River. Saks and Neiman Marcus do not open branches in predominantly black suburbs nor do Fortune 500 headquarters locate there. Likewise, the edge city and edgeless commercial development in northeastern Illinois has gravitated primarily to Chicago's northern and western suburbs where the money is. Farther west, affluent Bellevue and the well-heeled eastside suburbs of Seattle are the natural locale for corporate offices and upscale retailing in the Puget Sound region.

In like manner, business has moved outward in pursuit of talent, for the suburbs are home to a disproportionate share of the reliable, skilled, middle-class clerical workers necessary to corporate offices and the engineers and scientists essential to burgeoning high-tech industries. Seattle's eastside suburbs, Chicago's northern and western satellites, and Fairfax County are rich in these human resources. Throughout America, high-tech businesses have flourished along the fringe taking advantage of the educated middle class. The string of suburbs constituting California's Silicon Valley is a world-famous incubator of computer technology, Tempe, Arizona, has labeled itself the Tech Oasis, whereas the Denver Technology Center sprawls into the affluent suburbs south of Colorado's capital city. DuPage County, west of Chicago, boasts of being the Silicon Prairie, Oakland County north of Detroit is Automation Alley, the hub of robotics technology in the United States, and Route 128 forms a high-tech arc through the western suburbs of Boston.

With much-traveled highways, wealth, and talent, the most favored suburbs have become dynamic centers of American business. They offer maximum access, money, and skills, and that is what attracts business. Commercial decentralization may take various forms—edge city, edgeless, or some hybrid of the two. Suburbs may also suffer momentary business setbacks owing to recession or the miscalculations of developers. Yet with the trinity of highways, wealth, and talent, the best suburban locations should continue their commercial preeminence.

The Varied World of Suburban Retailing

Perhaps no sector of American business is more suburban than retailing. With the decline of the great downtown department stores during the second half of the twentieth century, suburbia has emerged as the preeminent place to shop. It is the mother lode of modern consumerism, the destination for Americans seeking to satisfy their passion for spending. In America, shopping is a suburban pursuit.

During the last decades of the twentieth century the inescapable symbol of suburban shopping was the mall. Ridicule of the suburbs invariably included jabs at soulless malls, blank-faced hulks surrounded by vast parking lots where Americans accumulated consumer debt in the bland, climate-controlled environment of chain stores. The pinnacle of mall development was the gigantic Mall of America, which opened in Bloomington, Minnesota, south of Minneapolis in 1992. With 520 stores, this megamall was the largest enclosed shopping space in the United States, attracting over 42 million visitors each year; the Bloomington Convention and Visitors Bureau claimed it was "the nation's #1 visited attraction."[41] At the center of the mall was the seven-acre Camp Snoopy, the nation's largest indoor theme park, boasting two roller coasters.

Yet the opening of Mall of America did not mark the beginning of a new golden age for the suburban enclosed mall. Though the Mall of America attracted hordes of visitors its performance as a business investment was less than spectacular. In 1998 it earned $36 million for its owners, and the following year the operating income was up to $40 million. "That's a very shallow return for a project that cost $650 million to build," observed one leader in the shopping center industry. Ten years after its opening, two real estate experts estimated that the mall was worth at most $550 million, $100 million less than its cost of construction. "The Mall of America marked the culmination of the trend toward ever-larger enclosed malls," observed another expert in 2002. "I don't think we're going to see anything that big again."[42]

In the eyes of many knowledgeable observers, the Mall of America actually marked the beginning of the end of the nation's love affair with the enclosed suburban shopping center. By the turn of the twenty-first century, once-prosperous enclosed malls across America were losing customers and tenants. Americans were spending less time in malls; according to a New York real estate firm the average mall visit was down to only 40 minutes in 1999 as compared with an earlier average of 1.5 hours.[43] The International Council of Shopping Centers estimated that the giant regional malls were the site of 40 percent of all retail sales in the early 1990s, but that by 2005 this was down to only 20 percent.[44] In 1999 one student of retailing predicted that 15 to 20 percent of the nation's 2,200 enclosed malls would soon close. In 2002 a leader in the retail real estate industry offered an even more dire prognostication when he claimed, "a thousand older shopping centers with a staggering 7 to 11 million square feet of commercial space will be taken off the market in the next 10 years." Confronted by the prospect of widespread mall closures, in 2000 the National Endowment for the Arts sponsored a conference on "redressing the mall," with participants sharing their views on how to reconfigure the giant suburban hulks that were expected to blight the American landscape. "A substantial percentage of shopping centers have become architecturally, economically, and socially obsolete," reported one participant. "Abandoned, boarded up, or still in their death throes, these malls no longer generate profits, no longer serve their communities, and worse, drain the financial base and social spirit from their neighborhoods."[45]

Indicative of the change in American retailing was the website deadmalls.com, which first appeared in October 2000. Dedicated to recording the gradual demise of the mall and the preservation of mall history, by 2006 deadmalls.com listed more than 220 dead or dying shopping centers across the nation with information and memories contributed by nostalgic mall aficionados. "I want to try and preserve what they were," confessed one of the website's creators who grew up during the heyday of the malls. "I'm a product of my generation."[46] Though many retailing experts felt the dead mall eulogies were premature, even the International Council of Shopping Centers had to admit that the mainstay of its organization was no longer on the cutting edge of American retailing. The organization reported that only one new enclosed mall opened in the entire nation in 2006. An executive of the corporation developing this lone shopping center expressed hope, however, that an era was not ending. "Let's remember that the best-producing centers are still the enclosed malls," he observed. "Hopefully, in time the pendulum will swing back into more equilibrium."[47]

Contributing to the decline of the enclosed mall was the slow death of the department store. America's great department stores had served as the mall anchors; they were expected to draw the customers who would not only buy their merchandise but that of the smaller specialty shops located between the big general merchandising emporiums. By the first decade of the twenty-first century many department stores had disappeared; others were consolidating, circling the wagons for a unified resistance to the assaults on their once impregnable status. "Major department stores are a train wreck now," commented one expert on consumer shopping patterns. "When you see major department store shopping is down, and they can only sell things when they're 40 percent off, that is not a formula of success. That is a disaster." The consequences were evident in Atlanta-area malls. In 2003 Lord & Taylor announced the closing of its Atlanta-area stores and Macy's and Rich's department stores merged, closing three Macy's mall sites and leaving one half-filled. More than 1.3 million square feet of empty department store space brought gloom to eight of the sixteen metropolitan-area malls, the vacant sites constituting nearly one-seventh of the total space in those shopping centers.[48]

Perhaps the chief enemies of the beleaguered department stores were the rapidly proliferating big-box stores that were becoming ubiquitous features of the suburban landscape. Among these were the huge discount retailers Wal-Mart and Target, which offered an even greater range of merchandise than the old department stores and at bargain prices. Others were mega–specialty stores known as *category killers* because their massive inventories and lower prices precluded the need for smaller competitors. Notable examples were the home improvement centers Home Depot and Lowes, and the office suppliers Office Depot and Staples. Wal-Mart, however, was the preeminent big-box retailer, having secured first place among world retailers with nearly four times the revenues in 2004 as the second largest American chain, Home Depot.[49] By 2004, 82 percent of American households shopped at Wal-Mart; it was the largest private employer in the United States with 1.2 million workers and the largest owner of corporate real estate with 911 million square feet of space, equal to about 215 Malls of America.[50]

Yet the giant discounter and other big-box retailers have not won accolades from all suburban Americans. Wal-Mart's enormous warehouselike superstores of 200,000 to 250,000 square feet, the size of five or six football fields, surrounded by acres of asphalt are too often deemed aesthetic eyesores that attract unwanted traffic, drive established retailers out of business, and underpay their nonunionized employees. To limit the behemoths, a number of communities have capped the size of retail establishments. Suburban Contra Costa County, northeast of San Francisco, effectively forbid construction of Wal-Mart superstores by limiting the size of such stores to 90,000 square feet.[51] In 2004, voters in Inglewood, California, outside of Los Angeles, defeated a referendum measure that would have permitted a 200,000-square-foot Wal-Mart superstore in that suburb.[52] That same year the founder of Sprawl-Busters, a group dedicated to curbing Wal-Mart, observed: "Ten years ago, fighting Wal-Mart was so unusual it was a national story—small town beats Goliath. Today, these battles are all over." Moreover, the Sprawl Busters website listed nearly 200 communities that had "beaten big-box stores" between 1998 and 2004.[53] Despite these supposed successes Wal-Mart, Target, Home Depot, and their ilk remain an ever-increasing feature of the suburban scene. Some localities may force modifications in size and design, but the big-box juggernaut has continued to sweep across suburbia, and suburban Americans continue to fill the Wal-Mart cash registers with their earnings.

Though Wal-Mart generally opts for freestanding stores, many of the big-box retailers locate in what are known as *power centers*. The International Council of Shopping Centers defines a power center as "a center dominated by several large anchors, including discount department stores, off-price stores, warehouse clubs, or 'category killers.'" with "only a minimum amount of small specialty tenants."[54] These meccas for bargain hunters are among the most formidable rivals to the enclosed mall. At a power center the shopper can find more for less, taking advantage of the prices and inventory offered by the hulking giants of twenty-first-century retailing.

Further undermining the enclosed mall is the *lifestyle center*. During the first decade of the twenty-first century, these open-air centers of upscale chain specialty stores with an ample supply of restaurants and entertainment venues became the latest rage in American retailing and a new feature of the nation's suburbs. The first of these lifestyle centers was Saddle Creek, which opened in 1987 in the Memphis suburb of Germantown. It, however, spawned few imitators until the first five years of the twenty-first century when the format attracted development dollars throughout the United States. By the close of 2005 there were 147 lifestyle centers nationwide, 17 having opened that year, and 50 more were planned or under construction.[55]

Basic to the lifestyle concept is the creation of a pleasurable ambience of well-designed and tastefully landscaped outdoor plazas and walkways. The centers are intended to be reminiscent of the small town main streets of yesterday, but with such upscale retailers as Ann Taylor, Banana Republic, and Pottery Barn never found in those small towns. In addition, they have plenty of parking, thus correcting a flaw that destroyed main street retailing. "The concept is a modernized version of the traditional marketplace," according to two leading retail developers writing in *Urban Land*. It is "a return to the character and ambience of a small town with enhanced offerings that include in-demand retailers, restaurants, entertainment, and services for a complete shopping 'experience.'"[56] A Massachusetts developer reiterated this when he explained that his lifestyle center was "designed to give the customer a sense of place that is more than just a place to shop. It creates something of a downtown feel."[57] Clay Terrace, a lifestyle center in suburban Carmel north of Indianapolis, attempts to recreate a small-town main street by producing façades that seem to date from periods of the past. "The idea was to create a small-town streetscape from an architectural series of prototypical buildings that represent different eras of architecture," remarked the center's designer. Moreover, the center includes a village green, "a place to sit on a bench and have lunch, or for the kids to stop and play."[58]

Not everyone is enamored with the lifestyle centers. The president of a corporation that owns some of the nation's largest malls has called the lifestyle centers nothing more than "malls in sheep's clothing"; another mall owner labeled them "glorified strip centers."[59] And the emphasis on pedestrian space does not mean that the lifestyle centers are actually recreating the main streets of the past. "The lifestyle centers that work best for us are where significant convenient parking is available to our customer," explained one chain store tenant.[60] Shoppers may enjoy strolling past charming storefronts and sidewalk cafes, but they do not want to stroll too far from their car.

A variant of the lifestyle center is the *town center*. Like their lifestyle cousins, town centers are open air with attractive public spaces and a main street ambience. They are mixed-use centers including not only retailing and entertainment, but also offices, housing, and often public facilities such as libraries. They are intended to be 24-hour venues, places where people live, work, and play that will recreate the liveliest urban streets. "A true mixed-use town center brings together everything people want in one attractive, exciting place, often generating two or three times the draw of a traditional shopping center," explained one town center developer. According to him, "many people are hungry for homes in a true town center that allows them to walk to stores, restaurants, entertainment, even work."[61] In 2004 Crocker Park opened in Westlake, Ohio, west of Cleveland; in true town center fashion its plans called for offices and apartments located over first-story retail space along the project's main street. Its developers were adamant in their declaration that it was something more than a lifestyle center. "Crocker Park is very different from a mixed-use point of view," claimed its builder. "We basically are building the city's desire for a mix of uses with pedestrian connectivity."[62] In Plano, Texas, Legacy Town Center is a development of stores, restaurants, apartments, and tastefully landscaped open spaces dropped down in a preexisting mega–office park housing the headquarters of such corporate giants as Frito-Lay, J. C. Penney, and EDS computers. City Center Englewood in the Denver suburb of Englewood combines offices, retailing, apartments, and a civic center complete with a public library, city offices, the local courts, and a cultural and performance center.[63]

Though lifestyle and town centers seem to have upstaged the older malls during the first years of the twenty-first century, many mall owners are not passively accepting obsolescence and a place on the deadmalls website. Instead, across the country older malls have adapted to the new fashion for open-air centers by adding outdoor lifestyle streets to their existing enclosed facilities. The owner of Long Island's Smith Haven Mall launched its makeover in January 2006 with plans to demolish the mall's vacant Stern's department store building and replace it with an open-air center featuring such lifestyle mainstays as the Cheesecake Factory, Barnes and Noble, and Dick's Sporting Goods.[64] Meanwhile, the Atlanta area's gigantic Cumberland Mall was adding "a 77,000 square-foot lifestyle, pedestrian-friendly streetscape," and in suburban Skokie, north of Chicago, the venerable Old Orchard Mall was proposing to level the spaces once occupied by Lord & Taylor and Saks Fifth Avenue and replace them with a lifestyle center of specialty stores along "a Main Street-style shopping promenade."[65] In Lynnwood, Washington, north of Seattle, Alderwood Mall added an open-air lifestyle component in 2004 complete with Borders Books, Eddie Bauer Home, and Pottery Barn.[66]

The lifestyle and town center options seemed especially popular in the Denver suburbs where older enclosed malls were being bulldozed and rebuilt as open-air venues. City Center Englewood arose on the site of the obsolete Cinderella City Mall, a new town center arose in Lakewood, replacing the former Villa Italia Mall, and in Centennial Southglenn Mall was giving way to The Streets at Southglenn with 950,000 square feet of retail space and 350 loft residences. "In addition to offering a wide variety of today's most desired retail shops and restaurants," the developer promised, "everything at The Streets at Southglenn will be designed to provide residents with urban convenience in an accessible, suburban setting."[67]

This adaptation and restructuring has resulted in the hybrid center, yet another retailing format that promises to be increasingly significant in the future. As its name implies, the hybrid center is a shopping area that combines the features of the enclosed mall, the lifestyle center, and possibly the power center. Thus some older malls are not only adding open-air lifestyle components but attracting such big-box stores as Target and Old Navy, more often found in power centers, to fill spaces vacated by department stores. The newly constructed District at Tustin Legacy in Orange County, California, combines such power center mainstays as Costco and Lowe's Home Improvement with entertainment venues in an open-air format reminiscent of lifestyle centers. "We have introduced into the power center an entertainment component and lifestyle elements to create a regional power-lifestyle-entertainment center," explained the developer.[68] As retailing adapts to the decline of the department store and changing consumer preferences, the mélange of power center, enclosed mall, and lifestyle center will probably become more common or possibly spawn some new and as yet unknown format.

In any case, suburban retailing is continually reinventing itself. It is not dependent on the fortunes of the traditional enclosed mall. Instead, suburbs throughout the nation are breeding grounds for the shopping options of tomorrow. The enclosed mall may no longer be on the cutting edge of retailing, but the suburbs remain the shopping frontier. In suburbia Americans spend their money and developers and retailers experiment and innovate in a continuing attempt to get them to spend more. Rather than a bland environment of look-alike shopping centers offering more of the same, suburbia is the testing ground where investors are creating the something different that will be the next magnet for consumer cash.

The Fiscalization of Land Use

Shopping center developers are not the only parties interested in where suburbanites spend their money. This is a question equally important to local government officials struggling to balance municipal budgets. With a disproportionate number of homeowners, America's suburbs are inordinately concerned about property tax burdens. A successful suburban mayor is one who relieves the tax burden of his home-owning constituents, and the chief means of achieving this relief is through attracting tax-generating business. Consequently, throughout the nation suburban officials make land use decisions with an eye to reducing the residential tax burden and enhancing the commercial contribution to the public treasury.

This concern for accommodating revenue-generating businesses has been labeled the *fiscalization of land use*. In many American suburbs, fiscal policy in large measure determines land use decisions. The best use is that which produces the most tax revenues with the least costs—and that usually means commerce.

This fiscalization of land use is especially evident in suburban California. In 1978 California voters passed Proposition 13, which limited property taxes to no more than 1 percent of assessed valuation, and capped assessment hikes at 2 percent per year until sale of the property. With their ability to raise money through the property tax curbed, California municipalities turned to the local sales tax as an alternative. To enhance sales tax receipts they sought retail establishments, zoned for retailing and offered incentives to any business that could boost revenues. The math was simple; big retail sales meant a cash bonanza for a municipality and an end to budget woes. The result was an unseemly scramble for retailers, most notably big-box stores and giant auto malls. In fact, one author claimed that the auto mall "was invented in California—not by the auto industry trying to sell cars, but by local governments trying to capture sales taxes."[69]

Survey research supports such rhetoric. In a 1998 survey, top officials in California municipalities identified retailing as the most desirable use for both vacant land and redeveloped tracts. Local officials regarded residential and heavy industrial as the least favored uses. According to the municipal leaders, California communities were more likely to provide incentives for retailing than for any other form of development. The survey also found that the most important fact influencing development decisions was "new sales tax revenues generated."[70]

These findings are hardly surprising to anyone familiar with California local government. Well-publicized battles for sales tax dollars have erupted across the state. One example is the clash between Oxnard and Ventura over Ventura's plan to renovate and expand the Buenaventura Mall, a scheme that would draw anchor tenants from Oxnard's The Esplanade mall costing the city more than $500,000 annually in sales tax receipts. To ensure the survival and continuing profitability of the Buenaventura Mall, Ventura signed on to a $12.6 million incentive deal, agreeing to rebate to the mall developers 80 percent of the additional sales tax revenues generated by the remodeling and expansion. A Ventura city council member explained this generosity: "The bottom line is that people have got to understand that in our competitive society, if we do not improve our mall we are going to lose it." Oxnard responded by proposing a plan for sales tax sharing with its neighboring municipality, but Ventura rejected it. "Now because their shopping center has deteriorated ... they want to share," complained Ventura's mayor; "I haven't seen any movement from them wanting to share Wal-Mart and all those stores along the ... Freeway."[71] Lawsuits ensued as the rival municipalities fought for every available sales tax dollar.

The 2005 economic development plan of San Ramon, a fast-growing community east of San Francisco, also revealed the importance of retailing to California municipal leaders. The first goal listed was to "improve and expand upon San Ramon's retail services" and thus remedy the "significant amount of retail 'leakage'" that resulted from local residents shopping elsewhere. According to the plan, "cities with regional shopping centers and/or auto dealerships such as Walnut Creek, Dublin, Pleasanton, and Pleasant Hill, all generate far greater per capita sales than San Ramon" with per capita receipts ranging from $16,700 to $28,000 annually compared to San Ramon's $9,700. Because there was no need for another regional mall, the plan suggested development of a lifestyle center "with higher-end offerings" that would provide a "unique shopping environment" and "allow San Ramon to draw shoppers from the region and compete effectively with other retail centers along the I-680 corridor." Very importantly, a new retail center would "generate additional annual sales tax revenue for the City."[72] In other words, the lifestyle center was not only a means by which private developers could take on the aging Goliaths of the regional mall; it was also an option for municipalities seeking to carve out a sales tax niche and thereby profit. The burgeoning diversity of suburban retailing profited the public as well as the private sector, a fact well known to California public officials. Not only was the auto mall a municipal offspring, but if San Ramon leaders had their way, their city would also partner in the birth of yet another lifestyle center.

Municipal promotion of retailing, however, is not a phenomenon limited to California. By the beginning of the twenty-first century, thirty-three states had authorized local sales taxes, and they were especially significant in the West. Phoenix-area municipalities have equaled, if not surpassed, their California counterparts in their pursuit of sales tax dollars. During the first decade of the twenty-first century in Phoenix's Maricopa County, fewer than half of the twenty-four municipalities imposed a property tax, whereas all of them benefited from a sales tax. Receipts from the sales levy averaged 40 percent of the local operating revenues of the county's municipalities.[73]

With so much at stake, Phoenix-area municipalities have engaged in cutthroat competition for the most lucrative retailers. Gilbert and Chandler fought a costly auto mall tax war, each trying to outbid the other in incentives to prospective auto dealerships. In 2004 Gilbert secured a 100-acre auto mall in exchange for a rebate to the mall owner of half of all sales tax receipts up to $60 million. That same year, nearby Chandler agreed to a 50 percent sales tax rebate with an estimated value of $40 million as bait to lure a 90-acre auto park. Meanwhile, Mesa was negotiating a $12-million rebate deal to snare a 36-acre auto mall.[74] Yet Mesa seemed to be fighting a losing battle as more of its car dealerships departed for Chandler and Gilbert. "It's a significant concern for us," admitted Mesa's financial services manager in 2005. "As a market segment, they are a huge source of sales tax revenue."[75]

Some Arizonans were not pleased by the high price of attracting retailers. "[Phoenix-area] cities have been prostituting themselves for years for a hit of sales tax," complained one columnist. "Every week, the paper features a fresh orgy of incentives. So Glendale offered $17 million for Arrowhead Towne Center, ... Chandler has offered $42 million to land a mall ... Tempe has cobbled together $50 million for a mall that will help strangle its own downtown."[76] In response, state legislators proposed a ban on such retail subsidies. "Why is our money going to Wal-Mart, Costco and auto dealerships?" asked one lawmaker.[77] The answer was, Wal-Mart and auto malls meant money in municipal treasuries. As long as Phoenix-area municipalities received as much as half their local revenues from sales levies, they would do whatever was legal to lure big retailers to their communities. If barred from negotiating tax rebates, the bait might be in the form of zoning exceptions or expedited permitting. Retailers paid the city's bills, and thus in the minds of local budget makers they deserved favored treatment.

Utah's suburban municipalities have engaged in much the same pursuit for tax-rich retailing. In Utah half of sales tax revenues go to the municipality where the sale is made and the other half is distributed among localities according to population. Consequently, in Utah as in Arizona and California, municipalities have good reason to pursue big-box retailers and snatch them from neighboring competitors. "It's kind of a Cold War mentality," explained the vice president of the Utah Taxpayers Association. "Basically what you have is cities competing against each other for sales-tax dollars."[78] A poll of Utahns conducted in November 2004 showed that 55 percent would support the construction of a Wal-Mart in their city, and 80 percent said that a very important or somewhat important factor in permitting a big-box store in their community was the tax revenues generated.[79] Utahns were well aware that Wal-Mart meant not only lower prices but lower taxes.

In 2004 and 2005, the prospect of big-box tax revenues stirred a bitter conflict in the Salt Lake City suburb of Sandy. Sandy was a mature suburb with little undeveloped land other than a 107-acre former gravel pit. When a developer proposed a mixed-use project with a Wal-Mart and Lowe's Home Improvement store on the gravel-pit site, Sandy's tax-hungry city leaders proved amenable. An economic impact study reported a projected yield of more than $10 million in sales tax receipts over a 15-year period.[80]

Sandy's city council voted to rezone the tract to allow the big-box stores, and some council members were frank about their motives. "My reasoning has always been—and people hate me to say this—but we need the tax revenue it generates into our city," remarked one council member. "The bottom line is tax revenue," he continued. "We would never allow these types of businesses if we didn't need money from them."[81]

Some Sandy residents, however, were not convinced and organized Save Our Communities to fight the big-box invasion. Conducting a "park, not parking lot" campaign, these opponents preferred that the gravel pit remain open space and complained about city leaders' ill-considered fiscalization of land use. "I really think that the council is looking at the sales tax dollars, that this is all about money at this point," complained one foe. "I think that's a dangerous way to look at our community, and if you talk to residents, I don't think that is really why they moved to Sandy."[82] Yet it was a way suburban officials throughout the nation were thinking. Wal-Mart produced budget surpluses; whining homeowners produced deficits. In a referendum in November 2005, Sandy voters agreed with their tax-conscious council, approving the zoning change and opting for the fiscal benefits of big-box retailing.[83]

East of the Mississippi, Chicago-area suburbs likewise fashioned their land use and economic development policies based on the desire for sales tax revenues. Some municipalities, such as upscale Oak Brook with its giant Oakbrook Center mall, levied no property taxes, its homeowners being spared that expense owing to ample sales tax receipts. The opening of Stratford Square Mall in 1981 had a similar impact on the village of Bloomingdale. "The village portion of the retail sales tax eventually allowed us to drop the property tax from 50 cents to 9 cents," recalled a Bloomingdale official in 2003. "Basically the village can function without depending upon a property tax." But he realized that Bloomingdale had to be vigilant in its pursuit of retailing if it was to remain a low-tax domain. "For a lot of years we were blessed. A lot of retailers just came," he observed. "Now we need to be more proactive. They're not going to come here by themselves like they used to."[84]

Other Chicago-area municipalities shared this proactive stance and were straightforward in their preference for tax-producing retail over other uses. In 2004 the northern suburb of Buffalo Grove declared a moratorium on banks and other financial institutions. "What our board has indicated is that there is just so many banks taking up prime retail spots that could be generating sales tax for the village," explained Buffalo Grove's assistant village manager.[85] That same year the Hinsdale village board approved a moratorium on additional banks, barber shops, and beauty parlors—all businesses that did not pay off.[86] In 2005 the *Chicago Tribune* likewise reported that "a developer's proposal to add a non-revenue generating bank to the mix of businesses in a new building" in Winfield's downtown redevelopment area "drew heavy fire from the Village Board."[87] A village trustee of Oak Lawn explained the fiscal realities facing suburban officials throughout the Chicago area. "That's the key, to develop sales tax revenues," he asserted. "Every cent of sales tax that we bring in helps keep our property taxes down."[88] In 2003 the mayor of Palos Heights reiterated this argument. His community had recently lost two car dealerships that generated about $300,000 in annual sales tax revenues, and he was eager to lure upscale retailers to compensate for the loss. "The idea is to build a business base so we can shift some of that burden from the individual homeowner's property taxes and get revenue from sales tax," he argued. "It's not just to bring business to town—there's a logic to it."[89]

In some states, however, municipalities do not benefit from sales taxes and consequently fiscal realities do not dictate a pro-retail development policy. In Ohio and Pennsylvania, municipalities impose income taxes that together with property levies provide the largest portion of municipal funds. The result is an emphasis on the development of higher-wage office and manufacturing employment and a relative disdain for low-wage retailing. A 2004 survey asked Pennsylvania township officials, "What type of business would you like to see develop?" Service and technology was the preference of 31 percent, manufacturing was the choice of 29 percent, but retailing trailed with only 9 percent. When asked whether "development of new retail shopping centers [was] a high priority for your township," 77 percent answered no.[90] Similarly, a 2004 study of the fiscal impacts of land use in Ohio found that whereas office and industrial uses made money for municipalities, retailing was a drain on suburban treasuries. Because office employees had higher incomes than retail workers, office space generated substantially higher revenues than retail space.[91]

Ohio city planners were aware of this and devised their development priorities accordingly. The municipal income tax accounted for 43 percent of the revenues of the Cleveland suburb of Parma as compared to only 15 percent from the property and other taxes. Given this revenue structure, retailing was a fiscal loss to the community. Consequently, Parma's 2004 master plan proposed "to strengthen existing retail businesses, as opposed to constructing more retail space," because "retail businesses generally cost the city more in municipal services than the amount of tax revenues that they generate." The plan "recommended that the very small amount of vacant land which remains in Parma be devoted to uses which offer the City greater net fiscal benefits" such as "new industrial and regional office establishments." Parma planners noted with approval "the pending construction of the new Progressive Insurance processing center" and "the ongoing construction of new medical office buildings."[92] Under Ohio's municipal tax structure, these were the land uses that paid off. Physicians and insurance claims processors earned higher incomes than Wal-Mart employees, and office buildings generated less traffic-related expenses than big-box stores. The bottom line was that Parma should eschew retailing and embrace office buildings.

In the Northeast, the property tax has long been king, and any commercial establishment with a high assessed value is sought after by local officials. For example, in 2002 New Jersey ranked first among the states in per capita property taxes. Forty-nine percent of New Jersey's local government revenue derived from the property tax with most of the rest coming from state and federal aid. Moreover, it was widely believed that additional residential development did nothing to relieve this burden. A study found that for every dollar of revenue generated by new housing, the resultant costs to local government ranged from $1.14 to $1.51. Commercial and industrial development, however, cost only $0.17 to $0.34 for every dollar of tax receipts. According to a 2005 report on the property tax in New Jersey, these figures had "a significant effect on New Jersey's built environment. Municipalities overzone for commercial development, such as malls and office parks, and underzone for housing, especially multi-family housing."[93]

The same fiscal facts of life influence land use and development in New England. At the turn of the century in the upscale outer suburb of Littleton, Massachusetts, over 70 percent of all local revenues came from the property tax, and the town's 2002 master plan estimated that one dollar of residential development cost $1.16 in services, whereas one dollar of commercial development cost only $0.37 to the town government. The difference was largely owing to school expenditures that made up more than half the town's budget. Littleton's residences generated school expenditures of $7.6 million; its businesses cost the schools nothing.[94] Malls, office parks, and factories do not house children demanding a high-priced education—three- and four-bedroom homes do. For local budget makers in New England, this is an all-important distinction. To keep taxes low and meet payrolls, New England town governments have therefore pursued a no-children development policy.

Local officials have repeatedly expressed their preference for commerce over residential developments swarming with children. The town manager of Smithfield, Rhode Island, extolled a new shopping center in his town. "It's produced a lot of jobs; it's produced a considerable amount of revenue for our town, with a minimal impact," he explained. "There's very little service delivery that we provide for the revenue that we're getting." And he added, "They don't put kids in the schools."[95] In Johnston, Rhode Island, a town council advocate of a new BJ's Wholesale Club asserted, "It's a wonderful draw for the town," He claimed, "They use no police and fire, they don't put kids in the school system." Moreover, he contended that officials in neighboring towns would be happy to attract the megastore. "One official joked that he would gladly knock down a school to make room for the popular store."[96] Meanwhile, by 2004 Stoughton, a Massachusetts suburb south of Boston, was developing into a retail destination, offering incentives to the Swedish big-box furniture retailer IKEA and the discount giants Target and Kohl's. Some townspeople feared this would change the quality of life in the once peaceful community. But one longtime Stoughton resident expressed a sentiment that other suburbanites across the country would second: "Anything that brings in tax dollars that would decrease my taxes, I'm in favor of."[97]

The Northeast is actually not unique in its lack of enthusiasm for homes and children. Throughout the United States no matter the tax structure, commercial development is preferred to residential projects. In sales-tax-obsessed California suburbs, in the income tax domain of Ohio and Pennsylvania, in property-tax-dependent New Jersey and New England, housing is deemed a losing proposition from the standpoint of the municipal treasury and commerce a fiscal boon. As a result, suburban officials in every region pursued new business, and that transformed America in the decades following World War II. The exodus of business to the suburbs has not, then, been an unwanted invasion. This decentralization of commerce has not only shortened the suburbanite's commute to the office and trip to the store, it has relieved the suburban tax burden and proved a subsidy to beleaguered homeowners. The mall, the edgeless city office park, the big-box store, and the lifestyle center have all subsidized the suburban way of life and eased the otherwise awesome tax bill of homeowning residents.

Ironically, peripheral areas originally conceived as residential retreats of wholesome family life have developed into the domain of American commerce. They have sprouted edge cities, diffused into edgeless cities, and spawned a succession of enclosed malls, power centers, and lifestyle venues. By the early twenty-first century, many of these former bastions of the American family and home wanted nothing more than to be rid of child-producing families and housing subdivisions sucking cash from local treasuries. Changing patterns of work, shopping, and leisure, as well as the fiscal realities of American local government, have made a mockery of hoary stereotypes of suburbia. American suburbia of the early twenty-first century is not a haven or retreat. It is where Americans earn and spend as well as sleep. It is the twenty-four-hour focus of American life.

4

GOVERNING SUBURBIA

Governmental fragmentation is the essence of American suburbia.
By definition American suburbs are those areas that have eschewed
union with a larger hub and opted for a measure of autonomy.
They are independent principalities of local authority, and they
intend to remain so. Political division is the underlying principle of
suburbia, the basis for its being. The result is a confusing array of
municipalities, myriad Heights, Woods, Parks, and Forests, each
one jealous of its independence from the central city and from
each other. To those dedicated to orderly, centralized rule, this
jumble of often-conflicting governmental units may seem intolerable, but governmental disorder and discord are basic to American
suburban life, and anyone seeking to fathom suburbia must understand this devotion to disunion.

Throughout the twentieth century, a long list of academics
and civic reformers attacked this fragmentation, complaining that
it was inefficient and conducive to social inequity. Larger units
would supposedly deliver services more effectively and economically than the motley mass of suburban fragments. Moreover, these
fragments seemed to reinforce social segregation and inequality,

using zoning and other regulatory powers to keep out the poor and blacks and to attract and retain residential and commercial wealth to the detriment of their neighbors and the increasingly beleaguered central cities. Suburban government appeared to rest on a foundation of shortsighted parochialism and greed, a fact that critics deplored in articles, books, and policy reports. Yet the chorus of critics has hardly fazed the suburban structure of government. Most suburbanites view local self-determination not as selfish parochialism but as grassroots rule, authority in the hands of friends and neighbors in towns and villages tailored to their needs and concerns. It is power to the people, a perceived form of representative rule sacrosanct in the American system. And despite attacks, so far it seems invulnerable.

Fragmentation

Products of permissive incorporation laws and a desire for local self-rule, municipalities proliferated throughout the nineteenth and twentieth centuries, especially along the metropolitan fringe. According to the 2002 Census of Governments there were 19,429 municipal governments in the United States with Illinois, Texas, and Pennsylvania having more than 1,000 each. This does not include the town governments of New England, which the Census Bureau categorizes separately, but which are the primary units of local government in metropolitan Connecticut, Rhode Island, and Massachusetts. In Connecticut there are 149 of these near-sacred survivors from the colonial era, and Massachusetts claims 306 town bastions of local self-rule.

In addition, in 2002 there were 13,506 independent school districts in the United States, separate units of government charged with the oversight of public education. School districts are not necessarily coterminous with municipalities. In a single city there may be all or parts of two, three, four, or more school districts. Or within a single large school district there may be two, three, four, or more individual municipalities.

Adding to the confusion are special districts, 35,052 of which existed in 2002. Whereas the number of new municipalities has slowed considerably, special districts continue to proliferate. Between 1952 and 1972, the nation's inventory of municipal governments rose by 1,710, but from 1982 to 2002 there was an increase of only 353 new municipal units. By comparison, from 1982 to 2002 the number of special districts increased by nearly 7,000, a 25 percent rise in 20 years.

The burgeoning special districts are not general-purpose governments but usually focus on a single function. Especially common are fire protection, water supply, and drainage and flood control districts, but there are also library districts, park districts, cemetery districts, and special units providing a long list of additional services. Like school districts, special districts are not necessarily coterminous with other units of government. They can be charged with servicing only a small segment of suburbia or can be responsible for a multicounty regional domain. In California, the state with the largest number of special districts, County Service Area No. 2 in Los Angeles County comprises only 25 acres. In contrast, the Metropolitan Water District of Southern California extends over six counties and 5,200 square miles, serving 17 million people.[1]

Altogether the multitude of overlapping cities, towns, and districts add up to a complex structure of local rule unintelligible to many Americans. During the first decade of the twenty-first century in Chicago's Cook County there were, for example, 138 municipalities, the city of Chicago, and 137 suburban cities, towns, and villages. In addition, there were 30 suburban townships, 244 special districts, and 144 school districts. This included 38 fire protection districts, 47 library districts, and 92 park districts, each of these with a separate governing board and independent authority to levy property taxes and issue bonds.[2]

Immediately to the west of Cook County, suburban DuPage County included all or part of 38 separate municipalities, 26 fire protection districts, 34 park districts, and 42 school districts. Though some simple-minded citizens might believe that their village board was responsible for all local services, this was not the case. On its website, the Downers Grove Sanitary District made quite clear: "We are not part of the Village of Downers Grove." It was responsible for sanitary sewer service not only for the village of Downers Grove, but also for portions of the adjacent municipalities of Westmont, Woodridge, Lisle, Oak Brook, and Darien. And it was "a separate unit of local government, independent of the municipalities where we provide sewer service."[3] Similarly, the Lisle-Woodridge Fire District provided fire and medical emergency services for the village of Lisle and 80 percent of the village of Woodridge as well as some unincorporated areas, and the Carol Stream Fire District served the village of Carol Stream as well as portions of Bloomingdale, Winfield, and Glendale Heights and adjacent unincorporated territory.[4] In other words, residents of the village of Woodridge might receive their sanitary sewer service from the Downers Grove district but not receive their fire protection from the Lisle-Woodridge district. And a resident of Bloomingdale might receive fire protection from the Carol Stream district, which was a separate unit of government from the village of Carol Stream.

Confronted by the bewildering proliferation of local units, some states during the second half of the twentieth century sought to fashion a mechanism for the more orderly creation of governments and alteration of their boundaries. Minnesota pioneered this initiative. The rapid pace of post–World War II suburbanization produced in a single decade a total of 45 new villages in five of Minnesota's metropolitan counties. Nearly half of these new municipalities had fewer than 1,000 residents when incorporated. Seven actually had populations of less than 200, and one was home to only 43 people. Critical of this seemingly indiscriminate production of municipal governments, a 1959 legislative report argued that "multiplying villages, like rabbits, can outdistance all progress achieved by otherwise intelligent planning."[5] The Minnesota legislature responded in 1959 by creating the Minnesota Municipal Board, which was to conduct hearings to review and pass judgment on all incorporation and annexation requests in the state.

The board proved successful, and only two years after its creation a legislative commission reported that "the establishment of a statewide administrative commission to apply legislative standards in hearing and determining boundary change [was] indispensable to sound public policy in administering the future urban growth in Minnesota." Moreover, the commission had "found no expert that disagrees." The effect on the map of Minnesota was noteworthy. In the nine years before the board's formation, sixty-two cities with an average of 7.6 square miles had been incorporated in Minnesota; during the twenty years after 1959 there were only fifteen new municipalities organized averaging 30 square miles. Opting for fewer and larger units, the state board was clearly a deterrent to the proliferation of myriad small but autonomous fragments. In 1999 the duties of the municipal board were transferred to a state agency, Minnesota Planning, which continued the oversight of local government organization and boundary alteration. During the early twenty-first century the state agency processed an average of 350 to 400 boundary adjustments per year.[6]

California soon followed Minnesota's example in providing some supervision over the incorporation and annexation process. As in Minnesota the municipal birth rate troubled planners with ten new cities created in Los Angeles County alone in 1957. "At the present time, no one is charged with the responsibility of determining the effect of each one of hundreds of annexations or formations upon the future development of the entire county," wrote the executive director of the League of California Cities. "Lack of any coordinated review of such proposals has created many of our urban problems."[7] In other words, government formation in California was a free-for-all, and the state's metropolitan areas were suffering the adverse consequences. To remedy the situation, in 1963 California's legislature authorized the creation of a Local Agency Formation Commission (LAFCO) in each county, responsible for reviewing and approving or disapproving all requests for municipal incorporation, annexation, and the formation of special districts. The legislation as originally proposed called for a statewide oversight board, but owing to opposition from county officials, the final bill was amended to provide for a separate commission for each county made up of a mix of representatives from the county and cities within the county.

This structure has remained basically unchanged. Generally the LAFCOs have performed a reactive function, passing judgment on boundary changes proposed by municipalities and incorporation petitions submitted by residents. In the early twenty-first century, however, some LAFCOs have taken a more proactive stance to remedy the problem of small islands of unincorporated land surrounded by a city. Because of resistance from island residents or the unwillingness of cities to annex tax-poor tracts, the map of metropolitan California has been pockmarked with these tiny unincorporated areas embedded in municipalities. It has been difficult and costly for counties to provide services to the scattered pockets of territory, and in 2001 California's legislature authorized the annexation of islands of less than 75 acres by resolution of the surrounding city. Island residents were not able to block the annexation. In 2004 this was extended to pockets of less than 150 acres. To implement this law, LAFCOs actively pursued the elimination of the scattered pockets. In Santa Clara County south of San Francisco, the LAFCO issued a two-year fee waiver for island annexations, and elsewhere LAFCOs encouraged and facilitated the rationalization of municipal boundaries.[8]

However, the very existence of the multitude of unincorporated pockmarks forty years after the passage of the LAFCO legislation is damning evidence that the whole structure of oversight has had only limited impact on the ordering of local rule. In 2002 in the Southern California city of Orange, there were thirteen unincorporated islands comprising a total of 509 acres with about 350 homes.[9] As of 2005 there were approximately 180 such islands within fourteen cities in Santa Clara County.[10] These holes in California's municipalities were all-too-common reminders of the state's helter-skelter local government structure and the continuing problem of dealing with prevalent political fragmentation.

By the beginning of the twenty-first century, ten other states had created boundary review commissions. Some, such as Michigan, followed the Minnesota model authorizing a single board with statewide oversight of the development and alteration of local jurisdictions. Other states, such as Utah, emulated California with a separate board for each county. Missouri authorized a commission for only St. Louis County, a suburban area with a long history of controversy over incorporation, annexation, and local government structure in general.

In part because of the work of these oversight commissions, the competition for territory and power is not as ferocious during the early twenty-first century as in the wild, unfettered 1950s. New incorporations are less common and annexation squabbles generally less strident. Even more important, however, has been the role of special districts and counties in providing municipal services and thus precluding the need for incorporation and annexation. During the late twentieth century the growing number of special districts offered homeowners in unincorporated areas many of the services enjoyed by residents in municipalities. Similarly, suburban county governments assumed responsibility for municipal services in unincorporated areas, thereby discouraging residents from seeking incorporation. If the county provides adequate policing and parks, why incorporate, especially if tax rates are lower in the unincorporated county than in adjacent cities. Many suburban Americans have opted for county rule over municipal government, defeating annexation attempts and eschewing the option of creating yet another incorporated city or village along the metropolitan fringe.

Yet all is not quiet on the suburban front; battles over incorporation persist and the political fragmentation of suburban America continues to thwart the best-laid plans of advocates of unity and cooperation. For example, this has been true in Miami-Dade County, Florida. From 1950 through 1969, 114 new municipalities organized in the state of Florida, but from 1970 through 1989 this pace slowed markedly with a total of only 9 new governments. In the 1990s, however, the municipal birth rate picked up in part because of rising incorporation interest in the Miami area. Led by lawyer Gene Stearns, the wealthy communities of Key Biscayne, Aventura, and Pinecrest incorporated between 1991 and 1995, the first new municipalities in the county since 1960.[11] Sunny Isles Beach followed suit in 1997, and the pace quickened after the turn of the century with Miami Lakes voters approving municipal status in 2000, Palmetto Bay choosing incorporation in 2002, Miami Gardens and Doral both opting for cityhood in 2003, and Cutler Ridge residents doing so in 2005. This added up to a total of thirty-five municipalities in the county, more than one-quarter of which had formed in the period from 1990 to 2005.

Though the county provided municipal services to these areas prior to incorporation, advocates of cityhood repeatedly expressed a desire for greater local control and rule by friends and neighbors. An incorporation supporter in Cutler Ridge advised her neighbors: "Incorporation will provide residents with a local government consisting of members of the community, elected by the community." In its existing unincorporated state, "the county commission serves as both the county commission AND your city commission, yet [Cutler Ridge] voters can only vote for one of the 13 commissioners." Moreover, "all [county commission] meetings are held during the week, during the day, [in] downtown Miami, making attendance nearly impossible for local residents." And very importantly she insisted, "incorporation will provide for all taxes and fees currently being paid by area residents to REMAIN in the new city."[12] Advising Cutler Ridge voters, a resident of newly incorporated Palmetto Bay compared the response time of four hours by Miami-Dade police and five minutes for Palmetto Bay officers. "The question should be do you want service or not?" he stated to the Cutler Ridge electorate. "Incorporation provides you with local elected officials and local City employees who work to make your area the best it can be."[13]

The desire for suburban municipal autonomy cut across ethnic lines. The instigator of Doral's independence was Morgan Levy, but the work was carried on by Jose "Pepe" Cancio, and the first mayor was Juan Carlos Bermudez. Freshly minted Miami Gardens boasted of being the largest predominantly African American city in Florida, whereas other newcomers to municipal status were largely inhabited by white Anglos. At the tenth anniversary celebration of the creation of the city of Pinecrest, the mayor exclaimed that the municipality's dreams of becoming a "small, hometown community" had come true.[14] This was a dream being realized for a broad range of South Floridians.

Still other Miami-area residents sought to achieve hometown rule and struggled during the first decade of the twenty-first century to escape the thralldom of county authorities. The battle to incorporate The Falls began in 2003 when local residents rebelled at the inclusion of their community within the boundaries of a proposed 100,000-resident municipality of East Kendall. An incorporation advocate explained: "We thought we ought to be more similar in size to Pinecrest, Palmetto Bay," both of which had fewer than

25,000 residents.[15] Proponents of jettisoning county rule claimed that $3,536,878 raised from taxes in The Falls was spent in other areas of the county. "This tax money should stay in the local area," they argued. "The 'Village of The Falls' voters should decide locally how the money is spent."[16] In 2005 a resident reiterated this when he contended: "We want to bring government to us …. We want to be able to have a say how our dollars are spent" and "we want to control zoning of our neighborhood to maintain and improve our quality of life."[17] Not everyone in The Falls community agreed. "We are completely happy with Miami-Dade County running our area," remarked one fifteen-year resident. "This will be one more layer of government to dip its hands in taxpayers' pockets."[18]

Meanwhile, Biscayne Gardens was also considering incorporation as was miniscule but wealthy Fisher Island, an exclusive gated community of only 467 residents. "Is this a real city or a private city?" asked one county commissioner about the Fisher Island proposal in 2005. "I don't want to create a city that has different standings for the rich and the beautiful and at the other end the poor."[19] Equally interested in municipal status were the predominantly black communities of Goulds and Plant, but they were embroiled in a boundary dispute with the proposed municipality of Redland, where small farmers were seeking incorporation to prevent development of one of the last rural areas in the county. The wealthy, the small farmers, and the African Americans were all seeking municipal autonomy to pursue their separate destinies. The consequence was further political fragmentation of the metropolitan area.

As Miami-Dade fragmented into separate municipalities, the county commission became increasingly wary. Concerned about coordinated planning in the county's transit corridors, one commissioner warned: "If they all become incorporated and municipalities retain control of all zoning, we're going to have a very difficult time."[20] This was a fact of life throughout fragmented suburbia. How could the region as a whole realize its goals, if power was in the hands of myriad municipalities? Miami-Dade faced that conflict as it shattered into conflicting jurisdictions. The Florida metropolis, however, was not alone in its continuing struggle with fragmentation. A similar scenario was transpiring in Atlanta's Fulton County. Until 2005 Fulton County Democrats had blocked the incorporation of the community of Sandy Springs, a predominantly white area in the northern part of the county with 90,000 well-to-do residents. Incorporation would relieve Sandy Springs of having to pay taxes for county-provided services; in the past these taxes had not only financed public facilities and employees in Sandy Springs, but had subsidized services in the less affluent and predominantly black southern part of the county. Democrats favored this transfer of wealth and thus opposed municipal status for Sandy Springs, but when the Republicans took control of the state legislature in 2005, they authorized a referendum on incorporation in response to mounting grievances. Sandy Springs residents not only complained that the county was siphoning money from their pockets to subsidize services in poor areas, they claimed that county authorities had permitted too much development, particularly "tacky retail clutter" along Roswell Road.[21] Others criticized the poor services provided by the county. "I've called the police, and you could get a takeout order here faster than the time it took them to get to my house," reported one resident.[22]

In June 2005 Sandy Springs voters finally had their say with 94 percent of those casting ballots opting for cityhood and an end to dependence on county municipal services and land use regulation. "Sandy Springs can control its own destiny," proclaimed one exultant supporter of incorporation. "To have a city is a wonderful thing." Another resident reiterated what opponents of county rule had said in Cutler Ridge. "My major thing is, let's make the decisions here rather than downtown" in the county building in

Atlanta.[23] In Georgia as in Florida and the rest of the nation, suburbanites wanted rule close to home. Government by neighbors was better than government by distant county officials.

The Sandy Springs triumph ignited an avalanche of incorporation proposals as disgruntled Fulton Countians sought greater control over their destiny and perhaps more importantly over their tax dollars. In 2006 North Fulton state legislators introduced bills to create the cities of Johns Creek and Milton. The legislator sponsoring the proposed city of Milton claimed, "Fulton County, with 850,000 residents ... cannot provide true local government and local representation no matter how hard it tries." She argued: "A smaller, more local government allows for more meaningful participation by citizens."[24] Critics of the North Fulton independence movement claimed the motive was racism. North County whites did not want to pay for South Fulton blacks, but a leader of the Johns Creek incorporation effort emphasized that county opponents of municipal independence were more concerned about money than racial justice. "The color of this argument is green. It always has been and it always will be." He further contended that Johns Creek residents were fighting for nothing more than grassroots rule. "People want the decisions that are affecting their lives to be made by people they know and people they can talk to."[25]

Adding to the confusion, the existing city of Roswell was meanwhile seeking to annex the Newtown section of the proposed city of Johns Creek. Appealing to the prevailing sympathy for hometown rule, Roswell assured Newtown residents that "we have never lost our small town charm and our sense of family and community." In Roswell, progress was "in keeping with the neighborhood emphasis of the town."[26]

Faced with the threatened loss of North County subsidies and the seeming impossibility of the hard-pressed county treasury to continue to finance municipal services, South Fulton residents joined the free-for-all for survival, proposing the creation of new municipalities in their region. Consequently, in 2006 a South Fulton state legislator introduced bills to create the cities of Chattahoochee Hill Country and South Fulton. Basically, Fulton County was coming apart and every fragment was seeking the safety of municipal status. The multirace, multiclass unit of 850,000 people was yielding its municipal responsibilities to smaller governmental units presided over by officials deemed less alien and less distant.

This hasty and chaotic reordering of government was not necessarily the norm nationwide. Some county governments were attempting to withdraw from the costly business of providing municipal services in a more orderly fashion, and were actually promoting total coverage of the county by municipalities. Too often counties were left with the task of providing for those financially burdensome areas that no municipality wanted and that could not afford independent municipal status. The solution to this financial dilemma was to ensure that the entire county was within municipal boundaries; thus municipalities would be the sole providers of municipal services such as police, trash collection, and local parks, whereas the county would assume such regional responsibilities as the courts, prison facilities, regional parks, and possibly a regional airport.

During the first decade of the twenty-first century, Broward County, Florida, immediately north of Miami-Dade, attempted to realize this functional division by pursuing a policy to eliminate all unincorporated areas. Between 2000 and 2005 this resulted in the creation of two new municipalities, semirural Southwest Ranches and the predominantly black city of West Park. Existing municipalities were expected to annex the remaining unincorporated fragments. Broward generally proved successful in this effort, the unincorporated population in the county of 1.6 million residents dropping from 128,305 in 2000, and to 22,950 in October 2005.[27]

Yet Broward faced the same obstacles to orderly government organization that confronted policymakers throughout the nation. A disproportionate share of the unincorporated tracts was poor and black, and had remained beyond city limits because no municipality found it advantageous to annex them. Even though Broward's legislative delegation pushed through state legislation requiring the absorption of these tracts, some municipalities fought vigorously against annexation. The original draft of an annexation bill had determined that the white suburb of Plantation should absorb the black Melrose Park tract. Plantation, however, forced lawmakers to change their minds, and Melrose Park became part of Fort Lauderdale instead. "Unfortunately, Lady Justice is not wearing a blindfold, and it was pretty clear that race was an issue," commented one state senator. Plantation's city council president claimed the concern was financial. "Fort Lauderdale's got a broader tax base to lay the cost over than we do," he contended.[28] In any case, the often indistinguishable factors of money and race were clearly as significant in the more orderly division of local rule in Broward County as in the harried contest for survival in Fulton County.

Seattle's King County was also pursuing a policy of complete municipalization. In 1990 the Washington legislature passed the Growth Management Act, which directed that future growth in metropolitan areas remain within urban growth boundaries, and established that cities, not counties, were to provide basic municipal services. Counties were to be responsible for regional functions. Thus the act sought to combat sprawl and envisioned higher population densities as well as proposing the elimination of unincorporated areas within the urban growth boundaries. The consequence was a wave of new incorporations in King County as localities realized that they had better secure greater local control over land use to combat plans for undesirable high-density development. Moreover, the creation of municipalities seemed a wise step given the apparent future cutbacks in municipal services from the county. From 1962 through 1989, not one new municipality incorporated in King County, and only five did so in the entire state of Washington. During the 1990s, however, ten municipalities were created in King County alone.

Perhaps most important in the incorporation campaigns of the 1990s was the desire for local control over land use. The Citizens for Incorporation of Kenmore argued that "as a city, we can negotiate growth and density targets …. Although we will still have to accept some growth, we can better control how, when and where it goes and what it looks like."[29] In Woodinville, residents also recognized the need to take charge before outsiders indifferent to the community's wishes destroyed their bucolic domain. "It was just starting to get away from us," a community leader said of preincorporation development. "When I realized King County planners hadn't actually been here, I realized we needed more control," explained a member of the incorporation committee, Citizens for Home Rule. Ten years after incorporation, Woodinville's drive for self-determination had paid off, the community having successfully pursued a plan to "preserve the city's friendly, small-town identity and protect open spaces, historic buildings and traditions."[30]

In 2000 much of King County, however, remained unincorporated. Consequently, King County launched the Annexation Initiative with an "ideal scenario" of municipal rule over the entire urbanized area by 2006.[31] Yet by February of that year, 200,000 county residents still lived outside municipal boundaries as municipalities balked at the financial burden of absorbing tax-poor areas.[32] In 2004 the city of Kirkland claimed that annexation of the Juanita/Finn Hill district might produce a $3- to $4-million deficit, and Kent estimated an equal drain on its treasury if it absorbed the Kent Northeast/Panther Lake territory.[33]

Moreover, in some areas the question of annexation versus incorporation stalled the transition to municipal rule. This was the case in the Fairwood community. In 2004 a Fairwood task force filed a request for incorporation. "We want to be able to control our own zoning so we can keep the community quiet and laid-back, which is how it is now," explained the task force president.[34] The county executive's office applauded the action, which would be one more step toward blanket municipal coverage of King County. "This is basically the direction the executive has wanted to move in for a couple of years," a county spokesperson commented. "They really stepped up to the plate. We want to work with them to make sure it works."[35] But they had stepped up to the plate prematurely because serious doubts arose as to the financial feasibility of the largely residential area, which had few retailers generating sales tax revenue. Meanwhile another group, A Greater Renton—A Better Fairwood, favored annexation of the community to the suburban city of Renton. Though somewhat interested in the possible annexation, Renton estimated that absorption of Fairwood would entail a loss of $9 million per year to the city treasury.[36] In 2006 the Renton city council president advised "that the people of Fairwood would be wise before they incorporate to at least take a wait-and-see, and see what Renton has to offer in the coming years."[37]

Wait and see what is most advantageous to one's own frag-ment—that is the suburban credo. Localities will incorporate and annex if there is something in it for them. Otherwise they will drag their heels and thwart county or state schemes for the supposed rationalization of local rule. Throughout the nation, the interest of the fragment appears to prevail as cries of local control, grassroots rule, and hometown governance are as loud and commonplace in the twenty-first century as in the twentieth. A columnist in Salt Lake City called it "municipal Darwinism," communities "gobbling up the most attractive, tax-rich unincorporated areas and squirreling them away into cities."[38] In Salt Lake County as in Miami-Dade, Fulton County, and King County, it is a battle of survival for the fittest. Prosperous Sandy Springs withdrew its assets and let South Fulton fend for itself. Kirkland and Kent guarded their assets and balked at King County's initiative to abdicate responsibility for municipal services. The American tradition of fragmented local rule is alive and well in the twenty-first century.

Despite the criticisms of fragmentation, it does reflect the predilection of Americans to keep government close to home. African Americans, Hispanics, and Anglos all seem to share the view that hometown rule is best. It allows them to fashion their enclaves, evicting the tacky development along Roswell Road, preserving the farmlands of Redland, and protecting and perpetuating the small-town environment of Woodinville. Through creation of a separate government, suburbanites can ensure that Fairwood remains quiet and laid-back. Though cynical observers may regard grassroots rule as simply a selfish ploy enabling suburbanites to ignore the larger problems of American society, local self-determination is a deep-seated American value that appears firmly rooted in the national psyche. When Sandy Springs finally embarked on its independent municipal destiny, a local state representative proclaimed, "This event marks the end of our struggle for self-determination and freedom."[39] Many suburban Americans would second this sentiment. Freedom and self-determination are the foundation of American political thought, and nowhere are the shortcomings as well as the benefits of those values more evident than in suburbia.

Consolidation

Fragmentation has not remained unchallenged. Another venerable tradition in metropolitan America has been the recurring cries for consolidation or at least cooperation among governmental units. In the nineteenth and early twentieth centuries this often resulted in large-scale annexation of suburban areas producing the behemoth municipalities of New York City, Chicago, and Los Angeles. But the desire for unification has also manifested itself in schemes for two-tiered federative metropolitan rule, which preserved existing municipalities but added an overarching government responsible for regional functions and formulating coherent regional policies. The many villages would continue to provide local police, street, and park services, for example, but the metropolitan government would draw the fragments together, draft large-scale plans, and guide the future of the region as a whole. In the late 1920s and early 1930s, voters in the Pittsburgh, Cleveland, and St. Louis metropolitan areas confronted proposals for such a dual-tiered metropolitan scheme, but each of the reform initiatives suffered defeat at the polls.

There followed a lull in reform interest during the late 1930s and 1940s followed by a resurgence in campaigns for unification during the 1950s and 1960s. In the late 1950s the Cleveland and St. Louis areas again considered proposals for federative metropolitan rule uniting the central city and suburbs under a new regional layer of government—and again voters rejected the reform schemes. Reformers did succeed in consolidating the city and county governments in Jacksonville, Nashville, and Indianapolis, placing the unincorporated areas of the counties under the authority of the central-city mayor and council.

In the late 1970s and the 1980s, however, enthusiasm for city-county consolidation appeared to wane with no additional major cities opting for this reform during these years. Moreover, the apparent futility of imposing a federative metropolitan structure further dampened hopes for fusing the fragments of the American metropolis. As African Americans gained power in central cities, they joined many suburban whites in opposition to unification. Metropolitanwide government promised to dilute the hard-won power of central-city blacks and threatened to return them to the status of an ignored minority. Their share of the metropolitan electorate was far less than their percentage of central-city voters, so simple math seemed to prove that regional government equaled a loss of power. Metropolitan reform, in fact, appeared to enhance the political clout of virtually no one. It threatened the suburbanite and inner-city dweller alike. Consequently, it remained largely the unrealized dream of academics and a small corps of stalwart government reformers.

In the 1990s and the first decade of the twenty-first century, however, metropolitan reform experienced yet another revival as calls for cooperation and unity have once again become fashionable, though now under the label of the *new regionalism*. The new regionalists are less sanguine about innovative structures of government, such as two-tiered federative rule. Instead, they emphasize the need for Americans to think regionally, consider larger regional needs, and form regional alliances and coalitions. Eventually this might lead to formal consolidation, but the new regionalists believe that suburbanites at the very least have to recognize the wisdom of viewing the larger metropolitan picture and working with the central city to effectively tackle the problems affecting all regional residents. Regional economic development, transportation, planning, and social inequality are issues of significance to all metropolitan voters, and the new regionalists argue that it is in the electorate's common interest to work together in a metropolitanwide alliance to confront these shared problems.

One of the leading new regionalists of the 1990s and early twenty-first century is David Rusk, the former mayor of Albuquerque and author of the influential *Cities without Suburbs* (published in 1993 with an updated third edition in 2003). In this work Rusk focuses primarily on the need for cities and suburbs to cooperate in overcoming racial and economic segregation. He presents twenty-four "lessons from urban America," the first of which is that "the real city is the total metropolitan area—city and suburb."

"Any attack on urban social and economic problems must treat suburb and city as indivisible parts of a whole," Rusk argues. Though he recognizes the possible merits of government schemes to aid the urban poor, Rusk believes "absent efforts at reunification, such programs will be unable to reverse the downward slide of the inner cities." Thus "redeeming inner cities and the urban underclass requires reintegration of city and suburb." To achieve this reintegration and remedy racial and economic segregation, Rusk urges state governments to "improve annexation laws" and thereby "facilitate continuous central city expansion ... enact laws to encourage city-county consolidation ... empower county government with all municipal powers so that they can act as de facto metro governments" and require all governments to provide their fair share of housing for low- and moderate-income families, and institute tax-sharing programs that would require wealthy suburbs to share revenues with less affluent central cities.[40]

Other prominent new regionalists share Rusk's commitment to the necessity for cooperative action. In a series of "citistate reports" usually commissioned by the leading local newspaper, columnist Neal Peirce has assessed metropolitan problems and attempted to stimulate united action to ensure that each region can succeed in the competitive global economy. "Political boundaries are increasingly outmoded," Peirce wrote in his 2004 report on greater Boston. "A modern citistate ... is organic. It's a labor market, the reach of leading newspapers and TV stations, a medical marketplace, a 'commutershed.'" Thus he urged residents of eastern Massachusetts to think beyond their individual towns and acknowledge the shared interests of the Boston citistate. "Now the people of the region need to actually act on this reality," Peirce asserted.[41]

A third new regionalist crusader is Myron Orfield, a former Minnesota legislator who has emphasized the opportunity to build coalitions between central cities and stagnant first-tier suburbs suffering competition from growing outer-ring communities. Like

Rusk he has preached the need for redistribution of revenues from rich suburbs to poor areas, the provision of affordable housing in every suburb rather than concentration of the poor in the hub city and inner-ring communities, and the development of regional leadership to guide future growth. Like both Rusk and Peirce, Orfield has spread his gospel throughout the United States, speaking to civic leaders and preparing a long list of "metropatterns" studies presenting "a regional agenda for community and stability" for regions from Boston to Los Angeles.[42]

Rusk, Peirce, and Orfield have won powerful allies, including the prestigious Brookings Institution. In 2000 this respected think tank sponsored the publication of a collection of essays, *Reflections on Regionalism*, with a foreword by Vice President Al Gore who endorsed regionalism as "a powerful way of thinking and acting."[43] The momentum for change seemed to be mounting by the dawn of the twenty-first century with many vocal observers making the case for the desirability and even necessity of piecing together the fragmented map of metropolitan America.

Adding to the enthusiasm was the successful city-county consolidation campaign in Louisville, Kentucky. Between 1960 and 1990 the city's population dropped from 390,639 to 269,063, and from 64 percent of the Jefferson County total to only 40 percent. In the late 1990s, city leaders were all too aware that Louisville was a classic example of an older faltering hub in a fragmented metropolitan area. Making matters even worse was the humiliating prospect that Lexington would surpass Louisville as Kentucky's largest city in the 2000 census.

Faced with this dismal fate, a broad-based coalition of local government and business leaders secured state legislative authorization for a merger of the city and surrounding Jefferson County, subject to voter approval. Both Louisville's mayor and Jefferson County's executive endorsed the union, but the most vocal backer was the charismatic former mayor Jerry Abramson, who emphasized the need to boost Louisville's position in the census rankings and ensure its big-city status. If Louisville jumped from sixty-fifth largest city in the nation to the sixteenth position, businesses would supposedly take notice and relocate to the statistically enhanced Kentucky metropolis. The slogan of consolidation backers was "America's Newest Top Twenty City."[44]

To allay suburban fears and maximize voter support for the merger in the November 2000 referendum, the consolidation proposal actually provided for limited changes in the structure of government. The law authorizing the merger specified that "all taxing districts, fire protection districts, sanitation districts, water districts, and any other special taxing or service districts of any kind ... shall continue to exercise all the powers and functions permitted by the Commonwealth of Kentucky."[45] Thus all eighty-five small suburban cities would survive as independent municipalities and the twenty-one suburban fire districts would also remain in business. Highly fragmented Jefferson County would remain divided among an abundance of local governments. The proposal did provide, however, for a single mayor and single council to guide both the city of Louisville government and the county agencies. Moreover, it placed a moratorium on all annexations in the county until 2015, putting on hold the threat of annexation wars among the many municipalities seeking tax-rich additions to their domains.

Though the structural changes were not revolutionary, friends of consolidation believed that voter approval of the plan would mark an end to stagnation and the beginning of a new and better era for the Kentucky metropolis. "Mayors, county judges, local businesses and corporate recruiters have said for years that our divided political leadership and divided governmental operations hurt economic development," editorialized the *Louisville Journal Courier*. According to this metropolitan daily, "unification will give us a better shot at shaping a better economic destiny." Moreover, the newspaper warned central-city residents that "an assertive and affirmative new suburban politics is on the rise," which portended "the very kind of competition that has cut off so many other cities from the engines of economic, social and political power they need to maintain their vitality." Consequently, Louisville voters were advised "to reunite with their former neighbors and become influential partners in a common metropolitan government."[46]

Not everyone bought this argument. Black leaders feared a loss of power and opposed the proposal. National civil rights leader Jesse Jackson came to Louisville and warned African Americans that "merger represents extending the walls we come to battle." Appealing to his listeners through a baseball analogy, Jackson claimed, "merger means that now that we're about to get to the plate, they want to move the fence back."[47] Some suburban officials were also wary, with sixteen of the county's suburban mayors publicly opposing consolidation. The mayor of suburban St. Matthews expressed fears that the new merged government might in some way deprive his community of some of its taxing authority. "That's our biggest fear—that we could be forced into joining the new government because we'd be out of business financially," he explained. Yet forty-one officials of the small suburban cities endorsed the proposal, regarding fears of possible skullduggery as ridiculous. The mayor of Anchorage argued, "there's nothing vague" about the consolidation scheme. "It was carefully crafted to protect small cities and the services they provide."[48]

On Election Day in November 2000, voters dismissed opposition fears and approved the consolidation plan by 54 percent to 46 percent. It won in both the city and the suburbs, though predictably lost by overwhelming margins in the black districts. Amid much fanfare, in January 2003 the plan took effect with the merger's biggest fan, Jerry Abramson, as first mayor of the consolidated city-county; one year later Abramson was still proclaiming the merits of the new bigger image. "You've got to be on the radar screen for decision-makers to think of you," the mayor argued. "Once we were the 16th largest city, we could make the list of the top 20 or 25 cities in America every time they did a list—*USA Today, Financial Times, Newsweek, The Courier-Journal*."[49]

Though some questioned whether the "new" Louisville was attracting that much more attention from corporate bigwigs, it certainly was on the radar screen of boosters in other beleaguered metropolitan areas. During the first year of consolidation, delegations came from Ohio, Alabama, and California to investigate what was going on in Louisville, and about fifteen communities wrote or called officials of the new city-county for further information. "Louisville and Jefferson County are known internationally for what they did with their consolidation," explained an interested Alabama leader, and a metropolitan reformer from Syracuse, New York, commented: "Louisville's success left some people here believing that it can be done."[50] In November 2005 Louisville hosted a conference "Collaborative Government: Is Your Community Ready?" An expected two hundred delegates would gather to learn, according to one Pennsylvania mayor, "how Louisville accomplished a successful merger ... [,] did it right, getting everybody on board and joining one vision."[51]

Among those most interested in the Louisville experiment were officials in the Pittsburgh area. Metropolitan Pittsburgh had the distinction of being both one of the most politically fragmented regions in the nation as well as the area with the most consistent decline in population. Pittsburgh's Allegheny County was home to 128 municipalities plus 43 school districts, and its population had dropped from 1,336,449 in 1990 to an estimated 1,250,867 in 2004. Many of its governments were also near bankruptcy. In December 2003 the state of Pennsylvania was forced to intervene and fashion a financial recovery plan for the fiscally distressed city of Pittsburgh. Recognizing the need for drastic action, in 2004 both Pittsburgh's mayor and the county executive broached the idea of merging the city and county. Louisville's Jerry Abramson came to Pittsburgh to tell his success story, and the Allegheny County executive told business leaders "to pay particular attention to Louisville because there is a model out there that works for us."[52] Like Abramson, the executive emphasized the economic payoff of a consolidation that would transform Pittsburgh into the seventh largest city in the nation. "We're going to make it a big city again," he explained. "Companies are going to want to be here."[53] A University of Pittsburgh expert on public administration joined the chorus for reform. "There is no way we can develop [a] shared vision the way we are now governed," he claimed. "We look like the Keystone Kops, running off in a thousand different directions."[54]

Rapid action, however, seemed unlikely. "I'm a voice for my suburban residents, and I'm not going to saddle them with the city's debts," protested one suburban county councilman.[55] A resident of Homestead also voiced the concerns of many suburbanites. "Every one of the small towns has its own character," he argued. "I think we have to revive our towns [rather than consolidate them]."[56] In 2005 the county council president summed up realities. "I think [a full merger] will not happen in the near future," he said. "I think it will be more that both entities see ways to save money and eliminate duplication."[57]

Meanwhile, the equally distressed Buffalo region was also exploring the option of city-county consolidation. In 2004 Erie County executive Joel Giambra proposed merging his domain with the city of Buffalo to create a regional government. "People are beginning to realize we can't continue to do business the way we've been doing it and survive," Giambra claimed. "There's no such thing as a successful suburb if you have a dying city."[58] A commission appointed to study the proposed merger reiterated the sentiment of consolidation advocates in Louisville and Pittsburgh, emphasizing the benefits of a new metropolis-on-the-rise image for the down-at-the-heels Buffalo region. "This merger would make 'Greater Buffalo' the 10th largest city in the United States and would show the nation and ourselves, that we are a world-class, progressive region," announced the commission.[59] Others were more skeptical. "It makes for better headlines than solutions," observed an official of suburban Amherst.[60] A poll conducted in May 2004 found that only 39 percent of suburban voters favored merger of the city and county. "Why should a voter in [suburban] Amherst or Waterloo care who runs the City of Buffalo, especially when the proposed merger does not seem to bring any new assets to the table?" asked one study of the consolidation effort.[61]

By mid-2005 enthusiasm for metropolitan reform in western New York had waned. "No one knows for sure, but Giambra's notion of a full-scale merger of city and county governments appears dead, or at least relegated to the back burner," commented a *Buffalo News* reporter.[62] In the fall of 2005 a candidate for mayor of Buffalo likewise concluded: "I think metro government would be hard to get to even in the next 20 years."[63]

The story was similar elsewhere in the nation. In November 2004 voters in Des Moines's Polk County defeated a proposal to merge the government of Des Moines and the county by an over-whelming margin of 65 percent against to 35 percent in favor. The Greater Des Moines Partnership declared, "Greater Des Moines shouldn't be viewed as a crazy quilt of 69 independent local governmental bodies with the city of Des Moines stitched in the middle but rather as a single community with an interwoven economy, housing market, retail network, transportation system, cultural and education opportunities."[64] The voters, however, opted for the crazy quilt rather than the single interwoven community.

Perhaps most embarrassing to new regionalists was the repeated defeat of city-county consolidation on David Rusk's home turf of Albuquerque. Rusk drafted a report supporting merger, claiming that Albuquerque's instant leap to twenty-sixth rank among the nation's cities "would open up vast new marketing opportunities for how the unified community projects itself to the world." Yet in November 2003 consolidation failed by a vote of 38.5 percent for and 61.5 percent against, and in November 2004 a second proposal won support from only 41 percent of those casting ballots. "Unification will not be happening in the bold stroke that was in this charter," observed one merger proponent after the 2004 election. Instead, he believed that "unification is inevitable, probably in smaller, more directed steps. By that I mean joint powers agreements and greater cooperation between the governments."[65] Albuquerque was not to be the Lexington and Concord of any new regionalist revolution; rather unification would proceed, if at all, through incremental measures. Deploring the expansionist policies of suburban Rio Rancho, the *Albuquerque Tribune* summed up the frustrations of fans of regional rule in an editorial appearing soon after the 2004 defeat. "We're all in this together," the newspaper contended. "We all need to cooperate through real, regional institutions that have real power." The *Tribune* concluded: "The sooner we all concede that the sun doesn't revolve independently around our meager patches of middle Rio Grande earth, the better off we will be."[66]

Louisville's merger has thus generated a good deal of discussion but less achievement. City-county consolidation seems destined to proceed at a limited pace in the future as the barriers to reform preclude rapid change. In addition, any modifications in the fragmented structure of rule might well be more a public relations ploy than an actual unification of governments. Louisville's much ballyhooed reform eliminated very few governments and proved successful at the polls because it maintained the status quo for so many area residents. If Jerry Abramson had actually tried to create a united countywide city without independent suburban municipalities, he would have confronted an insuperable veto. His reform was as much sleight of hand as reality, and did not deviate from the American suburban tradition of grassroots rule. In the

Louisville area, residents could have their fragmentation and their census rank as well.

Another notable characteristic of city-county consolidation efforts of the early twenty-first century was the lack of interest in questions of social equity. Though Rusk and other new regionalists might have urged unification to overcome racial and economic disparities, Louisville leaders promoted their merger scheme primarily as a means to boost the region's reputation in the business world. Investment was the motive, not equality. The chief opponents of consolidation were African Americans who favored perpetuating race-based fragmentation, believing that through division they could best secure power. Similarly in the Pittsburgh and Buffalo areas, social fragmentation was of little concern. Solving financial problems and boosting flagging economies were the chief selling points for consolidation. If the new regionalists expected suburban Americans to abandon their separate governments in the pursuit of social harmony, they were doomed to disappointment. In the early twenty-first century, social equity through government consolidation was a concept that appealed to few metropolitan voters.

City-county consolidation, however, was not the only option for metropolitan reform. New regionalists also admired the multi-county metropolitan authorities coordinating regional functions in the Twin Cities area of Minnesota and in Portland, Oregon. Both seemed to provide regional leadership and curb the worst consequences of fragmentation. Consequently, they merited emulation in metropolitan areas throughout the United States.

In 1967 the Minnesota legislature created the Twin Cities Metropolitan Council whose members would be appointed by the governor. The council's authority extended over the entire seven-county metropolitan area; by the beginning of the twenty-first century these counties contained 188 separate cities and townships. Originally a relatively weak agency dedicated to preparing reports on metropolitan problems and services, it gradually acquired additional responsibilities, and by 2000 it was in charge of regional parks, the regional wastewater and treatment system, the regional transit network, and metropolitan affordable housing efforts. Moreover, it set regional development goals and reviewed the comprehensive plans of local government units in the metropolitan area and required that they conform to the council's regional blueprint for growth.

The Twin Cities area has also won applause for its metropolitan tax base sharing scheme. Created by Minnesota's Fiscal Disparities Act of 1971, the program requires each area municipality to contribute 40 percent of the growth in its commercial and industrial property tax base to a common pool. The revenue from a metropolitanwide tax on the pooled assessed value is then distributed to area municipalities according to a formula based on population and per capita property value. This has reduced the disparities between tax-rich and tax-poor communities, and in the minds of metropolitan reformers represents an admirable step toward social and economic equity. According to the Metropolitan Council, "From a regional perspective the Twin Cities is one economy." Consequently, all the metropolitan cities should share the revenue benefits of "commercial-industrial development that is ... the result of the regional market and public investments made at the regional and state levels."[67]

Portland Metro dates from 1970 and is a multipurpose district whose jurisdiction extends over three metropolitan counties. By the beginning of the twenty-first century, the elected metro board was responsible for regional land use planning, metropolitanwide solid waste disposal, the region's air and water quality, and the metropolitan zoo, convention center, performing arts center, stadium, and coliseum. Especially known for its stringent land use policies, Portland Metro has led the battle to contain sprawl in Oregon's Willamette Valley. This broad planning authority has made it a revered icon among proponents of regional rule.

Together the Twin Cities and Portland areas are, according to metropolitan reformers, enlightened models of what might be in urban regions throughout the United States. They prove that even in America, a greater degree of regional governance is possible. Though possible, such regional regimes have not, however, proven popular nationwide. Despite all the laurels heaped upon them, the Twin Cities Metropolitan Council and Portland Metro have not spawned imitators throughout the nation. They were admired models of metropolitan reform in the 1970s when they first flourished, and they remained inspiring exceptions to the national norm in the early twenty-first century. They have attracted much attention because they are unusual, not because they are emulated. Even within Minnesota and Oregon they have aroused opposition, and especially in the case of the Twin Cities council they have suffered periodic setbacks. Metropolitan tax base sharing has not brought peace among revenue-greedy municipalities. Fiscal zoning and competition for commercial properties continue. The Twin Cities council may provide some regional coordination, but municipal independence is jealously guarded and fissure often seems to prevail over fusion.

New regionalism has not, then, transformed the map of metropolitan America or defeated the American tradition of suburban fragmentation. In part this may be owing to the false assumptions and outmoded thinking underlying much of metropolitan reform. Metropolitan reformers have long assumed that the real community of interest and natural domain for cooperative governance is the metropolitan area as a whole as defined by the federal census bureau. They adhere to the increasingly outdated notion that the historic hub city is still the shared heart of the metropolitan area and that suburbanites should recognize this reality. Rusk's real city is a combination of the central city and suburbs; Peirce's Boston citistate is all of eastern Massachusetts, what he deems the natural commutershed of Boston. Yet in the early twenty-first century the most common commute is from one suburb to another, not from a suburb to the central city; the most common shopping destination is in one's own suburb or in a neighboring suburban community; one goes to the movies at a multiplex close to home. One may occasionally go to the central city to attend a ball game, but that older hub is not one's home turf, the place where suburbanites spend any significant part of their lives. Their true region is the portion of the census-defined metropolitan area that they frequent; for the plurality of Americans their real city is not the central city and suburbs, but the group of suburbs where they spend their lives. New regionalists claim that the larger area, a creation of the census bureau, forms one economy, one social unit, which should command the united loyalty of all area residents. Yet the everyday realities of life seem to indicate otherwise. For Long Islanders, New Jersey is alien territory, and regionalist rhetoric has not, and probably will not, change that fact of life.

Given this narrower conception of the real city, it is not surprising that the most common and possibly most significant examples of intermunicipal cooperation have been at the subregional level. Though observers may emphasize the governmental conflict and fragmentation of suburban America, in fact there is a long history of cooperation between neighboring communities and cooperative effort appears to be increasing. Suburbanites may shun big schemes of regional reform, but they will readily embrace pragmatic ties that promise to reduce taxes, improve services, and boost the quality of life of the area they perceive as their true region.

Signs of subregional cooperation are evident in eastern Massachusetts, an area known for the jealously guarded self-determination of its vaunted town governments. A survey of officials in the area's 101 towns and cities conducted in 2002 found that "virtually no respondents conceived of the Boston metropolitan region as having a common identity." But "to the extent that respondents looked upon regionalization favorably—as some did—they tended to identify with sub-regions within the region, areas that often encompassed no more than the several towns or cities adjacent to their own."[68] One example of this subregional identity is the emerging 495/MetroWest Corridor Partnership, comprising thirty-two communities with 539,000 residents on the western edge of what new regionalists would deem the Boston metropolitan area. Faced with the need to revitalize the area economically, and recognizing that a Boston-centric approach would not suffice, the thirty-two towns are cooperatively heading out on their own. According to its strategic plan, the partnership has sought to "develop a region brand/identity[,] ... to promote the region as a single cohesive entity," and to "identify 495/MetroWest as a distinct planning region."[69] The 2000 census reported that only 8 percent of the resident labor force of the thirty-two communities commuted to jobs in Boston; 57 percent commuted within the MetroWest corridor. The existing Boston-centric regional transit authorities thus do not adequately serve MetroWest commuters, and one of the partnership's initiatives has been to lobby for the creation of a MetroWest Regional Transportation Authority.[70] Basically, the partnership is saying to the state of Massachusetts and the world that these thirty-two towns are not best served if regarded as fringe suburbs of Boston. They constitute their own region, and they are acting cooperatively to market that separate identity. They are seceding from Peirce's Boston citistate and working together with neighbors who share common interests.

In the highly fragmented Pittsburgh region, cooperative effort is also prominent in a number of subregions of the census-defined metropolitan area. In December 2003, for example, the fourteen suburban municipalities that constituted the Twin Rivers Council of Governments submitted a joint comprehensive plan for future development, "the first, halting step, on a long-term, dynamic exercise in cooperative community planning."[71] According to its bylaws, the suburban South Hills Area Council of Governments

(SHACOG) is "a voluntary organization of municipal governments" that "combine our total resources for regional challenges beyond our individual capabilities while retaining and strengthening local home rule." SHACOG has lived up to this promise. Its purchasing alliance buys in bulk everything from police ammunition to rock salt, thus saving alliance municipalities millions of dollars. In 1998 it developed the specifications for a joint bid for solid waste collection for thirteen member municipalities with an expected five-year savings of $1 million.[72] Meanwhile, four suburban municipalities in the Turtle Creek Valley Council of Governments share all public works equipment and maintain such joint public works services as snow removal and street repairs. There may be 128 municipalities in Allegheny County, but that does not mean they are all going off in their own directions. Subregional councils are the means for voluntary cooperation that saves money and improves services.

Subregional cooperation has also breached the fissures in the fragmented Chicago metropolitan area. As of 2005 there were seven villages and two townships in the Barrington Area Council of Governments (BACOG), which described itself as "a regional planning organization that serves to foster discussion, to study area needs, and to promote coordination of activities to solve problems of a regional nature." The member governments share a common comprehensive plan that ensures none will suffer from adverse development in neighboring jurisdictions. Because it safeguards against inflammatory conflicts over land use policy, BACOG has been described as "an insurance policy for each one of the member villages, who never know when a fire may break out in or adjacent to their villages."[73] Each municipality maintains its own government, but they work together to ensure a compatible small-town, low-density lifestyle and lobby jointly before the state legislature to protect their mutual interests.

The West Central Municipal Conference is another Chicago-area subregional group that exemplifies cooperative effort among more mature, inner-ring suburbs. An alliance of thirty-seven municipalities and one township with a diverse population of 550,000 in west suburban Cook County, the West Central Conference, like SHACOG, engages in group purchasing, thereby cutting the expenditures of its members. And like BACOG it lobbies at the county, state, and federal levels to ensure an enhanced voice for its communities. Predominantly Hispanic Cicero joins with African American Maywood and upscale, Anglo Riverside in a common mission to save money, improve services, and get the most favorable treatment they can from the higher levels of government. The desire for cash and power transcend ethnic lines, and the diverse communities of western Cook County are united in the cause of protecting and perpetuating themselves.

Perhaps nowhere are subregional units as prominent as in Southern California. The Southern California Association of Governments had served as a regionwide planning organization in the late twentieth century, but the vast expanse of the Los Angeles metropolitan area seemed to demand the formation of more effective subregional bodies. Created in 1994, the San Gabriel Valley Council of Governments joined thirty-one cities east of Los Angeles in a common effort to deal with issues that transcended municipal boundaries such as transportation, air quality, land use, and solid waste. In addition, it has sought to raise awareness of the separate identity of the San Gabriel Valley. According to a council publication, "one of its primary achievements is that the San Gabriel Valley now has its own name recognition and political identity."[74] But the San Gabriel Council is just one of a number of Southern California examples of the subregional phenomenon. The Gateway Cities Council of Governments serves a like function for the twenty-seven cities in southeast Los Angeles County, the South Bay Cities Council of Governments is an alliance of fifteen municipalities in the southwest part of the county, and the Ventura Council of Governments is a voluntary cooperative effort of ten cities and the Ventura County government in the suburban area northwest of Los Angeles. "While as cities we all value what makes us unique and independent, there are times when our collective endeavors get better results," explained the chair of the Ventura Council in 2005.[75]

Across the nation, then, alliances have formed and the apparent fragmentation of suburbia has not invariably produced a free-for-all with each municipality fending for itself. Metropolitan reformers have not fashioned giant conglomerates and eradicated governmental divisions, but piecemeal cooperation has produced efficiencies that have saved suburbanites money, and councils and conferences have opened channels of communication and joint action among neighboring cities. In suburbia there is not an uncompromising devotion to isolation and independence; pragmatism often prevails. "Where money is concerned," observes one Massachusetts suburban official, "there is always cooperation."[76]

The subregional phenomenon also suggests that suburbanites do not conceive of their true city as the hub metropolis and all surrounding suburbs, nor are they likely to do so in the future. Despite scholarly claims of regionwide interdependence, the typical suburbanite's zone of endeavor is more constricted. Suburban Americans live and work in the San Gabriel Valley or MetroWest. Residents of the working-class Gateway Cities region may never set foot in upscale Ventura County. Boston is a place that suburban residents of eastern Massachusetts may occasionally visit, but they have not chosen to live or work there. Suburbanites are not gullible; they will not sacrifice their interests or chosen way of life because some author or census bureau demographer says that they are part of a region. Instead, actual experience defines their regional vision and self-interest fixes the boundaries of cooperation. An official in suburban Malden, Massachusetts, sums up the American ideal: "On the regional issues, you pick and choose which relationships you want to be involved with; we don't need an all encompassing regional government."[77] Freedom and self-determination are the precepts underlying the fragmented structure of American suburban government, and American suburbs reserve the right to freely determine for themselves the regional alliances that serve their interests.

5

HOUSING SUBURBIA

A house in the suburbs—that has long been regarded as the American dream. In the minds of Americans, suburbia has been virtually synonymous with the single-family detached house resting on a green lawn. Americans have aspired and saved for a suburban manse, and a large portion of the population has realized that goal. In 2005, 68.9 percent of American householders owned their home with the suburban rate rising to 76.4 percent as compared to the central city figure of 54.2 percent. Homeowning is the chief form of investment for most Americans; their house is their nest egg. And they expect their suburban governments to protect that investment without draining the homeowners' pockets. Thus suburban governments are expected to keep property taxes as low as possible and home prices high. That is the optimal formula in American suburbia and the foundation of suburban public policy.

In applying this formula, municipalities make vigorous use of the zoning powers, excluding uses and people deemed detrimental to home values and welcoming newcomers, both commercial and residential, who impose the least tax burden or actually relieve that burden. The exclusionary effects of such zoning, however, have come under increasing fire. Though the nation has long given lip service to the ideal of equal opportunity, exclusionary zoning thwarts the efforts of some Americans to realize their desired place in suburbia. Will protective land use regulation deny many Americans the suburban dream? Is suburbia on a collision course with the suburban ideal of a house and yard for all? These questions are attracting increasing attention in the early twenty-first century. Whether suburbia can meet the housing challenge and realize the dreams of millions of Americans is a problem that policymakers cannot ignore.

Affordability Crisis?

Fueling concern about access to suburbia has been the rising problem of the affordability of housing in many metropolitan areas. In recent decades housing prices have soared in a number of major metropolitan regions, threatening to keep many prospective homebuyers out of the market. From 1980 to 2004 housing prices adjusted for inflation rose 251 percent in Nassau and Suffolk counties on Long Island, and 180 percent in the Middlesex County suburban region of Cambridge-Newton-Framingham west of Boston.[1] Moreover, the rate of increase accelerated in the early years of the twenty-first century. In current dollars, housing prices rose 43.2 percent nationwide from 1999 to 2004 and 123.4 percent in the sizzling real estate market of California.[2] Yet during these same years the median household income in the United States increased only slightly. As a result, Americans were forced to pay a larger share of their income to realize the suburban dream.

By 2006 the stratospheric housing prices in some areas were making real estate brokers rich and garnering headlines throughout the nation. Leading the nation in inflated housing values was the San Jose-Sunnyvale-Santa Clara metropolitan area in California's Silicon Valley where the median sale price of existing single-family homes was over $746,000. The median home prices in the San Francisco and Orange County metropolitan areas of California also topped $700,000. On the East Coast prices had not reached California levels, but they were nevertheless far beyond the reach of most first-time homebuyers. The figure for the Nassau-Suffolk area was $475,000; for the Bridgeport-Stamford-Norwalk market in pricey Fairfield County, Connecticut, it stood at $471,000, and the median sales price of an existing single-family dwelling in the Washington, DC, metropolitan area was $423,000.[3]

To measure the impact of such prices on the average purchaser, the National Association of Home Builders computed a housing opportunity index. According to this index, in the first quarter of 2006 Los Angeles was the least affordable major metropolitan area with only 1.9 percent of the houses sold falling within the price range of families earning the region's median annual income of $56,200. To the south in Orange County, the situation was not much better with only 2.5 percent of the housing within the reach of median-income families. Nassau-Suffolk offered the worst scenario on the East Coast with 6.1 percent of the housing affordable to median-income residents.[4] In the Boston area the situation was much the same. Home prices there rose by 10 percent or more each year from 1997 to 2004, reaching a median of $376,000. By 2004 a median-income family could afford the median price of a home in only 27 of the 161 cities and towns in the metropolitan area.[5] An increasing share of Greater Boston was off-limits to middle-income residents. For those with less than median income, the situation in the nation's most expensive metropolitan areas was even worse. Their only option might be an overcrowded, converted garage in the Hispanic suburb of Maywood, California, or an overpriced rental unit in Boston's inner suburb of Chelsea. They might live in suburbia, but it was a suburban existence far removed from the American dream.

Faced with inflated housing prices, some Americans were giving up and moving out to cheaper areas. Between July 2004 and July 2005 there was a net outward migration of 43,126 from San Diego County, California, resulting in an actual loss of population of 1,728. "This is pretty stunning," commented a demographer for the local association of governments. He added, "The net out-migration (domestically) is so powerfully high," and he had no doubt about the cause. "What's driving this is the cost of housing," he observed. "It's just pushing people further east," into inland Riverside County. "This is quite a change from San Diego's image as a dream environment, but now 43,000 people are saying no," remarked another demographer. "It's the price of the housing that's driving them away, so it's time to pay attention."[6] One family forced out of the county was the Burnetts, who found an "affordable" home in the $300,000 range in distant Hemet in Riverside County. "The 88-mile drive is nuts," Eric Burnett said of his commute to San Diego, but he believed it was worth it. "It can be a long drive, but just being able to come home to a house where the kids are safe and comfortable makes all the difference."[7]

Other Americans were unwilling to accept life in an overpriced metropolitan area. One Southern Californian considering a move explained, "We like L.A., but you get more value for your dollar out of state." A graduate student agreed, "I'd rather move to another city [outside of Southern California] that's more affordable and have a home."[8] High housing costs were also a deterrent to life in the Boston area. "You try to recruit somebody from St. Louis—they can't afford to live here," said the chair of the Greater Boston Chamber of Commerce housing task force. "We clearly have a marketplace in Massachusetts in which it has become very difficult for the people who [already] work for us to find reasonably affordable housing, let alone to find people to recruit from outside the area."[9]

Long Islanders also feared that high housing costs were driving away prospective residents and young educated people vital to the area's economy. "The Nassau-Suffolk real estate market is red-hot, and ever-escalating home prices are undermining the middle-class expectation of home ownership that has been the foundation of our cherished suburban lifestyle," warned a Long Island state legislator in 2005.[10] The result was a supposed "brain drain" of young skilled workers that Long Island needed but who could not afford the pricey region. A Suffolk County commission claimed, "Long Island's young people, tomorrow's workforce and core population, are leaving Long Island in droves." In his 2005 State of the County Address, the Suffolk County executive asserted, "so many of our young people are just giving up and leaving for cheaper pastures elsewhere." As a result, "Grandparents are robbed of the opportunity of seeing their grandchildren grow up. Companies lack skilled employees. And we created an outstanding school system only to see students go away to college and never come back."[11] Long Island residents agreed; a 2005 poll revealed that 89 percent were concerned about affordable housing and 42 percent extremely concerned. Seventy percent of Long Islanders surveyed were worried that housing costs would force family members to move out of their county.[12]

In many areas there was growing concern that necessary public employees would not be able to find housing. In 2003 in the Silicon Valley suburb of Santa Clara, teachers' salaries started at $47,500, but according to one reporter, "in a place where tiny fixer-upper houses sell for half a million dollars and few apartments rent for less than $1,400 a month, the paycheck is hardly enough to live on anywhere close to school." The local superintendent of schools contended, "Even starting at $47,500, you'll never own anything in Silicon Valley for 10 or 15 years," adding, "You'll never have a chance because you can't get the down payment."[13] In booming Loudoun County, Virginia, west of Washington, DC, where the average sales price for housing exceeded $600,000 in 2006, nearly half of the sheriff's deputies lived outside the county, with many commuting from West Virginia and some making the long daily trek from Pennsylvania. "Most of them are looking to have a single-family home. They have a wife and kids and their dream is to have a home," explained a spokesperson for the sheriff's office.[14] The same problem faced police officers in the more upscale suburbs of Chicago. In 2004, all twenty-eight of the police officers in expensive Hinsdale lived outside of town. "It's a very nice community and we enjoy working here, but we just simply can't afford it," admitted the police chief.[15]

This affordability crisis, however, was not universal. Across the nation housing prices differed markedly, and in many areas life in suburbia remained a relative bargain. The West Coast and Northeast were least affordable and the source for most of the horror stories regarding suburban housing costs. By comparison, housing in the South and Midwest was cheap. In 2005 the median existing home price in the West was $335,300, in the Northeast $271,300, in the South $181,700, and in the Midwest $170,600. This gap increased notably in the late twentieth and early twenty-first centuries. Whereas in 2005 the median figure for the Midwest was 51 percent of the figure for the West and 63 percent of the median price for the Northeast, in 1968 the median housing price in the nation's heartland was 80 percent the median price for the West and 85 percent of the figure for the Northeast. The disparity had widened substantially in the late 1970s and early 1980s, had narrowed somewhat during the early 1990s when California's housing market cooled, then widened again in the early years of the twenty-first century.[16] The regional differences were not, then, temporary phenomena reflecting the superheated California market of the period 2000 to 2005 or a momentary inflation of prices in the Northeast. Twenty-first-century regional disparities were the product of a long-term trend that would probably persist even after inflationary pressures eased on the West Coast and in the Northeast. Periodic bursts of the housing price bubble on the East or West Coasts might occasionally narrow the gap, but the disparity was a long-standing fact of suburban life.

As price data from the South and Midwest indicate, the economic barriers to owning a suburban house were not uniformly high, and in many areas the door to suburbia was open to millions of homebuyers. For the last two quarters of 2005 and the first quarter of 2006, the Indianapolis metropolitan area ranked as America's most affordable major housing market with a median home price of $113,000. An extraordinary 90.1 percent of all housing in the metropolitan area was within the price range of families earning the median household income.[17] In other words, middle-income residents could afford nine out of every ten houses in the metropolitan area, including the majority of homes in the Indianapolis suburbs. In June 2006 in the upscale suburb of Carmel, a 2-story, 4-bedroom, 2.5-bath house with a 2.5-car garage on a cul-de-sac and treed lot was offered for $234,500, and another 4-bedroom, 2.5-bath, 3,700-square-foot home was selling for $224,900.[18]

With ready access to suburbia, Hoosiers were heading out of Indianapolis's Marion County for the purported advantages of life on the fringe. Carmel's Hamilton County and nearby Hendricks County ranked as two of the fastest growing counties in the nation with a 26 percent increase in housing units in each county between April 2000 and July 2004. "Let's face it, last year 10,000 people moved out of Marion and we saw 8,000 new people move into Hamilton," commented one census expert. "I'd say it's a pretty good guess that people in Indianapolis are going to the surrounding counties." Presenting the classic arguments for suburbia, mortgage officer Ed Gracia explained his move to Hendricks County. "It's a nice area," he said. "There's little crime, and we figured it would be a good place to raise children."[19]

Ed Gracia's good life in central Indiana contrasted markedly with suburban housing problems in troubled Southern California. At the beginning of the twenty-first century the Los Angeles suburb of South Gate was a blue-collar, immigrant community of Hispanic newcomers where 42 percent of the households fit the census bureau classification of low income. The city's 2005 general plan described its housing stock as "older, smaller, two-bedroom units."[20] Yet the median sales price of the fifty-five single-family homes sold in South Gate in June 2006 was $450,000.[21] For $51,000 less than that price one could purchase a 4-bedroom, 3.5-bath home with hardwood floors, a gourmet kitchen, and two-story great room with fireplace in elite Carmel.[22] For the price of an aging, miniscule tract house in Southern California, a central Indiana resident could purchase a luxury lifestyle in the region's most expensive suburb.

The relatively low housing costs in the Indianapolis area were not owing to sluggish population and lack of demand. Between 1990 and 2000 the population of the Indianapolis metropolitan area increased 17.4 percent as compared to a 6.4 percent rise in the Boston region where suburban housing costs stymied first-time home purchasers. Among the other relatively inexpensive metropolitan areas, however, were a number of depressed rustbelt regions that were attracting few new residents. In 2006, 87 percent of the housing in the Detroit-Livonia-Dearborn areas was within the reach of median-income families, and the figure for the more prosperous Warren-Farmington Hills-Troy suburban area north of Detroit was 82 percent. The declining Buffalo region vied with metropolitan Indianapolis for the rank of most affordable, and in the St. Louis, Cleveland, and Pittsburgh metropolitan areas, over 75 percent of the housing was within the price range of median-income families.[23]

Yet housing was also relatively inexpensive in a number of rapidly growing Southern metropolitan areas. In the Atlanta-Sandy

Springs-Marietta market a median-income family could afford 73 percent of all homes, and throughout booming Texas housing was a bargain. In the Houston-Baytown-Sugar Land metropolitan market the median sales price of existing single-family homes in 2005 was $143,000, 35 percent below the national median of $219,000, and in Dallas-Fort Worth-Arlington it was $148,000.[24] Thus there was no perfect correlation between price and population growth. In some areas with relatively stagnant populations, such as eastern Massachusetts, prices were high; in others such as St. Louis they were low. In West Coast growth areas housing costs seemed to threaten the suburban dream, yet in Georgia and Texas the dream was alive and well.

The good news from Georgia, Texas, and Indiana, however, was little consolation for those barred from suburban homeownership in California and Massachusetts. If the dream of a house in the suburbs was to become realizable not only in Indiana but in the nation as a whole, policymakers would have to tackle the problem of affordable housing and increase access to outlying communities. In the late twentieth century many took up this challenge, combating exclusionary policies and practices, and in the early twenty-first century these efforts continue. The goal is to make life in suburbia an option available to all Americans.

The New Jersey Experience

The most notable battle over access to suburbia has been fought in that most suburban of all states, New Jersey. From the late 1960s on, New Jerseyans have clashed over the barriers that prevent many Americans from realizing the suburban dream and especially over exclusionary zoning practices. Zoning has been the chief weapon in the suburban arsenal and has effectively rebuffed invasion by unwanted people and uses. Through careful application of their zoning powers, New Jersey's suburban municipalities have attempted to keep tax rates low and home property values high. In the process, however, they have closed the door to many of the state's less affluent residents. This use of exclusionary zoning became increasingly evident in the 1960s. From 1960 to 1967, more than 150 New Jersey municipalities raised minimum lot size requirements; none reduced the minimum permissible area of residential lots. By 1966 in the sixteen counties containing the newly developing suburbs of New Jersey, less than 5 percent of vacant residential land was zoned for quarter-acre lots or smaller. Over half, however, was zoned for minimum lots of more than one acre. Less than 0.1 percent of the land was zoned for mobile homes. In addition, communities were imposing minimum floor space requirements for dwellings as well as minimum lot widths. The cumulative effect was to exclude residents who could only afford a small house on a small lot or a mobile home. According to a critic of such exclusionary measures, these arrangements "ruled out practically all of the land for housing within the economic reach of 80% of New Jersey's population."[25] Through their zoning provisions, many of New Jersey's newly developing suburbs were making clear that the less affluent were not welcome to live within their boundaries.

To enhance their tax bases, many New Jersey municipalities were happy to accommodate revenue-rich business, but permitting construction of new housing for the moderate-income employees of those businesses was another question. Mahwah refused to amend its zoning ordinances to permit subsidized housing for workers at the community's Ford plant. Similarly, Franklin Lakes would not permit the construction of garden apartments for employees of its large IBM facility. "There is lots of empty land and cheap housing further out," commented one opponent of the apartments. "There's no reason why people should feel that they have to live in Franklin Lakes just because they work here."[26]

Criticism of such exclusionary practices mounted in the late 1960s and early 1970s as state planners recognized that New Jerseyans had to have some place to live. Paul Ylvisaker, New Jersey's first commissioner of community affairs, was convinced that "a suburban entity with zoning powers in the hands of people who are going to maximize their economic position ... is a dangerous thing," and contended that exclusive suburbs had "to rejoin the American Union." New Jersey's governor also complained of zoning "in suburban areas where a half acre, and sometimes two and three acres are required to erect a home, which prices the house out of the pocketbook of the average man."[27]

Governors and commissioners, however, were unable to force change. Consequently, New Jersey opponents of exclusionary zoning turned to the courts for a remedy. The litigation challenging suburban exclusion arose in Mount Laurel Township, a developing community on the suburban fringe east of the declining and increasingly black city of Camden. A small black community had existed in Mount Laurel for generations. Seeking better housing, leaders of this community proposed construction of a subsidized project of about one hundred low-income dwelling units. The land for the project was zoned for minimum half-acre lots, and Mount Laurel authorities refused to amend the zoning. The African Americans had good reason to believe that township leaders would do nothing to accommodate a continuing poor, black presence in the suburb. According to one black resident, a town councilman told them in the late 1960s, "If you can't afford to live in Mount Laurel, pack up and move to Camden!"[28] Unwilling to comply with this judgment and cede suburbia to middle- and upper-income whites, Mount Laurel's African Americans with the support of the NAACP instead brought suit, taking their challenge to exclusionary zoning to the New Jersey Supreme Court.

Before the state supreme court, lawyers for Mount Laurel asserted that suburban authorities had a right and obligation to use their zoning powers to protect and promote the interests of their constituents. "The Mount Laurel fathers are trying to do their best for the people of Mount Laurel," argued one attorney.[29] A sympathetic lawyer representing another township contended, "I don't see how you can compel a community to provide any kind of housing." Opponents of exclusionary zoning thought otherwise. An attorney advocating equal access to suburbia proclaimed, "The issue is whether zoning is going to be used by a private club to determine who is going to live in a community, or for the public welfare."[30]

In March 1975 the New Jersey Supreme Court ruled that zoning indeed had to serve the broader public welfare, holding Mount Laurel's exclusionary practices to be a violation of the state constitution. The court decided that New Jersey municipalities had to "make realistically possible an appropriate variety and choice of housing" and could not "foreclose the opportunity ... for low and moderate income housing." Each suburb was obligated to accommodate "the municipality's fair share of the present and prospective regional need" for low- and moderate-income dwellings.[31] In other words, the court was telling the suburbs that they had to rejoin, if not the Union, than the state of New Jersey, and shoulder a fair proportion of the housing needs of their region. The townships could no longer regard themselves as independent islands without bridges to their neighbors. Mount Laurel leaders had to do their best not only for the people of Mount Laurel, but also for the people of the larger region, taking into consideration the housing needs of all the people in the New Jersey sector of the Philadelphia metropolitan area.

In a concurring opinion, Justice Morris Pashman warned that the New Jersey Supreme Court should have mandated a more specific implementation plan to force compliance. According to Pashman, the "experience of the nation over the past 20 years must serve as a caution that, however much we might wish it, we cannot expect rapid, voluntary reversal" of exclusionary attitudes.[32] He proved to be correct. Local leaders across the state were neither happy with the Mount Laurel decision nor willing to comply voluntarily. In 1976 New Jersey's governor tried to tie distribution of state funds to voluntary compliance with the Mount Laurel ruling, stirring the ire of state legislators. "This may be the bicentennial year, but that doesn't mean we have to bring back King George III," observed one foe of this infringement on municipal freedom. "It's another instance of kicking the middle class in the ass," complained another defender of suburbia. The head of the New Jersey Builders Association summed up the local response when he observed, "Most towns are simply building new defenses. They didn't want [zoning reform] to begin with, and they still don't want it."[33]

Frustrated by inaction, the New Jersey Supreme Court returned to the question in 1983 and mandated an implementation plan that would supposedly get results. In its 1983 ruling the court assigned three trial judges to create a fair share formula that would set the low- and moderate-income housing goals for each municipality. Municipalities were expected to take affirmative steps toward realizing those goals. Moreover, to thwart exclusionary practices in noncompliant communities, the court authorized the builder's remedy. If a developer who was denied permission to build demonstrated that the municipality was violating the court's inclusionary Mount Laurel doctrine, then the developer would be entitled to proceed with the project regardless of municipal zoning ordinances, provided that at least 20 percent of the proposed dwelling units were set aside for low- and moderate-income residents. Communities that resisted thus faced the prospect of developers' bulldozers and the possible onslaught of hundreds of units of low-income housing.

Just as the court was getting tougher, opponents of court dictation were growing angrier. "I don't believe that every municipality has got to be a carbon copy of another," announced Governor Thomas Kean in response to the 1983 decision; "That's a socialistic country, a Communistic country, a dictatorship." Picking up on this theme of judicial totalitarianism, a state senator claimed that if New Jersey accepted the court's ruling, "everything would be administered from the state level ... like Russia." And a township official complained: "I think it's a disgrace we're being forced to legislate the destruction of our town."[34]

Dedicated to curbing the intervention of the judiciary, Governor Kean and the legislature agreed on legislation that would remove administration of inclusionary housing programs from the courts. In 1985 the New Jersey legislature adopted the Fair Housing Act, which established the Council on Affordable Housing (COAH) to administer the remedy mandated by the court. The council consisted of eleven gubernatorial appointees and was an agency within the Department of Community Affairs. It would determine the fair share of low- and moderate-income housing expected of each municipality, and once the COAH certified a municipality's housing plan that community would be exempt from the builder's remedy. In addition, the 1985 act authorized Regional Contribution Agreements (RCAs) whereby a municipality could pay another municipality in its region to assume up to 50 percent of its fair share housing obligation. In other words, well-to-do suburbs could pay less affluent, inner-city communities to take part of their assigned share of low- and moderate-income housing and thereby keep at least some poor people out of their town.

New Jersey's beleaguered supreme court upheld the new legislation, and it has remained the foundation for the state's inclusionary housing initiatives. By 2006 the fair share program had produced more than 30,000 low- and moderate-income housing units throughout the state, most of which would never have been built without the intervention of the courts and the COAH.[35] The low- and moderate-income figure seems small compared to the 240,000 units of all types of housing built statewide during the single decade of the 1990s, but defenders of the program claim that it benefits thousands of less affluent New Jerseyans who would otherwise be without affordable housing.

Many, however, regard New Jersey's scheme as inadequate, falling woefully short of the ideal presented in the Mount Laurel rulings. It has not substantially promoted black integration into the suburbs. A disproportionate share of the fair-share housing in the suburbs has housed whites, not blacks. In fact, there is evidence that many poor suburban blacks have moved back into the inner cities to occupy fair-share housing there. Moreover, the suburbs have avoided accommodating large households; an inordinate portion of the low- and moderate-income housing has been for elderly whites. A study from the late 1990s reported that "white elderly females are exceptionally strongly represented in [COAH] housing, especially in the suburbs."[36] The suburban units have more often served moderate-income households rather than the poor. "The common wisdom, accepted even by ardent supporters of the Mt. Laurel doctrine," one observer has noted, "is that occupants of Mt. Laurel housing tend to be relatively high socioeconomic status but at a low point in their lifetime earning potential, e.g., 'junior yuppies, divorced persons, graduate students, the retired.'"[37]

COAH's implementation of the program has also come under fire. Its approval of Regional Contribution Agreements has been viewed as perpetuating social and racial divisions rather than breaching them. "RCAs have worked to concentrate poverty," complained one advocate of affordable housing. "We need to desegregate, you need to deconcentrate these social ills," agreed another critic. He was "very much appalled at how Mount Laurel has been implemented."[38] Eager to be free of local restraints on development, the New Jersey Builders Association joined in the criticisms. "Unfortunately, COAH has become little more than a state agency that is providing protective cover to municipalities that are seeking to avoid their constitutional obligation," complained the builders association in discussing its legislative recommendations for the 2006–2007 year. "It is now an impediment to the creation of affordable housing."[39]

Builders and affordable housing advocates felt COAH had not done enough; town officials felt it had done too much. Yet there was a consensus that New Jersey had not succeeded in solving its housing problems. By 2005 New Jersey housing was less affordable than ever, its housing among the most expensive in the nation. More than two hundred civic, business, and religious groups joined in a coalition, Homes for New Jersey, "united in the goal of putting safe, affordable and accessible homes within reach of everyone who lives in New Jersey." The organization warned, "It is no longer a problem only for the state's lowest-income residents," and added, "Soaring housing costs mean that growing numbers of middle-class people are now finding that they can't afford to live in New Jersey."[40] During the gubernatorial campaigns of 2005, the winning candidate embraced Homes for New Jersey's goal of 100,000 new affordable housing units, but many New Jerseyans recognized the obstacles to fulfillment of this promise. "Any program aimed at expanding the supply of affordable housing for both low- and middle-income residents must confront the issue of exclusionary zoning, which is practiced with abandon by developing communities throughout the state," warned a New Jersey newspaper in December 2005.[41]

Thirty years earlier the New Jersey Supreme Court had said much the same thing in its first Mount Laurel decision. Three decades had passed and the affordable housing problem had worsened. It was no longer simply a question of whether the poor or working class could afford to live in the suburbs; it was becoming an issue of whether anyone could afford to live in the entire state of New Jersey. And again the target of complaints was exclusionary zoning practiced with abandon throughout the state. New Jersey had created some affordable dwelling units, but it had made little if any progress in guaranteeing access to the suburban dream.

The Massachusetts Experiment

Second only to New Jersey, Massachusetts has won recognition for its attempts to open the suburbs. As in New Jersey, the fight against exclusionary suburban zoning became a major issue in Massachusetts during the late 1960s. A 1968 legislative report expressed concern that minimum lot size requirements and other land use restrictions were barring the poor from suburbia. "The interplay of these municipal regulations determines, in substantial degree," the report found, "the extent to which additional modest income housing is possible in relation to the local supply of 'buildable' land." The following year foes of exclusionary land-use controls introduced a bill intended to exempt builders of low- or moderate-income housing from the burdensome local restrictions. Opponents of the measure decried this proposed invasion of the prerogatives of local government. "Towns which establish two-acre zoning," argued one foe, "are simply trying to preserve the basic character and social structure of the community."[42] Despite the purported violation of home rule and the specter of state control, the legislature passed the bill in 1969, largely owing to united support from lawmakers representing the state's older cities.

Often called the Anti-Snob Zoning Law, but today generally referred to as Chapter 40B, the act provides that developers of subsidized housing can appeal local rejection of a building permit to a state board of zoning appeals, which can override the local veto and authorize construction to proceed regardless of municipal zoning requirements. Developers can qualify for the state override if at least 20 to 25 percent of the units in the proposed project are priced below market value. Thus the law opens towns to unwanted market-rate residential development if the builder includes the requisite share of subsidized housing. If more than 10 percent of a community's housing stock is deemed affordable by state standards, then the locality is immune from the appeals process. In other words, if suburban towns achieve their 10-percent affordable housing obligation, the state will no longer intervene.

As in New Jersey, the anti-snob legislation has produced thousands of housing units for the less affluent, which probably would not otherwise have been built, but it has not achieved a radical redistribution of the population or made most of suburbia affordable to the low-income masses. During the first thirty years of the law's existence, approximately 18,000 units of affordable housing were built as a result of Chapter 40B. Whereas in 1972 only 3 of the state's 351 municipalities exceeded the 10 percent goal, by 2002 this was up to 27.[43] Yet this also meant that after more than three decades, more than 90 percent of Massachusetts towns and cities had not attained the modest goal of 10 percent affordable housing. By the close of 2004, 21 of the 161 communities in the Boston metropolitan area had achieved the goal, yet even this limited accomplishment is misleading. The state counted market-rate units in rental projects that included subsidized housing toward the 10 percent goal. Consequently, some of the "affordable" units in the 10 percent total were actually not affordable. Counting only units truly affordable to households earning less than 80 percent of the region's median income, just 9 of the 161 cities and towns in the Boston area actually topped the 10 percent mark.[44]

Most of this Chapter 40B housing in the suburbs is for moderate-income residents rather than the very poor. A review of more than 2,000 affordable units constructed between 2002 and 2004 found that only 35 percent were reserved for households earning 60 percent or less of the region's median income, and a disproportionate share of the 35 percent was in the central city of Boston. A study of housing in Greater Boston concluded that "without additional subsidies," which were in short supply, the chapter 40B units "tend to serve households making between 70-80 percent of the area's median income rather than poorer households."[45]

More than three decades of life under Chapter 40B has not changed the attitude of suburban Massachusetts toward low- and moderate-income housing. In the early twenty-first century, Massachusetts suburban communities are as hostile and obstructive to state housing initiatives as they were in the late 1960s or early 1970s. During the first decade of the century, the fast-growing town of Bolton ranked tenth among Massachusetts towns in median income and had an affordable housing inventory of only fourteen units. In a 2002 survey Bolton residents were asked, "Do you favor the town actively engaging in the creation of 'affordable' and other housing options?" Fifty-eight percent answered no, with one respondent replying, "Affordable housing will put a huge tax burden on all property owners!" Another answered, "There should be no entitlement for anyone to live here .... People move all the time because they can or cannot afford a place—that's life."[46] Town leaders were just as resistant to state intervention as they had ever been. When in 2005 developers proposed a 20-unit Chapter 40B project (Minuteman Village in Arlington), one town official reacted in the spirit of 1776 against this state-imposed burden. "I find it offensive that they take the name of the Minuteman who stood up, fought and died against outside centralized authority cramming something down their throats," he remarked. "They wrap that cloak around this thing, which is the epitome of distant despotism telling local people what to do."[47]

By the early twenty-first century, Massachusetts suburban towns were not only hostile to low- and moderate-income housing, but to virtually all housing. In one town after another, residents opposed growth and especially any growth in the population of children. To avoid any increase in school expenditures, towns engaged in what one legislator call "vasectomy zoning." One-bedroom, moderate-income units were far preferable to three-bedroom, moderate-income homes, and housing restricted to senior citizens was welcome as an alternative to fertile families. "Our housing policies, if you can call them policies, have become very anti-child," admitted one suburban town administrator. "I joke that China at least has a one-child policy, because we don't want any," observed a town planner. Generally, housing was anathema to cost-conscious Massachusetts suburbs. One developer contended that any housing projects actually completed in the Boston metropolitan area amounted to "islands of success in a sea of failures."[48]

Given this antidevelopment attitude, Chapter 40B developments faced time- and money-consuming resistance that only added to the region's housing problems. The southern suburb of Scituate, for example, battled a 40B proposal for 250 homes. More than 100 citizens cheered when the town's zoning board chair told the project's developers that they had "a snowball's chance in hell" of obtaining permission to connect to Scituate's sewer system. The project site was hardly a natural beauty spot, having formerly accommodated an army artillery proving ground and a chemical lubricant factory, but residents preferred the vacant industrial wasteland to housing that would create traffic, burden the schools, and add more people to the area. "Residents are going to find multi-story buildings in their backyards," complained one resident referring to three proposed three-story apartment buildings. "The development is completely out of scale for the neighborhood," said another.[49]

The nearby town of Marshfield also engaged in an unsuccessful four-year battle to prevent a 98-unit 40B apartment complex from being built on the site of a former drive-in theater. "Anyone who thinks you can block 40Bs from coming and don't have to provide affordable housing—they're nuts," commented one Marshfield official in response to the opposition. "They want to pull the drawbridge up and say, 'I got mine.'"[50] Yet many Marshfield residents were irate and unwilling to yield to the state-imposed program. "Why does the State let builders destroy our ecosystem, pollute our wells and endanger children in the name of 40B?" asked a group called Marshfield Action. "Massachusetts isn't Communist Russia!! ... JOIN US TO SAVE OUR TOWNS!"[51]

Massachusetts towns, however, are not as defenseless in the face of housing development as opponents of 40B might imply. Deterring housing development is a mind-boggling array of regulations and restrictions. "I was amazed and appalled by the almost impenetrable thicket of barriers formed by Massachusetts state and local regulations," commented urban scholar Anthony Downs in 2003. "Those rules add to planning time requirements, create lengthy delays in gaining approvals, and demand costly additional construction steps." Downs contended that these regulations "all too often effectively block developers from building units that poor-to moderate-income households could afford to buy or rent."[52] A 2006 study agreed, claiming that "localities have demonstrated remarkable resilience and creativity in keeping the supply of housing low. If the state tries to limit the restrictions along any one dimension, communities will increase them on one or more other dimensions."[53] Among the creative devices for keeping people out of town is the traditional minimum lot size requirement. But communities have also imposed growth caps that limit the number of new dwellings built each year, wetland regulations more stringent than those of the state that prevent construction on any soggy patch town authorities might deem environmentally sensitive, and similarly strict septic-system rules that keep builders at bay.

By not providing a municipal sewer system and relying on septic tanks, towns can justify their low-density existence. For example, one sewerless community is Weston, the state's wealthiest town, where the median price of a single-family home in 2004 was $1.2 million. Though the town could afford sewers, their absence has excused Weston from accommodating many new residents. Weston's annual report for 2003 explained, "since there is no town sewage, each property must have its own septic system, which incidentally requires and legally justifies larger lots and setbacks." Thus the carefully zoned plutocratic refuge has avoided "haphazard overdevelopment" and "preserved a level of residential privacy."[54]

Given the high housing prices and resistance to residential development prevailing in early twenty-first century Massachusetts, exclusive Weston seems more the wave of the future than the inclusionary suburbs envisioned by anti-snob reformers of the late 1960s. In Massachusetts as in New Jersey, the state has made some dents in the exclusionary walls protecting suburbs, but it has not leveled those barriers or made life in Weston and similar towns available to many of the less affluent. The bottom line in Massachusetts, as in New Jersey, is that suburbia is less affordable in the early twenty-first century than it was in the late 1960s. Housing construction has declined not increased, and 40B has generated as much bitterness as building. Exclusionary policies survive in the guise of environmental measures, and wetlands take precedence over homes. The Massachusetts suburbs remain contested ground with residents doing their damnedest to keep newcomers out.

Affordable Housing Elsewhere

Elsewhere in the nation, states and localities have experimented with programs to make suburban housing available to all social classes. One of the most publicized schemes has been that of Montgomery County, Maryland, a generally upscale suburban area outside of Washington, DC. Like New Jersey and Massachusetts, Montgomery County has some of the most inflated housing prices in the United States, but affordable housing advocates have sought to provide a fair share of dwellings for the less affluent.

Montgomery County's moderately priced dwelling unit (MPDU) ordinance was enacted in 1974 and originally required that new housing developments of fifty or more units set aside 15 percent of the units as affordable. As compensation, developers received a density bonus of 20 percent, meaning they could build 20 percent more units on their land than the zoning ordinance permitted. The price and rents of units were to be controlled for five years. The duration of rent controls was later extended to twenty years, and the price of owner-occupied units was to be regulated for ten years. The required percentage of affordable units has changed over the years, as has the density bonus awarded developers, but the basic principle of the law has remained the same. New housing complexes must accommodate those who otherwise might be priced out of much of Montgomery County. During the first years of the twenty-first century the program was targeted specifically at households earning no more than 65 percent of the area's median income, which in 2000 was $82,800. In 2001 the county executive had fixed the annual income limits for beneficiaries of the program at $33,500 for a one-person household, and up to $52,000 for a family of five.[55] The program was not, then, for the poorest Americans.

During the first thirty years of the program, about 12,100 MPDU units were built in Montgomery County, earning the program accolades from affordable housing advocates nationwide. Yet production of the units peaked in the 1980s, dropping markedly after 1987 and remaining low in the early years of the twenty-first century. In 1984 the annual number completed reached a high of 1,224, but from 2000 to 2004 the annual figure ranged from 293 to 143. Meanwhile, in the thirty years from 1974 to 2004 more than 130,000 market-rate homes were constructed; in 2003 the 143 new MPDU units contrasted to the 3,940 market-rate dwellings produced.[56] Thus, as in New Jersey and Massachusetts, there has not been a flood of moderate-income Americans to the suburbs. Instead, with rapidly increasing home prices, life in Montgomery County has become less affordable.

Moreover, because price and rent controls have lapsed on many of the MPDU units, the number of affordable dwellings in the program has actually declined in the 1990s and early twenty-first century. Though 10,572 units were created between 1974 and 1999, by the latter date only 3,805 were still regulated. The owners of the remaining units could charge whatever the market would bear. From 1992 to 1999 price controls expired on 2,135 owner-occupied units, yet only 1,598 additional such dwellings were produced.[57] Given the continuing low production rate in the early twenty-first century, there is little likelihood of accommodating an increasing number of less affluent residents in program housing.

In the early twenty-first century there was little enthusiasm among Montgomery County leaders for boosting housing production of any type. The county adopted a policy aimed at promoting a faster rate of job growth while allowing housing construction to lag. County officials realized what was all too evident to suburban leaders throughout much of the United States. Jobs cost less than residents, so places of employment were preferable to homes. "This policy is good for the tax base," contended the county executive. The county council president admitted, "We have a regional housing shortage because of hurdles put up by local governments." Yet he explained: "I get elected to represent the people of Montgomery County, not the region. I support broadening the tax base."[58] In the every-jurisdiction-for-itself fiscal world of suburban America, the pursuit of tax dollars was all important. The consequence in Montgomery County as elsewhere was to limit housing, especially for costly children, and promote business. In Maryland as in New Jersey and Massachusetts, parochial fiscal realities were trumping regional housing affordability.

Nowhere is housing less affordable than in California, and there too the state and local governments have made some barely effective efforts to accommodate low- and moderate-income households. In 1980 California's legislature passed the Housing Element Law requiring each city and county to include in its comprehensive plan a housing element. In this element the locality was to describe how it planned to meet its share of regional housing needs and provide dwellings for all income levels. It was up to the locality, however, to actually implement these plans, and implementation has fallen short of stated goals. In 2002 a state commission judged the law insufficient; it lacked "teeth" and focused "on planning, not performance." That same year a study of forty cities and counties in the San Francisco Bay Area found that from 1988 to 1998, these localities built only 32 percent of the affordable housing they had targeted to produce in their housing elements. Agreeing with the state commission, the Bay Area report argued that the California law "would be far more effective if targeted incentives and consequences were tied to localities actually meeting—not just planning for—their need for a full spectrum of housing."[59] Moreover, the Bay Area performance was not unique. The Southern California suburb of Thousand Oaks identified a need for the production of 2,827 very low-, low-, and moderate-income units over the years 1998 to 2005. Yet as of mid-2002 only 13 percent, 371 units, had been built.[60]

Some of the affordable housing constructed was only "low-income" by California standards. In 2004 in the upscale Ventura County community of Camarillo, northwest of Los Angeles, a family of four earning $57,500 was classified as low income. In one of Camarillo's affordable housing projects, the low-income units sold for $195,000, well above the median price for all homes in the Midwest and South.[61]

A more recent convert to affordable housing legislation is the state of Illinois. In 2003 Illinois lawmakers approved the Affordable Housing Planning and Appeals Act, which required counties and municipalities, where less than 10 percent of the housing was affordable, to adopt a plan to increase their affordable housing stock. If a community failed to comply with the law, then beginning in 2009 a developer denied local permission to build a project including affordable housing could appeal the denial to a state appeals board. In relatively affordable Illinois, most Chicago suburbs met the 10 percent minimum, but forty-nine of the most affluent communities fell short.[62]

As elsewhere, the affected localities were reluctant to cooperate, if not positively hostile. A number of older, expensive suburbs had little or no space for additional housing. "I don't know where we'd put that housing," commented the mayor of Lincolnshire. "We're basically built out."[63] "I believe that obtaining these required percentages will be impossible because of the value of our real estate and our lack of available property for development," observed the village president of Glencoe, where the average home sale price in 2003 was $1,081,582.[64] In the Barrington area, the law clashed with the residents' devotion to preserving a semirural environment protected by large-lot zoning. "I think it will be impossible to comply with the law," admitted the director of the Barrington Area Council of Governments whose organization lobbied to amend or repeal the act.[65] Other suburban officials echoed comments in New Jersey and Massachusetts regarding state dictation. "Communities should develop themselves for what they are," remarked the Oak Brook village president. "I don't want the state to interfere with local governance."[66]

Some angry residents were more outspoken in their opposition. A village trustee of usually sedate Glencoe claimed that since passage of the affordable housing act "all hell has broken loose." She described a village board meeting where "the room was filled with screaming, arm-waving opponents" who "personally attacked those who had expressed an interest in following the [housing] law." According to this official, "Fears spilled out: Parks would be filled with multistory buildings, the state board would overturn our zoning, our tranquil village would be transformed overnight."[67] A group of residents from the affluent North Shore suburbs organized the New Trier Neighbors, whose president attacked the law as "social engineering." If "the home values in the town that you live are too expensive," he asserted, "the options are you have to move somewhere else or you have to make more money."[68] Basically, the New Trier Neighbors believed that no one should expect the state of Illinois to guarantee them a home in Wilmette, Winnetka, or Glencoe. That was a privilege to be earned.

This was a stance that millions of suburbanites would second. They had fashioned their New England towns, New Jersey townships, and Illinois villages to conform to their desired way of life, and they did not appreciate the states dictating an increased level of housing production or the creation of government-guaranteed refuges for those who could not afford life in the suburbs. Local self-determination was a basic precept of suburban America, and that meant that each locality should determine its own land uses. Any violation of this principle might result in screaming and arm waving in Illinois, cries of communism in New Jersey, and creative resistance through the discovery of hitherto unknown wetlands in Massachusetts.

Given the resistance, foot-dragging, and often nominal nature of inclusionary programs, the affordable housing initiatives have not had a marked impact on the nature of suburbia. After more than thirty years of effort, the schemes have produced some housing but not much, and most of that has been for moderate-income Americans, especially senior citizens. Millions of African Americans live in suburbia, but not because of affordable housing programs. There are also many poor residents of suburbia, but again most are not beneficiaries of government-guaranteed housing units. They live in the less affluent suburbs where the market rate is affordable or where immigrant newcomers double up and crowd into any structure available.

The most affordable suburban areas are those where inclusionary housing programs do not exist and have never been seriously considered. In central Indiana, Texas, and the Atlanta metropolitan area, housing prices have remained below national levels without such programs. An antidevelopment ethos has not restrained build-ers, and thousands of dwelling units have spread across the coun-tryside. In these areas construction is not a dirty word. Nowhere has black suburbanization proceeded at such a rapid rate as in the Atlanta metropolitan area, and thousands of Hispanics are realiz-ing the American dream in single-family homes in the suburbs of Dallas. Seemingly the solution of affordability is to make houses and not laws. Layers of inclusionary measures applied to already existing layers of exclusionary provisions may enrich lawyers employed by developers or embattled towns, but they have not opened suburbia.

6

PLANNING SUBURBIA

America's suburbs have deep roots in the past, dominate the present, and appear to be the preferred place of residence, work, and leisure in the future. Given the nation's continuing suburban destiny, the question arises how best to create the suburbs of the future and recreate the inherited suburban landscape. Though planners have drafted careful blueprints for suburbs since the mid-nineteenth century, during the past fifty years an increasing number of observers have trumpeted the planning failures of suburbia, portraying it as a zone of uncontrolled growth blighting the countryside, the product of rampant and unthinking greed. And in the early twenty-first century complaints about ugly strip malls and soulless subdivisions appear to be mounting. A growing number of Americans seem to be demanding something better. Yet the precise nature of that something better is in doubt. What will be the nature of future suburbia? This question has spawned scores of books and articles in the past half century and promises to remain a matter of contention as Americans struggle to define their suburban utopia.

To Sprawl or Not to Sprawl?

At the heart of the debate over planning suburbia is the battle over sprawl. Though exact definitions of the phenomenon differ, the term sprawl is generally used to denote the low-density outward expansion of metropolitan areas often characterized by leapfrog development. Rather than laying out compact, contiguous, interconnected subdivisions, developers skip over vacant land to create housing tracts or commercial strips ever more distant from the metropolitan core. Sprawl also implies automobile-dependent development where everyone must drive to every destination because homes are isolated in homogeneous residential subdivisions rather than within walking distance of stores and offices. Sidewalks are rare and only the most venturesome pedestrian will attempt the trek from the Wal-Mart parking lot to a Home Depot store down the road. Highways are the lifelines of sprawl, the arteries that make it possible and that perpetuate this supposed blight.

The battle over sprawl dates from the 1950s when William H. Whyte authored an essay titled "Urban Sprawl" in which he established the template for antisprawl rhetoric in the decades to come. Expressing sentiments that would become all too familiar to students of metropolitan America, Whyte proclaimed that "huge patches of once-green countryside have been turned into vast, smog-filled deserts ... and each day—at the rate of some 3,000 acres a day—more countryside is being bulldozed under." He argued, "With this same kind of sprawl ... we are ruining the whole metropolitan area of the future," and "the result is a mess." He concluded that "Sprawl is bad aesthetics; it is bad economics. Five acres are being made to do the work of one, and do it very poorly."[1] A decade later Whyte called on Americans to preserve "the last landscape," reiterating his criticisms of sprawling development. "We have been the most prodigal of people with land," Whyte told his readers, "and for years we wasted it with impunity."[2]

In the 1970s, criticism of sprawl moved beyond rhetoric and into the realm of statistical analysis. In 1974 the Real Estate Research Corporation authored *The Costs of Sprawl*, an attempt to measure in dollars the price Americans were paying for low-density development. This study concluded: "Sprawl is the most expensive form of residential development in terms of economic costs, environmental costs, natural resource consumption, and many types of personal costs."[3] Though reviewers of the study soon exposed flaws in its methodology, this report was often cited by foes of sprawl and remained a landmark in the evolution of the mounting assault on expansive, low-density land use.

The attacks of the 1960s and 1970s, however, were minor skirmishes compared to the full-fledged war on sprawl declared during the 1990s. Even in the wide-open spaces of the Plains, commentators decried the wasteful consumption of land. In December 1995 the *Kansas City Star* published a six-part expose of sprawl in the metropolitan area along the Missouri–Kansas border. "Like most American cities, Kansas City has been seduced by all things new," reported the *Star*. "The resulting sprawl has left in its wake a chronic rot, eroding our region from the inside out." The newspaper proclaimed, "We cannot afford the continuing chaos of sprawl."[4] That same year the Bank of America joined the fight, sponsoring an antisprawl study. With big business on board, foes of sprawl gained new confidence. "If the banks finally realize that sprawl can no longer be tolerated," observed one study, "recognition of the impacts of differing land development patterns on society's resources has indeed hit the big time."[5] Equally encouraging was the imprimatur of the apostles of God. In the late 1990s the Roman Catholic archdiocese of Detroit joined an interfaith coalition, which according to one commentator, was "working hard not only to curb and contain urban sprawl, but also to approach it as a moral issue that demands a response of justice and equality for all people living in the region." The mobilized archdiocese was "contacting all its 314 parishes to join in this ministry against sprawl."[6]

At the beginning of the twenty-first century, the war on sprawl remained unrelenting. "'Sprawl'—the uncontrolled expansion of low-density, single-use suburban development into the country-side—presents itself as *the* single most significant and urgent issue in American land use around the turn of the century," asserted the editor of *Harvard Design Magazine*.[7] Supporting this conclusion was an accelerating stream of books and articles reiterating many of the same arguments made over the past five decades. To inform novice warriors about the vocabulary of the conflict and the forms of development promoted by the enemy, Dolores Hayden, profes-sor of architecture at Yale, authored an illustrated *Field Guide to Sprawl* (2004).[8] Like a chart for enemy plane spotters, the field guide was a necessary addition to the battle gear of any crusader in the campaign to curb suburban development.

By the early twenty-first century, sprawl foes had formulated a long list of indictments against low-density expansion. One signif-icant criticism is that sprawl increases public infrastructure expen-ditures because of the demand for new roads and longer water and sewer lines to service the ever-expanding populated area. "Sprawl can inflate the costs of these new water and sewer hookups by 20 to 40 percent," contends one study.[9] A 2000 report on the costs of sprawl estimates that nonsprawling, controlled growth would reap a savings of $12.6 billion in water and sewer infrastructure expen-ditures over the period 2000 to 2025, and a $109.7 billion sav-ings in road costs.[10] Even with controlled growth the United States would face the prospect of monumental infrastructure outlays, yet by eschewing sprawl there would be some financial benefits. In the minds of some critics these savings are essential. A survey of the economic impact of sprawl concludes that the American public is not unhappy with the existing land use pattern, but "it simply can no longer afford it."[11]

Among the other costs of sprawl is the unnecessary loss of farmland to development. Dan Glickman, secretary of agriculture in the Clinton administration, has warned, "As our cities sprawl into neighboring rural areas, our farms are in danger of becoming subdivisions or shopping malls. We can't sit back and take our farms, and the food they supply, for granted." Founded in 1980 the American Farmland Trust is dedicated to making sure Americans do not take farms for granted and has lobbied vigorously for the preservation of agricultural land. In the late 1990s it claimed that "the nation's best and most productive farmland is being needlessly destroyed by sprawling growth patterns," and consequently "we are losing around 1 million acres of productive farmland each year ... especially near ever-expanding metropolitan areas, where 79 percent of our fruits, 69 percent of our vegetables and 52 percent of our milk are produced."[12] In the early twenty-first century its message has not changed, with its website warning, "every minute of every day, we lose two acres of agricultural land to development."[13]

Not only are farms casualties of sprawl but so, purportedly, are cities. Sprawling development drains older central cities of their residents, their businesses, and their tax base. According to foes of uncontrolled expansion, sprawl accommodates those who can afford to move outward, whereas the poor remain segregated in the aging core. Moreover, antisprawl crusaders argue that the state and federal governments have subsidized the new highways and other infrastructure of ever-expanding suburbia at the expense of the central cities. The public ledger has supposedly favored the fringe and beggared the core. Aided and abetted by government, Americans have thrown away their older cities in exchange for a newer, lower-density alternative, thereby shamefully wasting their existing built environment.

Equally at risk in sprawling America is the natural environment. Such major environmental groups as the Sierra Club and

Audubon Society have signed on to the antisprawl crusade. The Sierra Club has specifically launched the Challenge to Sprawl Campaign, which "works to fight poorly planned runaway development."[14] Of special concern to environmentalists is the rate of land consumption. Antisprawl researchers predict that uncontrolled development will consume 18.8 million acres of land between 2000 and 2025; by curbing sprawl, however, the nation can save 1.5 million acres of "environmentally fragile land."[15] The Sierra Club claims that wetlands, vital for filtering pollutants in America's water supplies, are diminishing at the rate of 120,000 acres per year.[16] And a 2005 study contends that "rapid consumption of land could threaten the survival of nearly one out of every three imperiled species in the U.S."[17] Concerned that "entire landscapes, seacoasts, river valleys, and forests are disappearing, covered over by highways, housing developments, and shopping malls," former Secretary of the Interior Bruce Babbitt recommends using the federal Endangered Species Act to check sprawling growth. In a triumph for Babbitt and likeminded environmentalists, the fate of the endangered desert tortoise, for example, has curbed indiscriminate sprawl in the fast-growing Las Vegas region.[18]

Environmentalists also indict auto-dependent suburbia for polluting the air. "Although emission controls have reduced tailpipe emissions, increased driving has offset that benefit," observes one critique of unchecked development.[19] Another claims that Americans can "count on sprawl-related increases in car travel to make air pollution 30 percent worse in 2010 than in 1989."[20] Among the foes of suburban growth, the automobile is often viewed as sprawl's weapon of mass destruction. Its tailpipes pollute, the impervious surfaces of its highways, driveways, and parking lots prevent percolation of rainwater into vital underground aquifers, and its engines are rapidly depleting the world's natural fuel supplies. And without the automobile, Americans could not invade the hinterland and plant homes in once-virgin countryside. "Suburban sprawl is wildly destructive of the environment, in terms of the land it gobbles up as well as the pollution created by zillions of unnecessary automobile trips," writes the distinguished architecture critic Paul Goldberger. In a judgment many sprawl fighters would second, Goldberger proclaims, "There is a fundamental contradiction between the principles of a civilized community and the idea of the automobile."[21]

Not only are the nation's natural resources at risk, so are its historical treasures. The National Trust for Historic Preservation deems sprawl as one of its greatest enemies; according to preservationists, sprawl threatens historic sites and creates unwanted competition for traditional Main Street business districts. In 1994 the trust joined in the struggle to prevent the Disney Corporation from creating a history theme park on the fringes of northern Virginia's suburban sprawl within a 30-minute drive of eighteen Civil War battlefields. In a full-page advertisement in the *Washington Post* the trust claimed that the theme park would "stand as a superscaled specimen of the leapfrog development that, year after year and acre after acre, erases the American countryside—sapping the vitality from existing cities and towns, fueling automobile dependency and its devastating impact on the region's air quality."[22] A decade later the trust remained vigilant in its defense of remnants from the past and in June 2005 placed a history-rich corridor running from southern Pennsylvania to central Virginia on its list of most endangered historic places. "New subdivisions sprout in the midst of cornfields," the trust noted of the endangered corridor, "meandering country roads are straightened and widened to accommodate traffic, traditional 'Main Street' towns find their character threatened by incompatible new development, and venerable landmarks are engulfed by sprawl."[23]

Yet another purported casualty of sprawl is the nation's health. A number of studies argue that auto dependency in sprawling suburbia has promoted obesity and hypertension. One foe of sprawl contended, "Americans were turning into whales because they lived in a landscape that discouraged walking."[24] Using a sprawl index, a study found that "for every fifty-point increase in degree of sprawl, the average resident was likely to be one pound heavier." Moreover, for every additional half hour spent in an automobile each day, the likelihood of obesity supposedly increased by 3 percent.[25]

Residents of sprawling suburbia may be fat, but according to critics they are not happy. Sprawl has destroyed close-knit pedestrian communities, and some commentators contend it has left Americans isolated, alienated, and fearful. "America, which was once the land of the free, because of the alienation of sprawl has now become the land of the frightened," contends one foe of uncontrolled development. "Sprawl has turned neighbors into strangers, and strangers into threats."[26] Another claims that "the sanitized suburban enclaves where we sought privacy, exclusivity, and prestige proved shallow, empty substitutes for the intimate human connections our parents or grandparents once enjoyed."[27] Physically and socially unhealthy, America's victims of sprawl seem doomed to a bloated, empty existence.

Not everyone, however, has joined in the diatribes against sprawl. A band of contrarians has emerged to challenge the long list of indictments and question the merits of government-imposed limits on development. Especially prominent has been a group of free-market devotees who oppose interfering with consumer preference for expansive, low-density settlement patterns. They reject the notion that American is running out of land; developed acreage accounts for only about 4 or 5 percent of the nation's area. They also scoff at the fearmongering about loss of farmland. With continuing agricultural surpluses burdening the nation, there is no danger of starvation. In addition, they do not share the auto-phobia of sprawl haters, but instead recognize the merits of the automobile. No other means of transportation affords such mobility and convenience, and accommodating automobiles is considerably cheaper than constructing and operating the fixed rail transit systems favored by many sprawl foes. Trusting in the market mechanism and deferring to consumer demand for suburban homes and automotive transportation, these supporters of uncontrolled development depict the sprawl haters as foolish meddlers in the free market who threaten to impose an unwanted way of life on unwary Americans.[28]

Foes of sprawl might dismiss these doctrinaire devotees of Adam Smith as obstinate ideologues who would prefer hell on earth to tougher government regulation of land use. But in 2005 sprawl fighters faced a more formidable threat when Robert Bruegmann's *Sprawl: A Compact History* appeared. A professor of art history and resident of a gentrified inner-city Chicago neighborhood, Bruegmann is a most unlikely defender of suburbia with seemingly no ulterior motives for thumbing his nose at antisprawl dogma. In his book, Bruegmann claims that sprawl is nothing new; since ancient times those who could afford to escape from the city have done so. Outward expansion is not a modern American perversion but a normal expression of the human desire for space, privacy, and mobility. Moreover, he contends that "there is little evidence that suburban sprawl is accelerating and considerable evidence that the opposite is occurring." In most metropolitan areas the lot sizes of new suburban subdivisions are smaller than they were in the 1950s or 1970s, and "densities are rising in at least half of the largest urbanized areas." One by one he dismisses the antisprawl contentions and argues, "there is an obvious class bias in these [antisprawl] judgments." According to Bruegmann, "in very few cases have these indictments against sprawl targeted architecture or landscapes acceptable to upper-middle-class taste, no matter how scattered or low density.... Sprawl is subdivisions and strip malls intended for middle and lower-middle-class families." In the end he warns, "We should be very wary of any sweeping diagnoses or remedies."[29]

Though his work grated the sensibilities of those sprawl haters who abhorred the mass of fat, isolated suburbanites threatening Civil War battlefields and desert tortoises, Bruegmann's work elicited applause from many readers fed up with years of antisuburban browbeating. In Long Island's *Newsday* an economist wrote, "It's time for certain Long Islanders to put aside their snobbish, selfish prejudices and learn to love suburban sprawl."[30] A columnist in the *Atlanta Journal-Constitution* argued that government should "look at how people choose to live, and serve them. Don't try to force us to live in configurations satisfying to central planners or those who would have us suffer highway congestion as punishment for making the wrong lifestyle choice."[31] The distinguished Chicago architect Stanley Tigerman commended Bruegmann claiming, "the intellectual perception of sprawl is a snobbish one that says it's all crap."[32]

Not only does the antisprawl campaign smack of snobbery, it can be criticized for providing needed ammunition to the exclusionary forces of suburbia. An increasingly significant suburban phenomenon is the obstructionist notion of "not in my backyard" (NIMBY). For many suburbanites, the only answer to anything new seems to be a loud "no." NIMBYism is rampant and relies frequently on the antidevelopment rhetoric of sprawl haters. Every new subdivision in an adjacent meadow or nearby woods is seen as unwanted sprawl by incumbent homeowners who enjoy their existing low-density, semirural environment. By crying sprawl, foes of change can lead a charge against any intruders in search of a suburban home of their own. In the NIMBY world of the twenty-first century, a convenient wetland may be sufficient to keep unwanted neighbors at bay; a wildlife habitat can block an unwelcome habitat for humanity. Rarely do existing homeowners perceive themselves as sprawling; only newcomers pose that threat. Basically suburbanites only oppose the sprawl of others; one's own sprawl is the American dream.

Smart Growth

Though antisprawl arguments may lend themselves to NIMBY abuse, foes of uncontrolled growth are not simple obstructionists opposed to all development. Instead, they have created an alternative vision for the suburban future, which they call *smart growth*. The basic principles of smart growth are the creation of compact, dense, walkable, mixed-use communities; preservation of open space and farmland; promotion of public transit with a resulting decline in the use of the automobile; and provision of a range of housing options including affordable units. Dedicated to curbing sprawl and getting people out of their automobiles, smart growth proponents envision a world where Americans will waste less land and walk more. Smart growth will supposedly produce vibrant urban environments that will foster a sense of community and spare the environment the devastation wreaked by the bulldozer and exhaust pipe.

During the early twenty-first century, a wide range of groups have joined in the Smart Growth Network, a coalition of private- and public-sector bodies dedicated to realizing the antisprawl agenda. The network partners include such stalwart sprawl haters as the American Farmland Trust and the National Trust for Historic Preservation, as well as such influential organizations as the American Planning Association, the National Association of Counties, the United States Environmental Protection Agency, and the National Association of Realtors. Also promoting smart growth are such strange bedfellows as the Sierra Club and the National Association of Home Builders. The American Institute of Architects has endorsed the creation of "livable" communities with all the smart growth characteristics, and the Boston Society of Architects is one of the instigators and most devoted components of the Massachusetts Smart Growth Alliance.[33] With unusual accord the nation's major organizations have united behind smart growth slogans and eschewed the uncontrolled, low-density development known as sprawl.

Smart growth, however, is not simply a vision; in some parts of the country it has been translated into reality. The preeminent smart growth model, and a mecca for all sprawl haters, is Portland, Oregon. In 1973 Oregon's legislature adopted the Land Conservation and Development Act, which required cities and metropolitan areas to fix urban growth boundaries. All urban development had to take place within these boundaries; the great majority of the state outside the limits was to remain rural and exempt from sprawl. Metropolitan Portland's growth boundary has won applause throughout the nation for its seeming success in stanching uncontrolled growth. "Drive south on I-5 from Portland, a city of 1.3 million, to Salem, the state capital less than 50 miles away, and you won't see the typical commercial strip sprawl, runaway roadside development and far-flung subdivisions that characterize many other highly traveled corridors in the U.S.," wrote one admirer. "What you see instead are pastoral landscapes of farms and fields in the fertile Willamette Valley, broken by occasional copses of evergreens." According to this observer, "the fact that much of the countryside is still rural can largely be attributed to Oregon's statewide land use planning program."[34]

Statistical data supported these observations. From 1980 to 1994 Portland's metropolitan population increased 25 percent, whereas the area of developed land rose only 16 percent. The density of new housing climbed from five units per acre in 1994 to eight units per acre in 1998. By the latter year the average lot size for new housing was 6,200 square feet as compared to 12,800 square feet twenty years earlier.[35] Contributing to this increase in density was a state rule requiring municipalities to reserve at least half of vacant residential land for apartments or attached dwellings. In Oregon the planning mandate was clearly for compact, small-lot development in sharp contrast to the large-lot, leapfrog expansion despised by smart growth advocates.

Aiding in the densification of metropolitan Portland was the opening of new light rail transit lines. The state land commission mandated that local land use and development plans aim at a 10 percent reduction in per capita vehicle miles by 2016 and a 15 percent drop by 2026. To achieve this goal, metropolitan Portland planners have promoted the development of light rail and an increased reliance on public transit. Through growing dependence on public transit, the environmentally conscious residents of the Portland metropolitan area can eschew the hated automobile and realize yet another goal of antisprawl smart growth.

By the beginning of the twenty-first century an increasing number of governors were turning their attention to the Portland model and campaigning for smart growth agendas in their states. In the vanguard was Maryland's Parris Glendening. As governor from 1995 to 2003, Glendening established a state office of smart growth and lobbied for an end to wasteful development in heavily populated Maryland. "The act of sprawl pulls both the human vitality and the economic vitality out of existing communities," Glendening contended. Moreover, because of sprawl, "The sense of community is being lost. We put ourselves in gated communities with five-acre lots, and then we say, 'I wonder why we've lost the strength.'"[36] To remedy the state's sprawl problem, in 1997 Glendening secured legislative approval of the Smart Growth Areas Act. This measure restricted state infrastructure spending to areas designated for urban development. In other words, the state would not finance new roads or sewer or water lines wherever developers chose to build. Funds would go to established communities with the hope of creating a denser, more compact pattern of settlement.

Following Glendening's example was Governor James McGreevey of New Jersey. New Jersey had a history of state-level planning, publishing its first state development plan in 1951. In

2002 under the new governor, however, its Office of State Planning was renamed the Office of Smart Growth, indicative of the administration's belief that smart growth was the one correct planning path to follow. In his 2003 state of the state address, McGreevey declared, "There is no single greater threat to our way of life in New Jersey than unrestrained, uncontrolled development." McGreevey later explained, "Sprawl is terribly expensive," and added, "In an era of almost universal state deficits, states will be increasingly hard-pressed to supply the infrastructure for suburban sprawl."[37] The Office of Smart Growth newsletter proclaimed that the McGreevey administration was working "every day so New Jerseyans can enjoy our state's landscapes, own a home, spend less time commuting to work and visit one of our state's quaint, revitalized downtowns."[38]

Most notably the McGreevey administration drafted the Blueprint for Intelligent Growth (BIG) complete with a color-coded map of the state. The older built-up areas were green, a signal to developers that they could proceed to build in those zones. In yellow districts, developers could move ahead but only with caution. In the red areas, which constituted most of New Jersey, the McGreevey administration was dedicated to bringing development to a dead stop. State infrastructure money for roads, schools, and sewers were to go to the green areas; no money would subsidize development in the red mass. Only the color-blind could miss the simple message. The state of New Jersey intended to promote compact, dense development in existing communities and preserve open space. "It's not realistic to think we should build homes for 1 million people and use up every square inch of open space to do it," argued the New Jersey commissioner of community affairs. "All over the world people love to live in cities. Look at New York, or Paris—even Hoboken."[39] In that most suburban of states the leadership was opting for urbanity over sprawl, and density over large-lot spaciousness.

Both Glendening and McGreevey were Democrats, but when Massachusetts's Republican Governor Mitt Romney embraced smart growth it proved that the antisprawl initiative could transcend party lines. On taking office in 2003 Romney appointed Douglas Foy, the environmentalist head of the Conservation Law Foundation and a leading smart growth advocate, as chief of commonwealth development charged with overseeing transportation, housing, community development, and environmental affairs throughout the state. "I very much believe in the concept known as smart growth," explained the governor. "You do not want to deplete your greenspace and air and water [in order] to grow, and the only way that's possible is if your growth is done in a thoughtful, coherent, strategic way." Soon after taking office, Foy reiterated this more forcefully in a speech before a group of office and industrial property developers. "We're not going to be able to continue to just sprawl across the landscape," he asserted. "We're not going to be able to help you go out and buy the cheapest piece of land you can find and then hope that we're going to run highways to it."[40]

In 2004 the Massachusetts legislature endorsed the Romney/Foy initiative when it approved Chapter 40R authorizing incentive payments to communities that established zoning districts mandating dense, mixed-use development in town centers or near transit stations. To receive state funds, towns or cities had to require a density within the zone of at least eight single-family homes per acre or twenty apartment units per acre, and 20 percent of the dwelling units had to be affordable. According to Romney, 40R was the "quintessential smart-growth strategy."[41] It boosted density, tied development to transit, and ensured a mix of uses and housing options.

Not only was smart growth influencing state policy, its impact was evident in local plans throughout the nation. In one community after another the blueprints for future development envisioned the creation of mixed-use town centers, pedestrian gathering places that would instill a new sense of community and serve as an antidote to sprawl. One of the most thoroughgoing smart growth plans was that for Alabama's fastest growing area, suburban Shelby County, east of Birmingham. By 2004 Shelby's population had reached 166,000, up 67 percent since 1990, and fears of rampant sprawl pervade the 2004 comprehensive plan. The plan seeks to create a "community of communities" with new construction "targeted to designated development areas ... so that growth takes place in a controlled manner without spreading into a dispersed, sprawling pattern." The county's communities are expected to grow "through concentration and redevelopment in their Core ... with as many activities as possible located within walking distance." These centers will "grow by infilling under-developed and vacant areas rather than simply growing outward." This containment of growth is necessary because "the rural heritage and economy that has given Shelby its truly unique character must be preserved and enhanced." The plan aims quite definitely at "the creation of pedestrian friendly communities." According to this model smart growth blueprint, "An auto-dominated transportation infrastructure should not control citizens' lives or the landscape."[42] In a comment to a local newspaper, the county's planning services supervisor reiterated this when he observed, "People are tired of driving. People want things more convenient."[43]

Local planners in Alabama, governors in Maryland, New Jersey, and Massachusetts, and the molders of metropolitan Portland were all in agreement. Sprawl was the malady and smart growth the cure. In the first years of the twenty-first century the smart growth panacea swept the nation and left its mark on public policy.

An ally in this antisprawl assault is smart growth's close cousin, the *new urbanism*. The husband-and-wife architect team of Andres Duany and Elizabeth Plater-Zyberk are the godparents and the principal protagonists of this movement; their firm

DPZ has designed many of the most notable new urbanist projects. Reflecting its origins in architecture, new urbanism focuses more on design principles than does the smart growth agenda, but basically the two movements share the same goals. According to its charter, the Congress of the New Urbanism, founded in 1994, stands for "the restoration of existing urban centers and towns .... the reconfiguration of sprawling suburbs into communities of real neighborhoods and diverse districts, the conservation of natural environments, and the preservation of our built legacy." The charter further states, "neighborhoods should be diverse in use and population; communities should be designed for the pedestrian and transit as well as the car; [and] urban places should be framed by architecture and landscape design that celebrate local history, climate, ecology, and building practice."[44] In other words, new urbanist projects should be walkable communities with a mix of uses and economic classes and a sense of place rooted in the indigenous natural and built environment. They should not be mass subdivisions consisting solely of homes in a single price range and resembling every other subdivision in the nation regardless of region.

Duany and Plater-Zyberk and their followers, however, are not design revolutionaries dedicated to overturning tradition. They seek to create old-fashioned neighborhoods like those developed before World War II. According to Duany and Plater-Zyberk, "What seems to work best is a historic model—the traditional neighborhood—adapted as necessary to serve the needs of modern man."[45] They embrace traditional styles of architecture and the grid street plan that was the standard layout for nineteenth-century American cities. They abhor the cul-de-sacs typical of post–World War II subdivisions, prefer prewar alleys, and praise the front porches of the past. New urbanism is, then, a variation on old urbanism. Narrow lots, small front yards, sidewalks, corner stores, and garages carefully hidden from view along back alleys add up to the new urbanist formula for a better future. Through new urbanism, Americans can supposedly recapture an older, happier way of life destroyed by sprawl.

Perhaps the most notable suburban example of the new urbanism precepts of Duany and Plater-Zyberk is Kentlands in Montgomery County, Maryland, outside of Washington, DC. Construction of Kentlands began in 1989 and by 2003 there were about 6,000 residents of the 356-acre, DPZ-designed community. With Georgian, Federal, and vernacular-style buildings reminiscent of the eighteenth and nineteenth centuries, Kentlands, in the words of one observer, is "equal parts Beacon Hill and Mayberry."[46] Moreover, it is walkable. "We didn't even look anywhere but Kentlands because we were attracted to its walkability," commented one contented resident. "To live where we could walk to things, we'd have to buy a pre–World War house and then we'd have to spend money to renovate it." Though Kentlands includes a range of housing types, it is out of the reach of the poorer half of American society. In 2003 two-bedroom condominiums started at $230,000, townhouses sold for $300,000 to $500,000, and single-family homes were bringing $600,000 to $700,000.[47] "Yes, they are expensive," admitted Duany. "It's a matter of supply and demand. People are desperate to live in places like Kentlands, as an alternative to lifeless, mindless, frustrating sprawl."[48]

Kentlands has spawned many imitators. In December 2003 the *New Urban News* claimed there were 648 new urbanist communities completed, under construction, or in the planning stage. They were located in forty-two of the fifty states. Only Vermont, New Hampshire, Maine, Hawaii, Idaho, Wyoming, and the Dakotas had escaped the new urbanist onslaught, but these less-populous states had largely evaded all urbanism.[49]

In the Midwest one of the principal beneficiaries of new urbanism is the upscale Indianapolis suburb of Carmel. Among its subdivisions is the 686-acre Village of WestClay, a development intended to resemble a nineteenth-century town complete with a range of pre-1920 architectural styles. Among the housing options are brick "brownstones" reminiscent of old New York, Second Empire houses topped with mansard roofs, Southern plantation-style manses, and front-porch cottages. At its core is a village center planned to contain apartments, a large park, and retailing. Applauding its new urbanist design, some residents praise the resulting small town sense of community. "My old house was in a Carmel subdivision, and in eight years, I spoke to my neighbor next door maybe five times," comments one WestClay resident. "Now, I see my neighbors daily. They come sit on my porch or I sit on theirs. It's a nice sense of community I haven't found anywhere else." Carmel's proud mayor James Brainard claims WestClay is the "best new urbanism development in the country."[50]

As an ardent advocate of new urbanism, Brainard is in a good position to judge the relative merits of the project. In interviews he respectfully quotes from the writings of Duany and Plater-Zyberk, and he openly eschews suburbia's automobile-dominated lifestyle. "Sixty-five percent of the country lives in a suburban setting, and they can't walk anywhere," Brainard laments. "It's resulted in very empty lives, spending hours in a car every day, not knowing your neighbors because everyone's off driving around."[51] To remedy this sense of placelessness in unfocused Carmel, Brainard has launched a design program intended to transform his community from an all-too-familiar American suburb to a city with a distinctive urban quality. Essential to this transition is the creation of a downtown, a pedestrian core that will transform the sprawling suburb into a community with a heart. In 2006 Brainard broke ground for Carmel City Center, which at completion will include retailing, offices, apartments, restaurants, a boutique hotel, and a performing arts center. On the site of a deteriorating strip mall anchored by a vacant Kroger's supermarket, the center is the crown jewel in Brainard's new urbanist initiative. "The New

Urbanism design principles that are being used in this development will make this a very pedestrian friendly project with a very welcoming atmosphere," Brainard has promised.[52]

Carmel may hope to become the new urbanist showplace of the Midwest, but the largest new urbanist project is rising far from Indiana on the site of a former copper mine in Utah. Over the course of seventy-five years the Kennecott Copper Company plans to transform its huge landholdings west of Salt Lake City into 162,800 houses and 58 million square feet of commercial space providing 100,000 jobs. Ultimately the company envisions a string of walkable, compact communities linked by light rail lines to Salt Lake City. The first of these communities, Daybreak, opened in 2004 with small lots and building styles reminiscent of early-twentieth-century Salt Lake City neighborhoods. In Daybreak there are garage-lined alleys but no cul-de-sacs. Plenty of sidewalks provide pedestrian access to the shops in the village center. One new resident sold his home on a half-acre lot in a nearby subdivision, opting instead for "a nice small yard" in Daybreak. "My wife always wanted a front porch," he explained.[53]

One variant of smart growth and new urbanism attracting increasing attention is *transit-oriented development* (TOD). This refers to dense, mixed use projects within easy walking distance of transit stations. Ideally TOD would significantly reduce reliance on the automobile and create a vibrant pedestrian-friendly environment. Advocates for such projects claim, "TOD could be nothing less than the defining armature for a fundamental rethinking about how we build communities."[54] Another has claimed, "the new 'transit town' is intended to be the new model community for the new millennium."[55]

What Portland is for smart growth in general, Arlington, Virginia, is for transit-oriented development. This inner suburb south of Washington, DC, has pioneered such development along the Rosslyn-Ballston Metrorail corridor. Between 1972 and the close of 2002, TOD added 11,000 dwelling units to the corridor as well as 16 million square feet of office space, 1,900 hotel rooms, and almost one million square feet of retailing. Symbolic of the devotion to density are the 18- to 20-story apartment towers clustering around the Metro stations. According to the 2000 census, 47.2 percent of the corridor's residents relied on transit or other nonautomotive means to get to work.[56] With a lifestyle approximating Manhattan rather than stereotypical suburbia, the Arlington corridor is the ultimate antisprawl environment.

Together transit-oriented development, new urbanism, and the smart growth of Parris Glendening and Portland planners add up to a well-publicized rejection of the sprawl usually associated with suburbia. Clearly some people are dissatisfied with a low-density, auto-oriented suburban lifestyle and are either proposing or imposing an alternative for metropolitan Americans. In response to complaints about uncontrolled growth, the forces for control are massed with plans in hand for a compact, walkable future.

Smart Growth Setbacks

During the first decade of the twenty-first century, however, smart growth has suffered as many setbacks as victories, calling into question whether it actually constitutes an acceptable alternative for most Americans. Density is a dirty word for many suburbanites, and the idea of building compact settlements flies in the face of their conception of a suburban lifestyle. Coercive planning that prevents landowners from doing what they wish with their property likewise offends the freedom-loving spirit of many Americans. Smart growth is predicated on the notion that government plans should determine what areas should be dense and what should be open space, what should be developed and what should lie fallow. Given that agenda, the implementation of smart growth is bound to offend many, and perhaps prove to be so unpopular as to remain unrealistic.

In Parris Glendening's Maryland the smart growth juggernaut has not won universal applause. Marylanders have balked at plans to create dense developments near their homes and have forced planners to reduce proposed densities. For example, the 508-acre Maple Farms development in suburban Howard County was intended to be a smart growth, new urbanist project with a minimum density of four or five houses per acre. Local protests forced a reduction to only 2.2 houses per acre, a figure in accord with traditional sprawl settlement. When confronted with the original proposal, the president of a neighboring homeowners association commented, "Each and every Fulton Manor homeowner spent a considerable amount of money to buy their property, build their dream home and raise their families in an idyllic country setting. Today our dreams appear to be turning into a nightmare." Even the former chair of the local chapter of the Sierra Club deviated from the group's smart growth agenda in order to defend his home located a mile from the proposed project. "My area has mostly five acre or larger lots," he argued. "We expected to see the area population grow with like development." Howard County's planning director summed up the situation when she observed, "Smart growth is something people want. They just don't want it in their own neighborhood."[57]

Overall, Maryland's smart growth policy does not seem to have had much impact on development. After adoption of the program in 1997, development outside the smart growth designated areas continued unabated. In November 2002, Glendening administration smart growth planners expressed reservations about the effectiveness of the program. "The rate at which farm and forest land is being developed has not slowed," they concluded. "Our current smart growth laws and programs may not be sufficient to overcome the many obstacles that have made sprawl the dominant form of development." The executive director of the Maryland Association of Counties was more outspoken in his criticism of the Glendening initiative. "Smart growth is inconsistent with the American dream of a big home on a five-acre lot," he contended. Moreover, he objected to state attempts to impose a single planning panacea on Maryland's localities. "The concept of a higher authority, of a Big Brother, is inconsistent with the democratic principles that have to be intertwined with land use management."[58]

Governor McGreevey's BIG map faced similar criticism. Areas colored green protested against the notion of denser development. "What's appropriate in New York City may not work in Bergen County," commented a planner in a major suburban county in northern New Jersey. Builders also expressed doubts: "You can't force all the development into those green areas," objected a spokesperson for a major builder. "Not everyone wants to live there." The simplicity of McGreevey's smart growth solution stirred additional criticism. "There's just three colors," observed one stubborn planner. "But in planning, there's so many shades of gray."[59] In late 2003 McGreevey resigned as governor following revelations of a homosexual relationship with an aide, and no more was heard of his BIG proposal. The state's Office of Smart Growth, however, survived, distributing grants to communities that promoted smart growth planning.

Meanwhile in Massachusetts, smart growth seemed to move only slowly forward. Between 2001 and 2005 residents in Kingston, Holbrook, and Malden all rejected proposals for compact transit villages. A suburb south of Boston, Kingston, had a two-acre minimum lot requirement for new houses and a construction cap that permitted the building of no more than seventy new homes per year. Yet the proposed Village at Kingston was a dense, mixed-use project with 800 dwelling units as well as retailing. "There was enormous resistance because people saw it as changing the character of the town," explained one local resident in 2003. "In my mind, it was voted down because of fear more than anything else." Another claimed that Massachusetts citizens had not yet found the smart growth message convincing. "They say they're interested, and they talk about planning, but they don't really want it."[60]

Reflecting this reluctance, Romney's 40R program got off to a slow start. In May 2006 a news article reported that state officials were "frustrated with the unpopularity of [the] highly touted program."[61] During the summer of 2006, however, towns expressed growing interest in the creation of smart growth overlay districts as authorized by 40R. They were beginning to act not so much because of a devotion to smart growth but owing to a perception that 40R was a preferable option to the 40B housing mandate. Under 40R smart growth projects were to include affordable housing, but towns had greater control over proposed developments and could dictate to developers the design and composition of what was built. Recognizing this, in June 2006 Kingston's selectmen approved a smart growth district to include 730 housing units as well as parks and stores in the long-contested zone near their transit station.[62] In another Massachusetts town, officials seemed to regard 40R as yet another tool for slowing development rather than increasing density. A newspaper account of a proposed 72-unit condominium project in Spencer reported that the selectmen "urged residents to research ways to fight the proposal, but also said they had to approve the 40R request, which would slow the project down about a year."[63]

Not only were state smart growth programs confronting problems, so were local initiatives. This was evident in one of the nation's fastest growing areas, suburban Loudoun County, Virginia, west of Washington, DC. In 1999 Loudoun residents reacted to rampant growth by electing the Voters to Stop Sprawl slate of candidates to the governing board of supervisors. Embracing smart growth, the new supervisors adopted a policy of keeping development out of the western half of the county, thus protecting the estates and horse farms of the plutocrats who had been major financial contributors to Voters to Stop Sprawl. Growth was to be confined to the already suburbanizing eastern half of the county inhabited by middle-class commuters. The easterners who had cast ballots to halt development in their own backyards felt betrayed. "When people in the east voted for smart growth, they thought it meant development would slow down in their own neighborhoods," commented a state legislator in 2001. "But what happened is the planning commission and board of supervisors are trying to shift all of the growth and put it into the suburbs. That's density packing." When county planners attempted to raise permissible density levels in the eastern part of the county to five houses per acre, the outcry was loud and strong. "Residents in the east are as entitled to green space and open space as anywhere else," insisted one non–smart growth supervisor. "We are not going to become the dumping ground for all density in the county."[64]

Joining in the complaints were the less affluent farmers in the west who had planned some day to cash in on their farms by selling them to developers. These westerners organized Citizens for Property Rights, protesting the downzoning of their farms from minimum residential lots of three acres to minimum tracts of twenty or fifty acres per dwelling. They complained that the smart growth supervisors were "beholden to ... elitist Western Loudoun Interests," and the multimillionaire estate owners had conducted a "carefully orchestrated and concerted campaign to curtail the property rights of other landowners within the county."[65] One owner of twenty-one acres complained, "I went from being able to build six additional houses someday ... to zero.... . This isn't Russia, is it? You don't want people taking stuff away from you without saying 'please.'"[66] Another property rights advocate arrived at the county government center dressed as revolutionary patriot Patrick Henry and led other foes of controlled growth in the singing of a revised version of "God Bless America": "God bless our property, Land that we love …".[67]

In the 2003 supervisors election, growth management was again the chief issue. One candidate from the east contended, "the 'smart-growth' package rammed through Loudoun County's Board of Supervisors … uses density packing to force most of Loudoun's growth to take place in our community or in the area immediately around it."[68] The voters seemed to buy this argument and those of the property rights advocates. They elected a new board of supervisors pledged to relaxing growth controls. One eastern resident seemed to sum up the views of her neighbors when she observed, "A lot of the slow-growth is protecting western Loudoun, not here where we live. I think we got the short end of the stick."[69]

The election did not end debate over growth. Most Loudoun Countians favored controlled growth, but they favored keeping additional people out of both the eastern and western halves of the county. They did not want smart growth; they wanted no growth. Developers and landowners continued to threaten lawsuits, and supervisors and residents continued to bicker over where to permit homes and how many could be built. In the end Loudoun Countians forced many potential new residents to move ever farther from the metropolitan core and find homes across the state line in West Virginia. "The land use regulations in Loudoun … have done nothing to stop sprawl," complained the planner for Jefferson County, West Virginia. "They've only accelerated it. They've pushed it out here."[70]

Some of the complaints about property rights heard in Loudoun County have been repeated in Shelby County, Alabama, drawing into question whether its model plan will prove successful in guiding development. Resenting the imposition of zoning restrictions on his land, one Shelby resident contended, "If you read the plan, you'll see how they talk about stripping us of our rights …. This plan will strip us of our freedoms." Another argued, "You do not take private landowners' rights away from them .... Yes, there needs to be a stop to the growth, but don't take it out on the private landowners."[71]

Meanwhile, not everyone in Shelby was buying into the plan's concept of compact village centers. Since the incorporated municipalities within Shelby were not subject to the county's planning authority, they could each head off in their own direction. Pelham was embracing commercial strip development along Alabama Highway 119, but nearby Indian Springs Village had been incorporated to protect its horse-farm ambience from development. One editorial from 2006 claimed, "in Montevallo, there is evidence of growth out of control."[72] That community was approving new housing subdivisions without provision for adequate sewage disposal. Shelby County was, in fact, a "community of communities," but the communities were each going their separate way. Given conflicting agendas, county planners seemed unlikely to realize their dreams of walkable village nodes dispersed carefully amid the preserved greenery of sylvan Shelby County.

In one area after another, smart growth planners were having a difficult time selling the proposition of density to suburbanites who wanted fewer neighbors rather than more. They were also confronting irate landowners who did not want to sacrifice prospective profits to realize visions of pedestrian villages surrounded by ample open space. The Sierra Club chair in Howard County wanted five-acre lots not encroaching new urbanism; the Kingston resident wanted a two-acre minimum not a transit village; and Loudoun Countians preferred to export prospective residents to West Virginia. Meanwhile, Loudoun farmers as well as some Shelby Countians were raising the banner of property rights, viewing smart growth as a violation of American liberty. During the first years of the twenty-first century, the course of smart growth has not been smooth. Suburban Americans have too often blocked the roadway, forcing detours or retreat.

Perhaps the greatest smart growth setback was suffered in that citadel of controlled growth, the state of Oregon. Rebelling against the state's draconian land-use restrictions, property rights advocates placed Measure 37 on the 2004 ballot. It required state and local agencies to compensate owners for any reduction in the value of their land resulting from land-use laws or rules. If the governmental body did not compensate the landowner, then the land in question was exempt from the regulations. "I'm 91 years old, my husband is dead, and I don't know how much longer I can fight," lamented Dorothy English in radio ads for the initiative.[73] The owner of nineteen acres outside of Portland, English was not permitted to build houses on her tract; not even her grandson could construct a home adjacent to the aged widow. English's appeal convinced many listeners; in November 2004 61 percent of Oregonians casting ballots voted for Measure 37. In February 2006 the measure was upheld by the Oregon Supreme Court, confirming victory for opponents of Oregon's controlled growth policies. Because the state and locality would not be able to compensate the thousands of claims brought by landowners, a waiver of land regulations was the only alternative. Oregon moved from the most restrictive state in the nation to a laissez-faire regime where landowners could not suffer loss at the hands of planning bureaucrats.

The events in Oregon stunned smart growth advocates. It was somewhat akin to the Visigoths sacking imperial Rome; the barbarians of development had overpowered the forces of civilized planning in the capital of smart growth. The executive director of the environmentalist 1000 Friends of Oregon warned, "without these safeguards, the land rush to develop Oregon's natural places and family farms begins." He reported that there were claims for exemptions on 30,000 acres of the Willamette Valley, including a proposal to develop an 850-house subdivision on 850 acres of forested land south of Portland.[74] In suburban Clackamas County, officials admitted that the granting of land restriction waivers was the only course open to them. "Where would you get the rather astronomical sums to pay owners?" the county board chair asked. "The answer is we have no source at this point, and I wouldn't anticipate there would be enough support in the community for paying the millions at stake."[75] The consequence was a long list of housing subdivisions with one-acre lots approved for development beyond the Portland Metro urban growth boundary. The vaunted growth boundary appeared to be sprouting leaks, and some residents of the metropolitan area were not saddened by the faltering fortunes of smart growth. "A decade ago, we said we didn't want sprawl, so we enacted ordinances that have led to higher densities inside the urban growth boundary," observed the mayor of suburban Tualatin. "Now, as we see what that's brought us, people are saying a little sprawl might not be so bad after all."[76]

The Oregon victory stirred interest in property rights elsewhere. Just to the north of Oregon, the Washington Farm Bureau directly assaulted land-use restrictions by placing Initiative 933 on the state ballot in November 2006. This proposition, like its Oregon predecessor, required compensation for losses owing to government regulation of land. Responding to the initiative, friends and foes of controlled growth repeated some of the same arguments heard in Oregon and Loudoun County. "It's about restoring balance between the need of government to regulate land use and the right of citizens to own and use their property," the farm bureau president said of Initiative 933. "For many people, it's about protecting the American Dream."[77] A controlled growth advocate rebutted, "it's really about creating loopholes for big developers at the expense of communities."[78] Writing in a California newspaper, a property rights activist summed up the attitude of his movement: "If 'smart growth'—i.e., cramming development into urban areas to leave rural areas open—is so 'smart' ... then the public will surely be willing to pay for some of its costs. If not, this will be because the public has consciously decided ... that some growth restrictions are a luxury, not a necessity."[79]

Thus the battle lines have been drawn, and smart growth has both advanced and retreated. Though many Americans claim to deplore sprawl, even more appear to hate density. In the end, most seem to favor their existing suburban environment, so much so that they oppose any change in the form of additional people or traffic. Meanwhile, they favor zoning to protect their home and lot, but are understandably outraged by zoning that depreciates the value of their property. Smart growth may be a clever formula for future development, but so far smart growth advocates are not smart enough to sell their whole package of reform to suburban Americans. Academics may compute the costs of sprawl and planners chart boundaries of growth, but they seem to have failed to accurately compute the preferred lifestyle of the suburban majority or chart the limits of American tolerance for infringement on their freedom to build where they want and on whatever size lot they desire.

7
THE BASICS

As the heart of America, the nation's home and office, suburbia is too significant to remain encumbered by well-worn myths and misleading stereotypes. It is time for everyone to acknowledge the basic facts of life of America's suburbs. Misconceptions, mindless diatribes, and impractical panaceas serve no useful purpose for either policymakers or the general citizenry.

First—American Suburbs Are Diverse

Suburbia is diverse and always has been. In the nineteenth and early twentieth centuries it was the site of estates for the gentry, homes for the middle class, and cottages for workers. It accommodated such noxious industries as slaughterhouses and tanneries and such land-extensive manufacturing establishments as steel mills and brickyards. Some suburbs preserved natural beauty and the American family; others perpetuated Polish traditions and lifestyle. Some were wet, replete with saloons; others were dry and kept the Sabbath holy. The near west-side suburbs of Chicago were the domain of both Frank Lloyd Wright and Al Capone, a land of world-famous innovative architecture and notorious mob lawlessness. Beltline railroads brought industry to some communities; commuter lines transported upper-middle-class businessmen to others. Riverside and Lake Forest had large homes along curving lanes; Cicero and Berwyn were laid out in a perpendicular grid pattern with rows of bungalows. Suburbia was not uniform in class, economics, morals, or appearance.

This remains true in the twenty-first century. There are straight suburbs and gay suburbs. There are suburbs for seniors and others for horses. Some suburbs are predominantly African American, others are overwhelmingly Hispanic, and still others are almost exclusively Anglo. American suburbia includes Little Saigon, Little Taipei, and Little Manila. It hosts appearances by Bollywood stars and offers a good selection of saris. A growing number of suburbs have a rich ethnic mix with residents whose ancestors haled from Europe, Africa, Latin America, and Asia. Some older, first-tier suburbs are rich; others are poor. Many have exemplary schools, but many also rank at the bottom of all educational rankings. Edge cities have more workers than residents; not far away, however, are communities with more bedrooms than businesses.

Nothing about suburbia precludes any form of endeavor or way of life. And as America becomes more suburban, the suburbs will continue to reflect the rich diversity of the nation. Suburbia is not bland or homogeneous. Only the most obtuse observers could seriously claim that America's suburbs offer a look-alike landscape with one suburban community indistinguishable from the next. A trip from Beverly Hills through West Hollywood south to Compton and out to Vernon, Maywood, and Monterey Park, then through the Inland Empire of San Bernardino and Riverside counties and back to Anaheim and Westminster encompasses an extraordinary range of ethnicity and social class. A tour of Boston's suburbs includes the physical remnants of four centuries of European settlement, with structures from the 1600s as well as landmarks of twentieth-century modernism, such as the home of famed architect Walter

Gropius. It offers the relics of America's earliest industry, the seventeenth-century Saugus Iron Works, mill structures remaining from the Industrial Revolution of the nineteenth century, and the research facilities of cutting edge twenty-first-century technology. In Foxborough, one can see the football field of the twenty-first century New England Patriots, and in Lexington and Concord, the fighting fields of eighteenth-century patriots who struck the first blows for American independence.

Suburbia thus includes not only the stereotypical shopping mall and housing subdivision, but virtually everything else as well. It is as varied as the nation as a whole, with landmarks from every century, people of all types, and a full range of businesses, employment, and shopping. Sneering comments about bland burbs reveal the prejudiced ignorance of the observer rather than the reality of suburbia.

Second—Suburbs Are an Expression of the American Desire for Freedom and the Right to Pursue One's Own Destiny

As perhaps the most libertarian nation in the world, it is appropriate that the United States is also the most suburban nation. American suburbs reflect the national commitment to freedom and self-determination. Whereas in America's close ideological cousins Canada and Great Britain central governments have forced consolidation of local units and imposed schemes of regional restructuring, in the United States a confusing multitude of suburban governments have survived and the citizenry has vigorously defended their prerogatives. Infringements on local self-rule are labeled as communistic, actions reminiscent of the old Soviet Union and most definitely un-American.

No matter what academic "experts" or government reformers may say, Americans cling to what they perceive as grassroots rule.

In New England the autonomy of the ancient towns is sacrosanct; in Georgia suburbanites clamor for self-determination and independence from county officials perceived as distant and unrepresentative; in New Jersey, Illinois, California, and Washington, suburban residents seek to define the destiny of their own communities free from state meddling. From the standpoint of efficiency or equity, American suburbia may not make any sense. Yet Americans perceive suburban self-determination as a vital component of the nation's heritage of liberty. The political fragmentation of suburbia is as American as apple pie, hot dogs, and the flag.

Not only do suburbanites seek to fulfill their craving for freedom through perpetuating multitudinous suburban governments, they also do so through the purchase of suburban homes. Owning one's own home is the American dream. Thereby Americans can claim a share of the nation's turf as their own domain. And it is a domain that is to be protected at all costs. In suburbia, homeowners claim to find the autonomy, privacy, and space denied them in an inner-city rental apartment. Invasions of that privacy and space elicit the vigorous waves of NIMBYism so prevalent in contemporary America. The gut devotion to property rights evident in Oregon and elsewhere also reflects this deep-seated American notion of the sanctity of ownership. Ideally in suburbia one's family can pursue its own destiny on its protected plot of earth in a municipality whose services and policies are tailored to its needs and desires. From the working-class families raising chickens in Chagrin Falls Park and South Gate to residents of twenty-first-century upscale subdivisions, Americans have regarded a suburban home as an expression of their individual autonomy, a manifestation of what Thomas Jefferson meant by the right to the pursuit of happiness.

Contributing to the supposed freedom and autonomy associated with suburban life is the automobile. No other mode of transportation has ever afforded people such a degree of individual mobility. Behind the wheel of a car one can go anywhere at any time.

Auto-borne Americans are not confined to a fixed rail pathway or a transit schedule. They can roam far beyond walking distance. Like political fragmentation and home ownership, the automobile seems to enhance one's ability to pursue one's own destiny to the maximum degree possible. Traffic and congestion are a threat to this freedom of mobility, and are thus the chief complaints among suburban foes of development. No-growth suburbanites want empty fields behind their houses and empty highways in front of their cars. Too many buildings and too many automobiles threaten the very freedom they associate with life along the fringe.

Third—The Greatest Threat to Suburban Life Is from the No-Growth, Low-Density Prejudices of Incumbent Suburbanites

Perhaps the greatest obstacles to future suburbanization are the suburbanites themselves. Despite all the ballyhoo about smart growth, relatively few really buy into all its tenets. Most suburbanites are not willing to accept higher density development or affordable housing if it is anywhere near them. Preserving open space attracts adherents because it seemingly promises to keep newcomers out of the backyards of incumbent suburbanites. In too many areas of the United States the prevailing sentiment is slow growth or no growth. Suburbanites want to close the door to their habitat and keep intruders out.

Especially undesirable are costly children who burden local school systems and drive up taxes, but in some areas the prevailing suburban policy appears to be antipeople, not just antichildren. Additional people are not welcome in protected suburban preserves across the nation, and land use policies aim to keep them out. If some people must be admitted, they will preferably be senior citizens who can be confined to their own retirement communities and not contribute youngsters to local schools or add to commuter traffic during the morning or evening rush hours.

This antihumanity sentiment has manifested itself in large-lot zoning and myriad "environmental" initiatives that drive up home prices and raise the economic barriers to an invasion of newcomers. Suburbanites spend billions on open space preservation in communities that already have ample open space and to protect the habitat of species about which few really care. What is important is to preserve the human habitat for existing residents and make sure that the suburban world they invested in a decade earlier will not change.

For many suburban residents, change appears to be the ultimate enemy. One must halt change, and the continuing evolution of history, by making sure that suburban tract houses are not visible from historical Civil War battlefields. One must prevent change that compromises the charm of New England towns and the rural atmosphere of equestrian retreats. When the upscale village of Franklin, Michigan, adopted the slogan "The Town That Time Forgot," it was embracing a sentiment dear to millions of suburbanites. Even the wealthy are not welcome newcomers if they threaten to introduce change. Teardown mansions may raise property values and boost tax revenues, but like affordable housing projects, they change the neighborhood cherished by incumbent homeowners whose sensibilities must not be offended. Suburban obstructionists raise aesthetic and environmental objections to justify their opposition to change. Yet their idea of optimal beauty and unsullied nature seems to be a world in which they exist but others are excluded.

These exclusionary naysayers conflict with the inclusive diversity presently characterizing suburbia. Given the fact that an ever-increasing portion of Americans are destined to live, shop, and work in suburbia, this diversity is bound to survive, but the forces of exclusion and inclusion seem destined to meet in many future clashes. Suburbia is the America of the present and the future; it is also the battleground of coming decades as the friction mounts between those who must be accommodated and those who dig in their heels. The most basic issue facing suburban Americans is how to balance the interests of the newcomers and naysayers and ensure the advantages of suburban life for both.

Notes

Introduction

1. In response to changing realities, in 2003 the census bureau dropped the category "central cities" and replaced it with "principal cities," which included former central cities plus certain other localities deemed significant but long regarded as suburban. Thus the New York City metropolitan area included the principal cities of New York City and Edison, New Jersey, and Thousand Oaks as well as Los Angeles was a principal city of the Los Angeles metropolitan area. This revision simply revealed the census bureau's ineptitude in confronting the existing world of edgeless cities sprawling across the landscape (see Chapter 3). No perceptive individual would ever conceive of Edison and New York City as like entities belonging in the same category, both equally world's apart from suburban northern New Jersey. The concept of central cities at least has a historical validity, and this examination will adhere to the older and more valid classifications, which may be largely obsolete in the twenty-first century, but were conceptually useful through much of the twentieth century.
2. Phyllis McGinley, "Suburbia: Of Thee I Sing," *Harper's Magazine*, December 1949, 79.

Chapter 1

1. Kenneth T. Jackson, *Crabgrass Frontier: The Suburbanization of the United States* (New York: Oxford University Press, 1985), 16.

2. Henry C. Binford, *The First Suburbs: Residential Communities on the Boston Periphery 1815–1860* (Chicago, IL: University of Chicago Press, 1985), 33–34, 39–40.

3. Jackson, *Crabgrass Frontier*, 27–28, 31–32.

4. Edward K. Spann, *The New Metropolis: New York City, 1840–1857* (New York: Columbia University Press, 1981), 184, 187.

5. Jackson, *Crabgrass Frontier*, 37.

6. Michael H. Ebner, *Creating Chicago's North Shore: A Suburban History* (Chicago, IL: University of Chicago Press, 1988), 21; Michael H. Ebner, "'In the Suburbes of Toun:' Chicago's North Shore to 1871," *Chicago History* 40 (summer 1982): 70.

7. Ebner, "In the Suburbes of Toun," 70.

8. Carl Abbott, "'Necessary Adjuncts to its Growth:' The Railroad Suburbs of Chicago, 1854–1875," *Journal of the Illinois State Historical Society* 73 (summer 1980): 117.

9. Everett Chamberlin, *Chicago and Its Suburbs* (Chicago, IL: T. A. Hungerford and Co., 1874), 188, 353, 425.

10. Sidney D. Maxwell, *The Suburbs of Cincinnati: Sketches Historical and Descriptive* (Cincinnati, OH: George E. Stevens and Co., 1870), 51–52.

11. Marc Lindner and Lawrence S. Zacharias, *Of Cabbages and Kings County: Agriculture and the Formation of Modern Brooklyn* (Iowa City: University of Iowa Press, 1999), 140.

12. Chamberlin, *Chicago and Its Suburbs*, 190, 356.

13. Homer Hoyt, *One Hundred Years of Land Values in Chicago* (Chicago, IL: University of Chicago Press, 1933), 100.

14. Jackson, *Crabgrass Frontier*, 77.

15. Ebner, *Creating Chicago's North Shore*, p.29.

16. Maxwell, *Suburbs of Cincinnati*, 77–78.

17. Abbott, "'Necessary Adjuncts of its Growth,'" 121.

18. John W. Reps, *The Making of Urban America: A History of City Planning in the United States* (Princeton, NJ: Princeton University Press, 1965), 344.

19. Dolores Hayden, *Building Suburbia: Green Fields and Urban Growth, 1820–2000* (New York: Pantheon Books, 2003), 62.

20. Louise Carroll Wade, *Chicago's Pride: The Stockyards, Packingtown, and Environs in the Nineteenth Century* (Urbana: University of Illinois Press, 1987), 47, 57, 271.

21. Jon C. Teaford, *City and Suburb: The Political Fragmentation of Metropolitan America, 1850–1970* (Baltimore: Johns Hopkins University Press, 1979), 16, 27; Richard Walker, "Industry Builds the City: The Suburbanization of Manufacturing in the San Francisco Bay Area, 1850–1940," *Journal of Historical Geography* 27 (January 2001): 42.

22. Teaford, *City and Suburb*, 27.

23. Edward K. Muller, "Industrial Suburbs and the Growth of Metropolitan Pittsburgh, 1870–1920," *Journal of Historical Geography* 27 (January 2001): 61–64; Robert Lewis, "Running Rings around the City: North American Industrial Suburbs, 1850–1950," in *Changing Suburbs: Foundation, Form and Function*, ed. Richard Harris and Peter J. Larkham (London: E & FN Spon, 1999), 149.

24. Muller, "Industrial Suburbs," 58–59.

25. Graham Romeyn Taylor, *Satellite Cities: A Study of Industrial Suburbs* (New York: D. Appleton and Company, 1915), 92–112, 138, 142, 151–160.

26. Helen Corbin Monchow, *Seventy Years of Real Estate Subdividing in the Region of Chicago* (Evanston, IL: Northwestern University, 1939), 103–104.

27. Teaford, *City and Suburb*, 23. See also Sundiata Keita Cha-Jua, *America's First Black Town: Brooklyn, Illinois, 1830–1915* (Urbana: University of Illinois Press, 2000).

28. Joseph C. Bigott, *From Cottage to Bungalow: Houses and the Working Class in Metropolitan Chicago, 1869–1929* (Chicago, IL: University of Chicago Press, 2001), 151.

29. Ronald Dale Karr, "Brookline and the Making of an Elite Suburb," *Chicago History* 13 (summer 1984): 45.

30. Taylor, *Satellite Cities*, 99–100.

31. Ibid., 141.

32. Robert M. Fogelson, *The Fragmented Metropolis: Los Angeles, 1850–1930* (Cambridge, Mass.: Harvard University Press, 1967), 89–93.

33. Teaford, *City and Suburb*, 8–9.

34. Richard Bigger and James D. Kitchen, *How the Cities Grew: A Century of Municipal Independence and Expansionism in Metropolitan Los Angeles* (Los Angeles: Bureau of Governmental Research, University of California, Los Angeles, 1952), 61.

35. Teaford, *City and Suburb*, 27–28.

36. Alan J. Karcher, *New Jersey's Multiple Municipal Madness* (New Brunswick, NJ: Rutgers University Press, 1998), 75–88.
37. Bigger and Kitchen, *How the Cities Grew*, 82–84.
38. Teaford, *City and Suburb*, 17.
39. Ebner, *Creating Chicago's North Shore*, 36.
40. Bigger and Kitchen, *How the Cities Grew*, 89.
41. Ebner, *Creating Chicago's North Shore*, 133.
42. Teaford, *City and Suburb*, 14–16.
43. Lindner and Zacharias, *Of Cabbages and Kings County*, 157.
44. Ann Durkin Keating, *Building Chicago: Suburban Developers and the Creation of a Divided Metropolis* (Columbus: Ohio State University Press, 1988), 105.
45. Teaford, *City and Suburb*, 40–47, 55–56.
46. Ibid., 41, 56. The East Cleveland mentioned here is not the same municipality as a second, surviving East Cleveland discussed in Chapter 2.
47. Keating, *Building Chicago*, 105.
48. R. D. McKenzie, *The Metropolitan Community* (New York: Russell and Russell, 1967), 271.
49. Teaford, *City and Suburb*, 77.
50. McKenzie, *Metropolitan Community*, 47.
51. Arthur A. Hagman, *Oakland County Book of History* (Pontiac, MI: Oakland County, 1970), 45, 175, 186, 195.
52. Andrew Wiese, *Places of Their Own: African American Suburbanization in the Twentieth Century* (Chicago: University of Chicago Press, 2004), 44–50.
53. Greg Hise, "'Nature's Workshop:' Industry and Urban Expansion in Southern California, 1900–1950," in *Manufacturing Suburbs: Building Work and Home on the Metropolitan Fringe*, ed. Robert Lewis (Philadelphia, PA: Temple University Press, 2004), 188.
54. Fred W. Viehe, "Black Gold Suburbs: The Influence of the Extractive Industry on the Suburbanization of Los Angeles, 1890–1930," *Journal of Urban History* 8 (November 1981): 15.
55. Hise, "Nature's Workshop," 188, 195, 197; Ricardo Romo, *East Los Angeles: History of a Barrio* (Austin: University of Texas Press, 1983), 81.
56. Viehe, "Black Gold Suburbs," 6, 8–9.
57. Bigger and Kitchen, *How the Cities Grew*, 91.

58. Harlan Paul Douglass, *The Suburban Trend* (New York: Century Company, 1925), 96.
59. Becky M. Nicolaides, *My Blue Heaven: Life and Politics in the Working-Class Suburbs of Los Angeles, 1920–1965* (Chicago, IL: University of Chicago Press, 2002), 20, 26.
60. Ibid., 30, 33.
61. Sharon Heiden, "Westmont," in *DuPage Roots*, ed. Richard A. Thompson (Wheaton, IL: DuPage County Historical Society, 1985), 247.
62. Jon C. Teaford, *Cities of the Heartland: The Rise and Fall of the Industrial Midwest* (Bloomington: Indiana University Press, 1993), 209.
63. Wiese, *Places of Their Own*, 73.
64. Ibid., 74, 82.
65. John Kobler, *Capone: The Life and World of Al Capone* (New York: Putnam, 1971), 119.
66. Ibid., 120.
67. Ibid., 126.
68. Arthur Evans Wood, *Hamtramck Then and Now: A Sociological Study of a Polish-American Community* (New York: Bookman Associates, 1955), 49.
69. George A. Lundberg, Mirra Komarovsky, and Mary Alice McInery, *Leisure: A Suburban Study* (New York: Columbia University Press, 1934), 45–46.
70. *Birmingham* (Michigan) *Eccentric*, 17 May 1928, 24; *New York Times*, 29 April 1928, Section 12, 4; Jon C. Teaford, *Post-Suburbia: Government and Politics in the Edge Cities* (Baltimore, MD: Johns Hopkins University Press, 1997), 9.
71. Carol A. O'Connor, *A Sort of Utopia: Scarsdale, 1891–1981* (Albany: State University of New York Press, 1983), 12–13.
72. Ibid., 48.
73. Ibid., 36–37, 41.
74. Ibid., 78–79.
75. John R. Stilgoe, *Borderland: Origins of the American Suburb, 1820–1939* (New Haven, CT: Yale University Press, 1988), 242, 246.
76. Teaford, *Cities of the Heartland*, 207.
77. Teaford, *Post-Suburbia*, 17–18.

78. Daniel J. Prosser, "Chicago and the Bungalow Boom of the 1920s," *Chicago History* 10 (summer 1981): 92.
79. Bigger and Kitchen, *How the Cities Grew*, 62.
80. Teaford, *Post-Suburbia*, 15.
81. McKenzie, *Metropolitan Community*, 71.
82. Teaford, *Post-Suburbia*, 25.
83. Bigger and Kitchen, *How the Cities Grew*, 175.
84. Teaford, *City and Suburb*, 90, 100, 104.
85. Bigger and Kitchen, *How the Cities Grew*, 190–191; Walter Wagner, *Beverly Hills: Inside the Golden Ghetto* (New York: Grosset and Dunlap, 1976), 19–21.
86. Teaford, *City and Suburb*, 95, 99–100, 103.
87. "Up from the Potato Fields," *Time*, 3 July 1950, 67–68.
88. Jackson, *Crabgrass Frontier*, 241.
89. William G. Weart, "Police Guard Site of Race Violence," *New York Times*, 15 August 1957, 14; William G. Weart, "Police Rout 400 at Negro's Home," *New York Times*, 20 August 1957, 29; Homer Bigart, "Negro Set to Stay in Levittown, Pa.," *New York Times,* 19 September 1957, 22; William G. Weart, "Home Is Guarded in Levittown, Pa.," *New York Times*, 25 September 1957, 19.
90. "A City of 30,000 Created on Coast in 2-Year Period," *New York Times*, 17 February 1952, Section 8, 1.
91. Teaford, *Post-Suburbia*, 47.
92. Dominic Paris, *Footpaths to Freeways: The Story of Livonia* (No place; No publisher, 1975), 223.
93. Esther Perica, *They Took the Challenge: The Story of Rolling Meadows* (Rolling Meadows, IL: Rolling Meadows Library, 1979), 47, 50.
94. Teaford, *Post-Suburbia*, 47.
95. Lundberg, Komarovsky, and McInerny, *Leisure*, 44.
96. John Keats, *The Crack in the Picture Window* (Boston, MA: Houghton Mifflin, 1956), xi–xii, 193.
97. David Riesman, "The Suburban Sadness," in *The Suburban Community*, ed. William M. Dobriner (New York: Putnam's, 1958), 376–377.
98. Gibson Winter, "The Church in Suburban Captivity," *Christian Century* 72 (28 September 1955): 1144.
99. Teaford, *Post-Suburbia*, 55.

100. "Too Many Shopping Centers?" *Business Week*, 17 November 1956, 136.

101. "Brisk Business for a Bright Shopping Center, *Fortune*, February 1957, 141.

102. Victor Gruen and Larry Smith, *Shopping Towns USA: The Planning of Shopping Centers* (New York: Reinhold Publishing, 1960), 23–24.

103. Clawson Plan Commission, *General Development Plan, City of Clawson, Michigan* (Clawson, MI: Clawson Plan Commission, 1956), 25.

104. Edgar Gray and William N. Leonard, "Park That Industry," *Long Island Business*, October 1957, 4.

105. Louise A. Mozingo, "The Corporate Estate in USA, 1954–64: 'Thoroughly Modern in Concept, but ... Down to Earth and Rugged,'" *Studies in the History of Garden and Designed Landscapes* 20 (spring 2000): 30.

106. Merrill Folsom, "Pepsi-Cola Planning to Leave City for Westchester," *New York Times*, 11 February 1967, 1, 19; Seth S. King, "American Can Co. Will Leave City," *New York Times*, 16 February 1967, 1, 25.

107. Earl W. Kersten, Jr. and D. Reid Ross, "Clayton: A New Metropolitan Focus in the St. Louis Area," *Annals of the Association of American Geographers* 58 (December 1968): 637.

108. Peter O. Muller, *Contemporary Suburban America* (Englewood Cliffs, NJ: Prentice-Hall, 1981), 121, 148–149.

109. Trout Pomeroy, *Oakland County: Making It Work in Michigan* (Chatsworth, CA: Windsor Publications, 1990), 46.

110. Teaford, *Post-Suburbia*, 170.

111. Ibid., 172.

112. Paul Goldberger, "Orange County: Tomorrowland—Wall to Wall," *New York Times*, 11 December 1988, Section 2, 32.

Chapter 2

1. Harlan Paul Douglass, *The Suburban Trend* (New York: Century Co., 1925), 74.

2. William H. Hudnut III, *Halfway to Everywhere: A Portrait of America's First-Tier Suburbs* (Washington, DC: Urban Land Institute, 2003), xii.

3. Robert Fishman, "The American Metropolis at Century's End: Past and Future Influences," *Housing Policy Debate* 11 (2000): 199, 211.

4. William H. Lucy and David L. Phillips, *Confronting Suburban Decline: Strategic Planning for Metropolitan Renewal* (Washington, DC: Island Press, 2000), 2.

5. Myron Orfield, *American Metropolitics: The New Suburban Reality* (Washington, DC: Brookings Institution Press, 2002), 2, 38–39.

6. Rachel Zinn, "Suburbs Look into Revitalization Group," *Toledo Blade*, 26 September 2004, http://uac.utoledo.edu/News/blade-9-26-04.htm (accessed 26 July 2006).

7. Mary Ann Barton, "A New Lease on Life," *American City and County*, 1 March 2004, http://americancityandcounty.com/mag/government_new_lease_life/ (accessed 26 July 2006).

8. *First Suburbs Handbook* (Kansas City, MO: Mid-America Regional Council, 2004), 3.

9. "Idea of the Week: Revitalizing 'First Suburbs,'" *DLC—New Dem Dispatch*, 20 May 2005, http://www.dlc.org/print.cfm?contentid=253339 (accessed 26 July 2006).

10. Hudnut, *Halfway to Everywhere*, 65.

11. *City of Chelsea Community Development Plan* (Chelsea, MA: City of Chelsea, 2004), 8, http://www.ci.chelsea.ma.us/Public_Documents/ChelseaMA_Planning/PublicationsFolder/ChelseaCDP.pdf (accessed 26 July 2006).

12. David R. Berman, "Takeovers of Local Governments: An Overview and Evaluation of State Policies," *Publius: The Journal of Federalism* 25 (summer 1995): 63.

13. *The Boston University/Chelsea Partnership: Thirteenth Annual Report to the Massachusetts Legislature*, 1 September 2004, http://www.bu.edu/chelsea.pdfs/2004LegReport.pdf (accessed 26 July 2006).

14. Jeffrey Cohan, "Shrinking Tax Bases Crippling Suburbs," *Pittsburgh Post-Gazette*, 7 March 2004, http://www.post-gazette.com/pg/04067/281673.stm (accessed 26 July 2006).

15. Ibid.

16. Hudnut, *Halfway to Everywhere*, 61.

17. Cuyahoga County Planning Commission, *City of East Cleveland Master Plan 2003*, 6.5, 6.16–6.17, 6.25, http://cpc.cuyahogacounty. us/docs/masterplans/eastcleveland.pdf (accessed 26 July 2006).

18. "East Cleveland City School District 2003–2004 School Year Report Card," http://www.ode.state.oh.us/reportcardfiles/2003-2004/DIST/043901.pdf (accessed 26 July 2006).

19. Southeast Michigan Council of Governments, *Fiscal Capacity of Southeast Michigan Communities: Taxable Value and Its Implications* (Detroit: Southeast Michigan Council of Governments, 2003), 10, 14, http://www.semcog.org/products/pdfs/taxablevalue. pdf (accessed 26 July 2006).

20. Governor's Highland Park Leadership Steering Committee, *Highland Park's Community Report to Governor Jennifer M. Granholm*, 18 February 2004, 3, http://cityofhighlandpark.us/ docs/2004governor.pdf (accessed 26 July 2006).

21. USC Center for Economic Development, School of Policy, Planning, and Development, University of Southern California, *Gateway Cities: A Profile at the Start of the 21st Century*, 9 February 2001, introduction page, http://www.usc.edu/schools/sppd/ced/ Gateway_Cities_Profile_2001.pdf (accessed 26 July 2006).

22. *Brookline Comprehensive Plan 2005–2015* (Brookline, MA: Town of Brookline, 2005), 18, http://www.townofbrooklinemass.com/ Planning/PDFs/BrooklineCompPlan0201.pdf (accessed 27 July 2006).

23. Bonnie Heudorfer and Barry Bluestone, *The Greater Boston Housing Report Card 2004: An Assessment of Progress in the Greater Boston Area* (Boston, MA: Boston Foundation, 2005), 56, http:// www.curp.neu.edu/pdfs/Housing%20Report%20Card%202004. pdf (accessed 27 July 2006).

24. *Brookline Comprehensive Plan*, 47.

25. Heudorfer and Bluestone, *Greater Boston Housing Report*, 56, 58.

26. Newton Framework Planning Committee, *A Framework for Newton's Planning* (Newton, MA: City of Newton, 2001), 8, 33, http:// www.ci.newton.ma.us/Planning/framework020503.pdf (accessed 27 July 2006).

27. "Bexley City School District 2003–2004 School Year Report Card," http://www.ode.state.oh.us/reportcardfiles/2003-2004/DIST/043620.pdf (accessed 27 July 2006); "Dublin City School District 2003–2004 School Year Report Card," http://www.ode.state.oh.us/reportcardfiles/2003-2004/DIST/047027.pdf (accessed 27 July 2006).

28. "Mayor's Comments," *The Columns*, summer 2005, 2; "About Mission Hills," http://ks-missionhills.civicplus.com/index.asp?ID=16 (accessed 3 November 2005).

29. Jane Adler, "House Prices Rise; Teardowns Increase," *Chicago Tribune*, 4 February 2004, Section 9, 34.

30. "Southern California Home Resale Activity," DQNews.com, http://www.dqnews.com/ZIPLAT.shtm (accessed 14 November 2005).

31. *The City of Grosse Pointe, Michigan Comprehensive Plan* (Grosse Pointe, MI: City of Grosse Pointe, 2003), 2, http://www.grossepointemi.us/f/master_plan.pdf (accessed 26 July 2006).

32. Adrian Scott Fine and Jim Lindberg, *Protecting America's Historic Neighborhoods: Taming the Teardown Trend* (Washington, DC: National Trust for Historic Preservation, 2002), 21.

33. *Wellesley Comprehensive Plan 2005–2015 Update Phase One* (Wellesley, MA: Wellesley Planning Board, 2005), 7, 24, 29, http://www.ci.wellesley.ma.us/Pages/WellesleyMA_Planning/DraftCompPlan.pdf (accessed 26 July 2006).

34. Diana Strzalka, "Teardowns Escalate Upscale Trend," *Chicago Tribune*, 6 October 2004, Section 9, 18.

35. Fine and Lindberg, *Protecting America's Historic Neighborhoods*, 19.

36. Adler, "House Prices Rise," 35.

37. Fine and Lindberg, *Protecting America's Historic Neighborhoods*, 19.

38. "Recent Teardowns in the Park Cities," http://preservationparkcities.org/Tear_Downs/pages/HP_Chart.html; http://preservationparkcities.org/Tear_Downs/pages/UP_Chart.html (accessed 28 October, 2005).

39. David Dillon, "Are Park Cities Getting Too Big for Their Britches?" *Dallas Morning News*, 19 May 2002, http://preservationparkcities.org/articles/pc27b.html (accessed 28 October 2005).

40. Leif Strickland, "Preservationists Go in Pursuit of Policies," *Dallas Morning News*, 1 January 2003, http://preservationparkcities.org/articles/pc39.html (accessed 28 October 2005).

41. Lee Zethraus, "Market Drives Tear-down Trend," *Dallas Morning News*, 8 August 2001, http://preservationparkcities.org/articles/pc56e.html (accessed 28 October 2005).

42. William H. Frey, "Melting Pot Suburbs: A Census 2000 Study of Suburban Diversity," The Brookings Institution Census 2000 Series, June 2001, http://www.brookings.edu/es/urban/census/frey.pdf (accessed 26 July 2006).

43. Andrew Wiese, *Places of Their Own: African American Suburbanization in the Twentieth Century* (Chicago, IL: University of Chicago Press, 2004), 269, 278.

44. "A Narrative Vision—Miami Gardens in Five to Ten Years, City of Miami Gardens, Florida, March 2005," 7, http://www.miami-gardens-fl.gov/cdmp/cdmp_draftvision.pdf (accessed 20 December 2005).

45. Hudnut, *Halfway to Everywhere*, 172.

46. *OPRHC: News from the Center*, spring 2005, 1.

47. Hudnut, *Halfway to Everywhere*, 171.

48. "Diversity Statement Adopted by President and Board of Trustees April 7, 2003," http://www.oak-park.us/public/pdfs/2003%20diversity%20statement.pdf (accessed 27 July 2006).

49. Hudnut, *Halfway to Everywhere*, 163, 166.

50. *The City of Moreno Valley Community & Economic Profile 2004* (Moreno Valley, CA: Moreno Valley Community and Economic Development Department, 2004), 4.

51. University City Department of Planning and Development, *City of University City Comprehensive Plan Update* (University City, MO: University City Department of Planning and Development, 1999, 58.

52. John R. Logan, "The New Ethnic Enclaves in America's Suburbs: A Report by the Lewis Mumford Center for Comparative Urban and Regional Research," 10, http://mumford.albany.edu/census/suburban/SuburbanReport/page1.html (accessed 27 July 2006).

53. John McCormick, "City Losing Immigrants to Suburbs," *Chicago Tribune*, 25 August 2003, Section 2, 4.

54. Frey, "Melting Post Suburbs," 11.

55. Ibid., 9, 11.

56. *Hialeah Garden News*, spring 2005, 1, 3–4.

57. Frey, "Melting Post Suburbs," 9, 11.

58. Blaine Harden, "Out West, A Paradox: Densely Packed Sprawl," *Washington Post*, 11 August 2005, A11.
59. Rick Hampson, "'New Brooklyns' Replace White Suburbs," *USA Today*, 19 May 2003, 1A.
60. Hans Johnson and Amanda Bailey, "California's Newest Homeowners: Affording the Unaffordable," *California Counts: Population Trends and Profiles* 7 (August 2005): 8.
61. Anthony Downs, "California's Inland Empire: The Leading Edge of Southern California Growth," *California Counts: Population Trends and Profiles* 7 (November 2005): 8.
62. Nicolas C. Vaca, *The Presumed Alliance: The Unspoken Conflict between Latinos and Blacks and What It Means for America* (New York: HarperCollins, 2004), 127.
63. David A. Badillo, "Mexicanos and Suburban Parish Communities: Religion, Space, and Identity in Contemporary Chicago," *Journal of Urban History* 31 (November 2004): 27, 35, 39.
64. Wei Li, "Building Ethnoburbia: The Emergence and Manifestation of the Chinese Ethnoburb in Los Angeles' San Gabriel Valley," *Journal of Asian American Studies* 2 (February 1999): 15. See also Wei Li, "Los Angeles's Chinese *Ethnoburb*: From Ethnic Service Center to Global Economy Outpost," *Urban Geography* 19 (1998): 502–517.
65. "Little Saigon," Westminster Chamber of Commerce, http://www.westminsterchamber.org/tourist/index.php (accessed 3 January 2006).
66. Ji Hyun Lim, "Finding Comfort in Daly City," *Asian Week*, 20–26 April 2001, http://www.asianweek.com/2001_04_20/feature_dalycity.html (accessed 28 July 2006).
67. John Maes, "Korean Newspaper Follows Its Readers," *Chicago Tribune*, 4 December 2000, Section 2-Northwest Ed., 3.
68. McCormick, "City Losing Immigrants to Suburbs," 4.
69. Marcelle S. Fischler, "Indian Culture Clash: Classical or Pop?" *New York Times*, 26 September 2004, Section 14-Long Island, 1.
70. S. Mitra Kalita, *Suburban Sahibs: Three Immigrant Families and Their Passage from India to America* (New Brunswick, NJ: Rutgers University Press, 2003), 12, 28.
71. James Allen and Eugene Turner, "The Most Ethnically Diverse Urban Places in the United States," *Urban Geography* 10 (1989): 523–539.

72. Andrew Kopkind, "Once Upon a Time in the West," *The Nation*, 1 June 1985, 672, 675; "A Gay City on the Hill?" *Newsweek*, 5 November 1984, 46; see also "In West Hollywood: Exotic Mix," *Time*, 16 December 1985, 7.

73. Sara Kocher Consulting, *City of West Hollywood Demographic Profile 2002*. 1–2, 4, 6, http://www.weho.org/download/index.cfm/fuseaction/download/cid/1969/ (accessed 27 July 2006).

74. "Welcome to WeHo!" http://www.gogaywesthollywood.com/ (accessed 2 December 2005).

75. "18th Annual West Hollywood Halloween Costume Carnaval," http://www.visitwesthollywood.com/halloween05/ (accessed 2 December 2005); *West Hollywood Vision 2020 Strategic Plan* (West Hollywood, CA: City of West Hollywood, 2003), 15.

76. A. J. Burton, "Wilton Manors: The New Gay Mecca?" 3 June 2004, The Gay Financial Network, http://www.gfn.com/realestate/story.phtml?sid=15726 (accessed 12 November 2005); "Welcome to Wilton Manors—The New Gay Mecca!" http://queereyehomes.com/wiltonmanors.asp (accessed 12 November 2005); "South Florida Pride & Gay Business Search—Relocating," http://www.southfloridapride.com/relocating/indexrelocating.htm (accessed 12 November 2005).

77. "South Florida Pride & Gay Business Search—Relocating."

78. Ginia Bellafante, "A Gay Boomtown Is More Mainstream and Less the Cliché," *New York Times*, 15 May 2004, A12.

79. Gary J. Gates, "Gay America," *Urban Land* 64 (February 2005): 79. See also Wayne Brekhus, *Peacocks, Chameleons, Centaurs: Gay Suburbia and the Grammar of Social Identity* (Chicago, IL: University of Chicago Press, 2003).

80. John M Findlay, *Magic Lands: Western Cityscapes and American Culture after 1940* (Berkeley: University of California Press, 1992), 207; James H. Andrews, "Leisure Power," *Planning* 65 (November 1999): 4, 6–7.

81. *City of Laguna Woods General Plan, Housing Element*, 2003, 12, 13, 35. 27, http://lagunawoodscity.org/images/lagunawoodscity/Housing%20Element%20rev.pdf (accessed July 2006); *Laguna Woods Wood Works*, winter 2003, 1.

82. Bonnie Heudorfer, *Age Restricted Active Adult Housing in Massachusetts: A Review of the Factors Fueling Its Explosive Growth and the Public Policy Issues It Raises* (No place: Citizens' Housing and Planning Association, 2005), 6, 10, http://www.chapa.org/AgeRestrictedHousinginMA.pdf (accessed 27 July 2006).

83. Donna Kutt Nahas, "Boom Market for Age-Restricted Housing," *New York Times*, 5 September 2004, Section 14-Long Island, 1.

84. Susan Warner, "Retired, Not Dead," *New York Times*, 19 December 2004, Section 14-New Jersey, 1, 11.

85. "Meet the Barringtons," *Chicago Tribune*, 31 July 2003, Section 5, 1.

86. *Comprehensive Plan Village of Barrington Hills, Public Hearing Draft*, October 2005, 3, 5, 18–19, http://www.ci.barrington-hills.il.us/pdf/BH_CompPlan101_26_05_text.pdf (accessed 27 July 2006).

87. "Town of Southwest Ranches." http://www.southwestranches.org/ (accessed 14 December 2005).

88. *The Official Town Newsletter Southwest Rancher*, October 2005, 3.

89. "City of Rolling Hills." http://www.palosverdes.com/rh/ (accessed 28 June 2005).

90. *Comprehensive Plan Bedford, New York*, July 2002, 4, http://www.bedfordny.info/html/pdf/01_introduction.pdf (accessed 27 July 2006).

91. *Franklin Village Master Plan Update 1997* (Franklin, MI: Franklin Village Planning Commission, 1997), 8, 22.

92. Catherine Kauffman, "Town of Paradise Valley History," 1, http://www.ci.paradise-valley.az.us/docs/HISTORY%20OF%20TOWN.pdf (accessed 27 July 2006).

93. *Paradise Valley General Plan*, adopted 21 November 2002, iii, http://www.ci.paradise-valley.az.us/docs/General_Plan/GP%20012703%20Preface.pdf (accessed 27 July 2006).

94. Robert E. Lang and Patrick A. Simmons, "'Boomburbs': The Emergence of Large, Fast-Growing Suburban Cities," in *Redefining Urban and Suburban America: Evidence from Census 2000, Volume One*, ed. Bruce Katz and Robert E. Lang (Washington, DC: Brookings Institution Press, 2003), 101, 103.

95. Robert E. Lang, "The Boomburbs at 'Buildout': Future Development in Large Fast-Growing Suburbs," Metropolitan Institute at Virginia Tech, January 2005, 2, http://www.mi.vt.edu/uploads/SGOE.pdf (accessed 28 July 2006).
96. *2005 Annual Report, McKinney, Texas* (McKinney, TX: City of McKinney, 2005), 2.
97. City of Frisco website, http://www.ci.frisco.tx.us/departments/Planning_Development/index.aspx?id=102 (accessed 15 November 2005).
98. *City of Surprise Community and Economic Development 2004 Annual Report* (Surprise, AZ: City of Surprise, 2005, 9; Shaun McKinnon, "W. Valley Is Shaping Growth," *Arizona Republic* (Phoenix), 14 May 2003, A1.
99. Mike Fimea, "Buckeye Poised for Growth," *Arizona Business Gazette*, 12 June 2003,, BG1; Buckeye Valley Chamber of Commerce website, http://www.buckeyevalleychamber.org/custom2.asp?pageid=308 (accessed 16 November 2005): McKinnon, "W. Valley Is Shaping Growth," A1; Marty Sauerzopf, "Buckeye OKs Massive Growth," *Arizona Republic* (Phoenix), 21 May 2003, A1.
100. Ibid.
101. Town of Buckeye website, http://www.buckeyeaz.gov/townabout/info.htm (accessed 16 November 2005).
102. *2005 Annual Report, McKinney, Texas*, 5.
103. Bonnie Rinaldi, "A Desert Dream," *Urban Land* 61 (September 2002): 80–81.
104. Lang, "Boomburb at 'Buildout,'" 10.
105. James B. Goodno, "Housing's 800-Pound Gorilla," *Planning* 71 (April 2005): 27. For more on homeowner associations and the small town politics of boomburbs, see Robert Lang and Jennifer LeFurgy, *Boomburbs: The Rise of America's Accidental Cities* (Washington, DC: Brookings Institution Press, 2007), chapter 6.
106. Cathy Clark, "The Boomburbs," *San Diego Magazine*, February 2004, http://www.sandiegomag.com/issues/february04/featurea0204.asp (accessed 6 January 2006).
107. Ted O'Callahan, "Cultures Come Together in Crossroads Area of Bellevue," *Seattle Times*, 17 September 2005, http://seattletimes.nwsource.com/html/eastsidenews/2002500467_neighborhood18.html (accessed 16 January 2006).

108. *City of Lakewood, Colorado Annual Budget 2006* (Lakewood, CO: City of Lakewood, 2005), 19–20, http://www.lakewood.org/FN/PDF_docs/2006bdgt1.pdf (accessed 29 July 2006).

109. Lang, "Boomburb at 'Buildout,'" 15–16.

110. *City of Tempe General Plan 2030* (Tempe, AZ: City of Tempe, 2003), 7, 125, http://www.tempe.gov/tdsi/gp2030/gp2030.pdf (accessed 29 July 2006).

111. Garin Groff, "Downtown Tempe Reaches for the Sky," *East Valley Tribune*, 14 November 2005, http://www.joelkotkin.com/Commentary/EVT%20Downtown%20Tempe%20reaches%20for%20the%20sky.htm (accessed 21 January 2006).

112. Mary Jo Waits and William Fulton, *Which Way Scottsdale?* (Tempe, AZ: Morrison Institute for Public Policy, 2003), 2, 6, 14.

Chapter 3

1. Joel Garreau, *Edge City: Life on the New Frontier* (New York: Doubleday, 1991), 3.

2. Ibid., 6–7.

3. Ibid., 426–438.

4. Robert E. Lang, *Edgeless Cities: Exploring the Elusive Metropolis* (Washington, DC: Brookings Institution Press, 2003), 1.

5. Ibid., 54–55, 60–62, 69–70; Robert E. Lang, Thomas Sanchez, and Jennifer LeFurgy, *Beyond Edgeless Cities: Office Geography in the New Metropolis* (Washington, DC: National Association of Realtors, 2006), 14.

6. Lang, *Edgeless Cities: Exploring the Elusive Metropolis*, 88, 99.

7. Garreau, *Edge City*, 425.

8. Ibid., 5.

9. Fairfax County Economic Development Authority, "Facts, Fairfax County, Virginia, USA," updated April 2006, http://www.fairfaxcountyeda.org/publications/fairfax_facts.pdf (accessed 29 July 2006).

10. "Real Estate Report, Fairfax County, Virginia, Midyear 2005," 2, http://www.fairfaxcountyeda.org/publications/my05rer.pdf (accessed 29 July 2006).

11. Fairfax County Economic Development Authority, "Facts," 2.

12. S. Mitra Kalita, "Fairfax's Point Man in India," *Washington Post*, 30 December 2005, D5.

13. Fairfax County Economic Development Authority, *Fairfax County Profile*, Updated May 2006, 2, http://www.fairfaxeda.org/publications/profile.pdf (accessed 29 July 2006).
14. Neil Irwin, "Change Around the Corner," *Washington Post*, 22 December 2003, E1–E2.
15. Elissa Silverman, "The Mall's New Mix," *Washington Post*, 30 September 2005, D1, D4.
16. "Lerner Enterprise: Tysons Galleria," http://www.lernerenterprises.com/retail/tysonsgalleria.html (accessed 3 January 2006).
17. "Area Business Report, Tysons Corner," updated May 2004, http://www.fairfaxcountyeda.org/publications/tysons.pdf (accessed 29 July 2006).
18. Peter Whoriskey, "Soaring View of Tysons Centers on a Downtown," *Washington Post*, 22 April 2005, A8.
19. Irwin, "Change around the Corner," E1.
20. Whoriskey, "Soaring View of Tysons," A8.
21. Peter Whoriskey, "Rebirth at Tysons Corner," *Washington Post*, 4 February 2005, Virginia Edition, B2.
22. "A Background on Reston Town Center," http://restontowncenter.com/featuresbotright.html (accessed 12 January 2006).
23. "Area Business Report, Reston-Herndon," updated May 2004, http://www.fairfaxcountyeda.org/publications/reston_herndon.pdf (accessed 29 July 2006).
24. Fairfax County Economic Development Authority, *Fairfax County Profile*, 7.
25. "Real Estate Report, Fairfax County, Midyear 2005," 1, 3.
26. Fairfax County Economic Development Authority, *Fairfax County Profile*, 6, 13.
27. "Area Business Report, Western Fairfax," updated May 2004, http://www.fairfaxcountyeda.org/publications/west_fairfax.pdf (accessed 29 July 2006).
28. Andy Klaff, Charles Dilks, and Casey Veatch, "Dulles Corridor Real Estate Overview," http://www.titanpubs.com/Greater_Reston/dulles.html (accessed 12 January 2006).
29. "Woodfield Shopping Center, Community Information," http://www.shopwoodfield.com/infodesk/community/135.html (accessed 4 January 2006); *Village of Schaumburg Community Profile* (Schaumburg, IL: Village of Schaumburg, 2002), 3, http://www.ci.schaumburg.il.us/vos.nsf/schaumburg/LLSN-5AYMWB (accessed 29 July 2006).

30. Village of Schaumburg, *Schaumburg Community Profile*, 16.
31. "Village of Schaumburg—New Developments in Last Five Years," http://www.ci.schaumburg.il.us/vos.nsf/schaumburg/JSCP-58UT29 (accessed 19 January 2006).
32. Village of Schaumburg, *Schaumburg Community Profile*, 3; "Village of Schaumburg, Economic Information," http://www.ci.schaumburg.il.us/vos.nsf/schaumburg/JSCP-58ZVFV (accessed 19 January 2006).
33. Department of Planning and Community Development, *Bellevue Economic Profile* (Bellevue, WA: City of Bellevue, 2005), 27, http://www.ci.bellevue.wa.us/departments/Development/pdf/Complete%20Economic%20Profile%206-1-2005.pdf (accessed 29 July 2006).
34. Ibid., 54.
35. Ibid., 55.
36. Ibid., 17; Clayton Park, "Is Bellevue the Epicenter of a Second Tech Boom?" *King County Journal*, 27 October 2005, http://www.kingcountyjournal.com/sited/story/html/221003 (accessed 16 January 2006).
37. David A. Grant, "Abandoned Projects Come Back to Life," *King County Journal*, 14 November 2005, http://www.kingcountyjournal.com/sited/story/html/222765 (accessed 16 January 2006).
38. Kristen Millares Bolt and John Cook, "A New Bellevue Rising: Big-thinking Kemper Freeman Jr. Thinking Even Bigger," *Seattle Post-Intelligencer*, 6 April 2005, http://seattlepi.nwsource.com/business/218982_kemper06.html (accessed 9 January 2006).
39. Lawrence Cheek, "On Architecture: Sleek New Lincoln Square Was Not What Bellevue Needed," *Seattle Post-Intelligencer*, 29 November 2005, http://seattlepi.nwsource.com/visualart/250008_architecture29.html (accessed 9 January 2006).
40. Bolt and Cook, "New Bellevue Rising."
41. "Mall of America," http://www.bloomingtonmn.org/mallofamerica.html (accessed 13 June, 2003).
42. Eric Wieffering, "10 Years Later, the Mall of America Still Stands Alone," *Minneapolis Star Tribune*, 4 August 2002, 1A.
43. Kevin Mattson, "Antidotes to Sprawl," in *Sprawl and Public Space: Redressing the Mall*, ed. David J. Smiley (Washington, DC: National Endowment for the Arts, 2002), 40.

44. H. Lee Murphy, "Retail Revisions: Mall Seek Lifestyle Change," *Crain's Chicago Business*, 28 March 2005, 36.
45. Mattson, "Antidotes to Sprawl," 40–41; "Roundtable: Obstacles to Development" in *Sprawl and Public Space*, 91; David Smiley, "Addressing Redress" in *Sprawl and Public Space*, 14.
46. Teresa F. Lindeman, "Dead Mall Shopping," *Pittsburgh Post-Gazette*, 10 May 2002, C3; see also http://www.deadmalls.com.
47. Donna Mitchell, "Turtle Creek Sole U.S. Enclosed Mall to Open During '06," http://www.icsc.org/srch/sct/sct0206/feat_turtle_creek_mall.php (accessed 4 April 2006).
48. Renee Degross, "Room at the Malls," *Atlanta Journal-Constitution*, 6 August 2003, 1D.
49. "State of the Industry," *Chain Store Age* 81 (August 2005): 6A.
50. Jennifer Evans-Cowley, *Meeting the Big-Box Challenge: Planning, Design, and Regulatory Strategies* (Chicago, IL: American Planning Association, 2006), 1; Marlon G. Boarnet, Randall Crane, Daniel G. Chatman, and Michael Manville, "Emerging Planning Challenges in Retail: The Case of Wal-Mart," *Journal of the American Planning Association* 71 (autumn 2005): 433.
51. John Ritter, "California Tries to Slam Lid on Big-Boxed Wal-Mart," *USA Today*, 2 March 2004, 2B.
52. Boarnet, et al., "Emerging Planning Challenges," 434.
53. Ritter, "California Tries to Slam Lid," 2B.
54. "ICSC Shopping Center Definitions," http://www.icsc.org/srch/lib/SCDefinitions.pdf (accessed 30 July, 2006).
55. Kristina Kessler, "Refining Retail," *Urban Land* 64 (October 2005): 87.
56. David C. Scholl and Robert B. Williams, "A Choice of Lifestyles," *Urban Land* 64 (October 2005): 89.
57. Robert Preer, "Sharing the Wealth in Hingham," *Boston Globe*, 28 November 2004, Globe South Section, 1.
58. Paula Widholm, "Indiana's Clay Terrace; Small-Town Charm Meets Upscale Shopping," *Midwest Construction* 8 (1 May 2005): 39.
59. Jennifer Waters, "Lifestyle Centers Offer It All," *Albany* (New York) *Times Union*, 20 June 2004, E1.
60. Ed McKinley, "These Centers Made for Walkin,' but Not Too Far Please," http://www.icsc.org/srch/sct/sct0206/feat_lifestyle_walk_park.php (accessed 4 April, 2006).

61. Charles Lockwood, "Raising the Bar," *Urban Land* 62 (February 2003): 77.

62. Sam Newberg, "Town Centers Open around the US," *New Urban News*, December 2004, http://www.newurbannews.com/TownCentersDec04.html (accessed 11 October 2005).

63. Lockwood, "Raising the Bar," 74. See also Janet H. Cho, "Westlake Complex Growing Up to Be Success," *Cleveland Plain Dealer*, 15 November 2005, C1.

64. Lauren Weber, "Smith Haven Mall Makeover," *Newsday* (Nassau and Suffolk Edition), 3 November 2005, A54.

65. "Cumberland Mall—About Us," http://www.cumberlandmall.com/html/MallInfo.asp (accessed 3 January, 2006); Sandra Jones, "Giant Expansion for Old Orchard," *Crain's Chicago Business*, 6 June 2005, 1.

66. Monica Soto Ouchi, "Alderwood Alters Retail Image," *Seattle Times*, 3 November 2004, F1.

67. "Southglenn Shopping Center Is Reinvented," News Release, Alberta Development Partners, http://www.newsouthglenn.com/Documents/AlbertaSouthglennAnnouncement.pdf (accessed 8 January, 2006).

68. Katherine Field, "Power Surge," *Chain Store Age* 82 (March 2006): 123.

69. Paul G. Lewis, "Retail Politics: Local Sales Taxes and the Fiscalization of Land Use," *Economic Development Quarterly* 15 (February 2001): 25.

70. Ibid., 26–28.

71. Jonathan Schwartz, "Prisoners of Proposition 13: Sales Taxes, Property Taxes, and the Fiscalization of Municipal Land Use Decisions," *Southern California Law Review* 71 (November 1997): 210–212.

72. Bay Area Economics, *City of San Ramon Economic Development Strategic Plan*, 12 August 2005, 2, 6–7, 9, http://www.ci.san-ramon.ca.us/econdev/images/edsp.pdf (accessed 30 July 2006).

73. Applied Economics, *Maricopa Association of Governments Growing Smarter Implementation: Historic Sales Tax Base—Final Report*, October 2001, 4, http://www.mag.maricopa.gov/pdf/cms.resource/Historic-Sales-Tax-Base.pdf (accessed 30 July 2006).

74. "Auto Mall Tax Wars—Our Stand: Subsidies Just Perpetuate the Bidding Contests Over Sales Revenues," *Arizona Republic* (Phoenix), 21 May 2004, Chandler/Sun Lakes and Ocotillo Community Section, 4.

75. Jim Walsh, "Car Dealerships Moving to Malls," *Arizona Republic* (Phoenix), 27 July 2005, Mesa/Apache Junction and Gold Canyon Community Section, 1.

76. Peter Aleshire, "Seductive Sales-Tax Deals Becoming Less Enticing," *Arizona Republic* (Phoenix), 28 May 2004, North Phoenix Community Section, 2.

77. Laurie Roberts, "Tax-Giveaway Politicians Star in 'Cities Gone Wild,'" *Arizona Republic* (Phoenix), 14 February 2004, B2.

78. Erin Stewart, Doug Smeath and Nicole Warburton, "Friend or Foe? Wal-Mart Alters Utah Landscape," *Deseret News* (Salt Lake City), 27 March 2005, A1.

79. Erin Stewart and Jenifer K. Nii, "Utahns Say Yes to Wal-Marts," *Deseret News* (Salt Lake City), 9 December 2004, B1.

80. Erin Stewart, "Sandy Plan Called Moneymaker," *Deseret News* (Salt Lake City), 14 September 2004, B1.

81. Stewart, Smeath and Warburton, "Friend or Foe?" A1; Stewart and Nii, "Utahns Say Yes to Wal-Marts," B1.

82. Kersten Swinyard, "Group Drops 'Park, Not Parking Lot' Angle," *Deseret News* (Salt Lake City), 8 September 2005, B3; Zack VanEyck, "Put Stores or Park in Sandy Pit,' *Deseret News*, 11 May 2004, B1.

83. Kersten Swinyard, "Voters Give Sandy Mayor His Fourth Term," *Deseret News* (Salt Lake City), 9 November 2005, A5.

84. Jodie Jacobs, "Two Officials Navigate Town's Growth Issue," *Chicago Tribune*, 5 March 2003, Section 9, 7; Joan Cary, "Bloomingdale Monitors Strong Business Centers," *Chicago Tribune*, 5 March 2003, Section 9, 10.

85. Michelle Groenke, "Good Retail Mix Key to Town's Success," *Chicago Tribune*, 23 June 2004, Section 9, 23.

86. Matt Baron, "Change Brings New Hurdles for 2 Towns," *Chicago Tribune*, 6 October 2004, Section 9, 7.

87. Warren Moulds, "New Mayors Must Now Tend to Community Issues," *Chicago Tribune*, 15 April 2005, Section 2, 4.

88. Ann R. Martin, "Makeover Is Making Economic Sense," *Chicago Tribune*, 17 September 2003, Section 9, 6.

89. Janice Neumann, "Palo Heights Mayor Steers away from Controversy," *Chicago Tribune*, 29 October 2003, Section 9, 12.
90. "Summer 2004 Pennsylvania Township Officials Survey," Lincoln Institute of Public Opinion, http://www.lincolninstitute.org/archives/surveys/2004Summer-Twp.html (accessed 14 February 2006).
91. Randall Gross, *Understanding the Fiscal Impacts of Land Use in Ohio*, 2 August 2004, http://www.regionalconnections.org/documents/pdf/fiscalimpacts.pdf (accessed 30 July 2006).
92. Cuyahoga County Planning Commission, *City of Parma 2004 Draft Master Plan*, 2.14, 4.13–4.14, http://cpc.cuyahogacounty.us/docs/masterplans/parma.pdf (accessed 30 July 2006).
93. Regional Plan Association, *Fundamental Property Tax Reform: Land Use Implications of New Jersey's Tax Debate*, October 2005, 6, 8, http://www.rpa.org/pdf/propertytax101705.pdf (accessed 30 July 2006).
94. *Littleton Master Plan 2002*, http://www.littletonma.org/Master%20Plan/chap%2010.htm (accessed 29 January 2006).
95. Randal Edgar, "Will It Be Trees or Stores On Exit 1, *Providence Journal*, 18 April 2004, A1.
96. Neil Shea, "Council Urges Zoning Board to Accept BJ's Proposal," *Providence Journal*, 20 October 2003, http://www.projo.com/northwest/content/projo_20031020_jletter.85ae8.html (accessed 15 February 2006).
97. Sandy Coleman, "Stoughton Adjusting to Role as Retail Mecca," *Boston Globe*, 6 June 2004, Globe South Section, 3.

Chapter 4

1. *What's So Special About Special Districts: A Citizen's Guide to Special Districts in California*, 3rd ed., http://www.sen.ca.gov/locgov/WSSASDREPORT.HTM (accessed 31 July 2006).
2. Illinois Commission on Intergovernmental Cooperation, *Legislator's Guide to Local Governments in Illinois: Special Districts* (Springfield, IL: State of Illinois, 2003), iv, 28–31, 47–49, 68–71, http://www.ilga.gov/commission/lru/SpecialDistricts.pdf (accessed 31 July 2006).
3. "Downers Grove Sanitary District," http://www.dgsd.org/index.html (accessed 24 May 2006).

4. "Lisle-Woodridge Fire District," http://www.lwfd.org/ (accessed 24 May 2006); "Carol Stream Fire Protection District," http://carolstreamfire.org/chief.htm (accessed 24 May 2006).

5. "History of Municipal Boundary in Minnesota," AdminMinnesota, Department of Administration, http://www.mba.state.mn.us/history.html (accessed 19 December 2005).

6. Ibid.; Minnesota Planning, *City Limits: A Report to the Minnesota Legislature on Municipal Boundary Adjustments*, February 2002, 6, http://www.mba.state.mn.us/pdfs/CityLimits.pdf (accessed 31 July 2006).

7. Commission on Local Governance for the 21st Century, *Growth within Bounds; Planning California Governance for the 21st Century* (Sacramento, CA: State of California, 2000), 25, http://www.opr.ca.gov/publications/PDFs/79515.pdf (accessed 31 July 2006).

8. Neelima Palacherla, "Proactive Island Annexation Program Adopted by Santa Clara LAFCo," *The Sphere: Newsletter of the California Association of Local Agency Formation Commissions*, May 2005, 1, 5, http://www.calafco.org/docs/Sphere/May2005.pdf (accessed 31 July 2006).

9. "Island Focus: Orange Islands," *LAFCO Unincorporated Islands Program*, Issue 2, summer 2002, 2, http://www.oclafco.ca.gov/islands/newsletter_sum02.pdf (accessed 31 July 2006).

10. Palacherla, "Proactive Island Annexation Program," 1.

11. Annette Steinacker, "Prospects for Regional Governance: Lessons from the Miami Abolition Vote," *Urban Affairs Review* 37 (September 2001): 109.

12. Nancy McCue, "Vote YES for a New City, Again," *Old Cutler Bay*, http://www.communitynewspapers.com/archives/2005/oldcutler/02_24_05/local1.htm (accessed 20 December, 2005).

13. Edward Ludovici, "A Tale of Two Cities," *Old Cutler Bay*, http://www.communitynewspapers.com/archives/2005/oldcutler/02_24_05/local5.htm (accessed 20 December 2005).

14. "Doral: The City and Its History," *Ciudad Doral Newspaper*, http://www.ciudaddoral.com/historia02.htm (accessed 23 March, 2006); Kathleen Fordyce, "Celebrating in Style," *MiamiHerald.com*, posted 23 March 2006, http://www.miami.com/mld/miamiherald/news/local/states/florida/counties/miami-dade/cities_neighborhoods/pinecrest/14155443.htm (accessed 23 March 2006).

15. Jennifer Mooney Piedra, "Incorporation Movement Gets New Life," *MiamiHerald.com*, posted 4 December 2005, http://www.miami.com/mld/miamiherald/news/local/states/florida/counties/miami-dade/cities_neighborhoods/Kendall/13317006.htm (accessed 20 December 2005).

16. "Does Incorporation of the Village of The Falls Make Dollars and 'Sense'?" http://www.jthtest.colonynet.com/images/file/0/686/Why_it_makes_sense.htm (accessed 20 December 2005).

17. "Cityhood Will Only Make Falls Better," *MiamiHerald.com*, posted 18 December 2005, http://www.miami.com/mld/miamiherald/news/local/states/florida/counties/miami-dade/cities_neighborhoods/pinecrest/13428225.htm (accessed 20 December 2005).

18. Piedra, "Incorporation Movement Gets New Life."

19. Suzy Valentine, "County OKs Study of Fisher Island Incorporation," Miamitodaynews.com, week of 20 October 2005, http://www.miamitodaynews.com/news/051020/story2.shtml (accessed 27 December 2005).

20. Suzy Valentine, "County Tightens Requirements for Municipal Incorporations," Miamitodaynews.com, week of 14 July 2005, http://www.miamitodaynews.com/news/050714/story6.shtml (accessed 20 December 2005).

21. Henry Farber, "Sandy Springs Could Be City Soon," *Atlanta Journal-Constitution*, 27 November 2004, B5.

22. Henry Farber, "Confidence High Ahead of City Vote," *Atlanta Journal-Constitution*, 20 June 2005, D5.

23. Henry Farber, "Sandy Springs a City at Last," *Atlanta Journal-Constitution*, 22 June 2005, A5; Marcia Langhenry and D. L. Bennett, "Sandy Springs Hopeful, Anxious," *Atlanta Journal-Constitution*, 23 June 2005, D3.

24. "Open Letter from Representative," New City of Milton website,. http://www.cityofmilton-ga.org/open_letter_from_representative.htm (accessed 2 August, 2006).

25. Debra Hunter, "Who Wants Out?" *Atlanta Magazine*, March 2006, 60.

26. "Welcome Home to the City of Roswell," December 2005, 2, http://www.roswellgov.com/docs/pdf/misc/annexation%202005/ROSWELL_HOMEINFO_BRO.pdf (accessed 31 July 2006).

27. "Unincorporated Broward," *Broward-by-the-Numbers*, December 2005, http://www.broward.org/planningservices/bbtn41.pdf (accessed 31 July 2006).

28. Brad Bennett, "Melrose Park Residents Place Hopes for Improvements in Ft. Lauderdale," *Miami Herald*, 12 November 2001, http://www.floridacdc.org/articles/011112-1.htm (accessed 27 December 2005).

29. William Fischel, *The Homevoter Hypothesis* (Cambridge, MA: Harvard University Press, 2001), 242.

30. J. Patrick Coolican, "Individualistic City to Celebrate," *Seattle Times*, 28 March 2003, East Zone Section, B3.

31. "About the Washington State Boundary Review Board for King County," http://www.metrokc.gov/annexations/about.aspx (accessed 30 January 2006).

32. Karen Gaudette, "Bill Would Help Cities Afford Annexations," *Seattle Times*, 15 February 2006, B5.

33. Keith Ervin, "Growing Interest in Annexation," *Seattle Times*, 9 September 2004, B3.

34. Liona Tannesen Burnham, "Area Ponders Incorporation," *Seattle Times*, 25 September 2005, G4.

35. Keith Ervin, "Fairwood Backers File Bid to Be City," *Seattle Times*, 20 November 2004, B1.

36. Keith Ervin, "Task Force Considers Fairwood's Future," *Seattle Times*, 10 June 2004, B3.

37. Keith Ervin, "Fairwood Annexation Sparks Debate," *Seattle Times*, 17 January 2006, B3.

38. Jay Evensen, "Darwinistic Carving Up of County Is Madness," *Deseret News*, 25 April 2004, AA1.

39. "Sandy Springs Open For Business," *Ledger-Enquirer.com*, posted 1 December 2005, http://www.ledger-enquirer.com/mld/ledgerenquirer/news/local/13300556.htm (accessed 20 December 2005).

40. David Rusk, *Cities without Suburbs* (Washington, DC: Woodrow Wilson Center Press, 1993), 5, 7, 121–122, 124.

41. Neal Peirce and Curtis Johnson, *Boston Unbound: Tapping Greater Boston's Assets and Talents to Create a World-Leading Citistate* (Boston, MA: Boston Globe, 2004), 4, http://www.tbf.org/uploadedFiles/Citistates_Final.pdf (accessed 31 July 2006).

42. See list of metropatterns studies at Myron Orfield website, University of Minnesota Law School, http://www.law.umn.edu/facultyprofiles/orfieldm.htm (accessed 2 August 2006). See also Myron Orfield, *American Metropolitics: The New Suburban Reality* (Washington, DC: Brookings Institution Press, 2002).

43. Bruce Katz, ed., *Reflections on Regionalism* (Washington, DC: Brookings Institution Press, 200), x.

44. Frank Gamrat and Jake Haulk, *Merging Governments: Lessons from Louisville, Indianapolis, and Philadelphia* (Pittsburgh, PA: Allegheny Institute for Public Policy, 2005), 4, http://www.alleghenyinstitute.org/reports/05_04.pdf (accessed 31 July 2006).

45. Ibid., 5.

46. "Merger and Growth," *Louisville Courier-Journal*, 2 November 2000, 12A: "What Merger Means for the City," *Louisville Courier-Journal*, 5 November 2000, 2D.

47. Al Cross, "Election 2000; Jackson Urges Blacks to Vote Against Merger," *Louisville Courier-Journal*, 13 October 2000, 1B.

48. Rick McDonough, "Officials of 41 Cities Back Merger," *Louisville Courier-Journal*, 29 September 2000, 1A.

49. Tompkins Wayne, "Big Merger Benefits Expected," *Louisville Courier-Journal*, 4 January 2004, 1E.

50. Shafer Sheldon, "Louisville Gladly Becomes Model for Merger," *Louisville Courier-Journal*, 2 January 2004, 1B.

51. Shafer Sheldon, "Session Set on Revamping Government," *Louisville Courier-Journal*, 21 March 2005, 1B.

52. Jeffrey Cohan, "Town Meeting: Louisville Mayor Offers Primer on Uniting City-County Government," *Post-Gazette.com*, 1 October 2004, http://www.post-gazette.com/pg/04275/388541.stm (accessed 2 August 2006).

53. Jerome L. Sherman, "City, County Heads Urge Consolidating," *Pittsburgh Post-Gazette*, 19 March 2005, A1.

54. Jeffrey Cohan, "Town Meeting Panelists Split on Consolidation," *Pittsburgh Post-Gazette*, 27 May 2004, B2.

55. Glenn May, "City-County Merger Still Distant," *Pittsburgh Tribune Review*, 31 January 2005.

56. Cohan, "Town Meeting Panelists Split on Consolidation," B2.

57. May, "City-County Merger Still Distant."

58. Michael O'Malley, "Erie County Executive Calls for Regional Government," *Cleveland Plain Dealer*, 11 February 2004, A9.

59. "Uniting for a Greater Buffalo—Information from the Greater Buffalo Commission on the Proposed City/County Merger," http://www.greaterbflo.org/process.asp (accessed 3 November 2005).

60. Phil Fairbanks and Brian Meyer, "Shall We Merge?" *Buffalo News*, 12 February 2004, A1.

61. Jason Feulner, Julien Hautier, Ben Walsh, *The Future of Government Consolidation in Upstate New York* (Syracuse, NY: Maxwell School of Citizenship and Public Affairs, Syracuse University, 2005), 40, http://www.suce.syr.edu/community/ocl/ocl_studies/2005/FutureofGovConsolidation.pdf (accessed 31 July 2006).

62. Phil Fairbanks, "Repairing County and City, Together or Apart," *Buffalo News*, 27 June 2005, A1.

63. Brian Meyer, "Merger Not Part of Mayoral Dialogue," *Buffalo News*, 31 October 2005, B1.

64. "Project Destiny Public Finance Task Force Report," The Greater Des Moines Partnership, 5 December 2003, http://www.desmoinesmetro.com/projectdestiny/pdfs/financemembers.pdf (accessed 31 July 2006).

65. David Rusk, *Governing Greater Albuquerque: A Report to the Unification Exploratory Group of the City of Albuquerque and Bernalillo County*, 18 October 2002, 2, http://www.gamaliel.org/DavidRusk/final%20report%2010-18-02.pdf (accessed 31 July 2006); Ed Asher, "Unification Rejected Again But Expected to Be Back," *Albuquerque Tribune*, 3 November 2004, A10.

66. "Cooperation Needed in Community Growth," *Albuquerque Tribune*, 18 November 2004, C2.

67. David Rusk, *Inside Game Outside Game: Winning Strategies for Saving Urban America* (Washington, DC: Brookings Institution Press, 1999), 239.

68. David J. Barron, Gerald E. Frug, and Rick T. Su, *Dispelling the Myth of Home Rule: Local Power in Greater Boston* (Cambridge, MA: Rappaport Institute for Greater Boston, 2004), xvii, http://www.ksg.harvard.edu/rappaport/downloads/home_rule/home_rule.pdf (accessed 1 August 2006).

69. *Strategic Plan—495/MetroWest Corridor Partnership* (2003), 11, http://www.arc-of-innovation.org/202492%20MWCC%20Brochure.pdf (accessed 28 July 2005).

70. "Why We Need a Regional Transportation Authority," *MetroWest Business*, June, July, August 2005, 1, 8.

71. *Twin Rivers Council of Governments Comprehensive Plan*, December 2003, 3, http://www.trcog.com/background.pdf (accessed 1 August 2006).
72. "SHACOG Preamble to By-Laws," http://www.shacog.com/shacoggeneral/preamble.htm (accessed 5 August 2005); "SHACOG Current Programs," http://www.shacog.com/shacoggeneral/programs.htm (accessed 5 August 2005).
73. *BACOG News*, 2005 Bi-annual No. 1, http://www.village.deerpark.il.us/board/Newsletters/Newsletters%202005/BACOGNewsletter2005-1FINAL.pdf (accessed 1 August 2006).
74. *Guide to the San Gabriel Valley Council of Governments*, 37, http://www.sgvcog.org/COG%20Orientation%203.pdf (accessed 1 August 2006).
75. "Chair's Message," Ventura Council of Governments website, ttp://www.venturacog.org/message.html (accessed 7 June 2006).
76. Barron, Frug, and Su, *Dispelling the Myth of Home Rule*, 79.
77. Ibid., 74.

Chapter 5

1. Edward L. Glaeser, Jenny Schuetz, and Bryce Ward, *Regulation and Rise of Housing Prices in Greater Boston* (Cambridge, MA: Rappaport Institute for Greater Boston, Harvard University and Boston: Pioneer Institute for Public Policy, 2006), 1.
2. Anthony Downs, "Break Down Those Barriers," *Planning* 71 (October 2005): 20–21.
3. National Association of Realtors, "Median Sales Price of Existing Single-Family Homes for Metropolitan Areas," http://www.realtor.org/Research.nsf/files/REL06Q1T.pdf/$FILE/REL06Q1T.pdf (accessed 9 June 2006).
4. Les Christie, "Most Affordable Housing Markets," CNNMoney.com, http://money.cnn.com/2006/05/18/real_estate/NAHB_housing_affordability_index/index.htm (accessed 11 June 2006).
5. Michael Jonas, "House Rules," *CommonWealth* 11 (Growth and Development Extra 2006): 39.
6. Lori Weisberg, "County Suffers Rare Population Exodus," *San Diego Union-Tribune*, 15 March 2006, A1.
7. Herbert Atienza, "A Place for Us," *Riverside Press Enterprise*, 26 February 2006, B1.

8. Diane Wedner, "To Live and Buy in L.A." *Los Angeles Times*, 4 June 2006, Part K, 1.
9. Jonas, "House Rules," 39.
10. Thomas DiNapoli, "Affordable-Housing Plan Is in Our Own Best Interest," *Newsday*, 13 September 2005, A41.
11. *Suffolk County Workforce Housing Commission Accomplishments and Recommendations 2005*, 2–3, http://www.co.suffolk.ny.us/Economic%20Development/ACFDF.pdf (accessed 2 August 2006).
12. Campbell Robertson, "As Housing Costs Rise, Nimbyism Is Slipping," *New York Times*, 30 January 2005, Section 14-Long Island, 1, 5.
13. Christopher Swope, "If You Lived Here, You'd Be Broke Now," *Governing* 17 (November 2003): 39.
14. Candace Rondeaux, "Va. Police Lament Recruiting Problems," *Washington Post*, 2 April 2006, C1.
15. Crystal Yednak, "Rich Suburbs Pushed on Affordable Homes," *Chicago Tribune*, 13 February 2004, Section 1, 28.
16. *U.S. Housing Market Conditions, 1st Quarter 2006* (May 2006), 71, http://www.huduser.org/periodicals/ushmc/spring06/USHMC_06Q1.pdf (accessed 2 August 2006).
17. "Indianapolis Remains Nation's Most Affordable Major Housing Market for Third Consecutive Quarter," National Association of Home Builders website, 17 May 2006, http://www.nahb.org/news_details.aspx?section ID=135&newsID=2595 (accessed 9 June 2006).; Christie, "Most Affordable Housing Markets."
18. *Indianapolis Star*, 11 June 2006, H15, H18.
19. Bill Ruthhart, "2 Counties Hit Top 25 for Growth in Housing," *Indianapolis Star*, 21 July 2005, A1, A12.
20. *City of South Gate General Plan Housing Element Update*, March 2005, 21, http://www.cityofsouthgate.org/Formatted%20Revision%208.pdf (accessed 2 August 2006).
21. "Southern California Home Resale Activity," DQNews.com, http://www.dqnews.com/ZIPLAT.shtm (accessed 3 August 2006).
22. *Indianapolis Star*, 11 June 2006, H15.
23. Christie, "Most Affordable Housing Markets."
24. Ibid.; National Association of Realtors, "Median Sales Price of Existing Homes."

25. Michael N. Danielson, *The Politics of Exclusion* (New York: Columbia University Press, 1976), 61, 63, 71.
26. Ibid., 41.
27. Ibid., 291, 293.
28. Charles M. Haar, *Suburbs under Siege: Race, Space, and Audacious Judges* (Princeton, NJ: Princeton University Press, 1996), 17–18.
29. Danielson, *Politics of Exclusion*, 40.
30. Haar, *Suburbs under Siege*, 21.
31. *Southern Burlington County NAACP v. Mount Laurel Township*, 67 N.J. 174 (1975).
32. Ibid., 197.
33. David L. Kirp, John Dwyer, and Larry A. Rosenthal, *Our Town: Race, Housing, and the Soul of Suburbia* (New Brunswick, NJ: Rutgers University Press, 1995), 117–118.
34. Ibid., 120–122.
35. John M. Payne, "The Paradox of Progress: Three Decades of the Mount Laurel Doctrine," *Journal of Planning History* 4 (May 2006): 134.
36. Naomi Bailin Wish and Stephen Eisendorfer, "Mount Laurel Housing Symposium: The Impact of Mount Laurel Initiatives: An Analysis of the Characteristic of Applicants and Occupants," *Seton Hall Law Review* 27 (1997): 1305.
37. Henry A. Span, "How the Courts Should Fight Exclusionary Zoning," *Seton Hall Law Review* 32 (2001):68.
38. Steven Strunsky, "To Integration Advocates, Mount Laurel Falls Short," Associated Press State and Local Wire, 18 January 2004, available on Lexis-Nexis.com.
39. *New Jersey Builders Association Legislative Program and Policy Statement 2006–2007*, 20, http://www.njba.org/lpps/NJBA_LPPS_final.pdf (accessed 2 August 2006).
40. *Within Reach: The Homes for New Jersey Housing Action Plan*, November 2005, 3, http://www.homesfornj.com/policypaper.html (accessed 14 June 2006).
41. "Housing Crisis: Raise the Roof," *Asbury Park Press*, 5 December 2005, http://www.app.com/apps/pbcs.dll/article?AID=/20051205/OPINION/512050310/1029 (accessed 14 June 2006).
42. Danielson, *Politics of Exclusion*, 301–302.

43. Stuart Meck, Rebecca Retzlaff, and James Schwab, *Regional Approaches to Affordable Housing* (Chicago, IL: American Planning Association, 2003), 142, 145–146.

44. Bonnie Heudorfer and Barry Bluestone, *The Greater Boston Housing Report Card 2004: An Assessment of Progress on Housing in the Greater Boston Area* (Boston, MA: Boston Foundation, 2005), 45, http://www.curp.neu.edu/pdfs/Housing%20Report%20Card%202004.pdf (accessed 27 July 2006).

45. Ibid., 41, 43.

46. "Report of the Affordable Housing Task Group, July 31, 2002," 2, 5, http://www.townofbolton.com/pages/BoltonMA_Planning/aff%20Housing%20Report,%20Phase%202.pdf (accessed 2 August 2006); "Bolton Town Survey January 2002," http://www.townofbolton.com/pages/BoltonMA_Planning/Town%20Survey%202002.pdf (accessed 2 August 2006).

47. Dorian Block, "Affordable-Housing Plan Chafes Residents," *Boston Globe*, 2 October 2005, Globe Northwest Section, 1.

48. Jonas, "House Rules," 43, 49.

49. Rick Collins, "'Snowball's Chance in Hell' Waiver Will Go to Developer," *Quincy Patriot Ledger*, 5 December 2003, 1.

50. Jonas, "House Rules," 46.

51. Christopher Courchesne, "What Regional Agenda?: Reconciling Massachusetts's Affordable Housing Law and Environmental Protection," *Harvard Environmental Law Review* 28 (2004): 232.

52. Charles C. Euchner with Elizabeth G. Frieze, *Getting Home: Overcoming Barriers to Housing in Greater Boston* (Boston: Pioneer Institute for Public Policy Research, 2003), v.

53. Glaeser, Schuetz, and Ward, *Regulation on Rise of Housing Prices*, v.

54. *Town of Weston Annual Report 2003* (Athol, MA: Athol Press, 2004), 26.

55. Karen Destorel Brown, *Expanding Affordable Housing through Inclusionary Zoning: Lessons from the Washington Metropolitan Area* (Washington, DC: Brookings Institution, 2001), 6, http://www.brookings.edu/es/urban/publications/inclusionary.pdf (accessed 2 August 2006).

56. "Neighbors for a Better Montgomery—Montgomery County's Affordable Housing Fraud," http://www.neighborspac.org/affordable-housing-fraud.htm (accessed 3 August 2006).

57. Brown, *Expanding Affordable Housing*, 16–17.
58. Peter Whoriskey, "Space for Employers, Not for Homes," *Washington Post*, 8 August 2004, A11.
59. Meck, Retzlaff, and Schwab, *Regional Approaches to Affordable Housing*, 43, 54–55.
60. *City of Thousand Oaks Affordable Housing Opportunities Assessment*, February 2003, 2, http://www.ci.thousand-oaks.ca.us/civica/filebank/blobdload.asp?BlobID=2757 (accessed 3 August 2006).
61. Randy Richardson, "Both Affluent and Affordable," *Planning* 70 (November 2004): 32–33.
62. Courtney Flynn and Susan Kuczka, "49 Towns Must Add Affordable Housing," *Chicago Tribune*, 12 August 2004, Section 2-Chicago, 1, 7.
63. Ibid., 1.
64. *The Glencoe Memo*, September/October 2004, 3.
65. Courtney Flynn and Trine Tsouderas, "State Grilled on Cheap Housing," *Chicago Tribune*, 26 August 2004, Section 2-North Shore, 9.
66. Yednak, "Rich Suburbs Pushed," Section 1, p.1.
67. Ellen Schubart, "My Town Comes to Terms with Affordable Housing," *Planning* 71 (October 2005): 16.
68. Trine Tsouderos, "North Shore Dwellers Target Housing Law," *Chicago Tribune*, 2 August 2004, Section 2-Chicagoland, 5.

Chapter 6

1. William H. Whyte, "Urban Sprawl," in *The Exploding Metropolis*, ed. Editors of *Fortune* (Garden City, NY: Doubleday and Company, 1958), 133–135.
2. William H. Whyte, *The Last Landscape* (Garden City, NY: Doubleday and Company, 1968), 1.
3. Robert W. Burchell et al., *The Costs of Sprawl—Revisited* (Washington, DC: National Academy Press, 1998), 11.
4. Chris Lester and Jeffrey Spivak, "The Test of Success: Teamwork," *Kansas City Star*, 22 December 1995, as quoted in Richard Moe and Carter Wilkie, *Changing Places: Rebuilding Community in the Age of Sprawl* (New York: Henry Holt and Company, 1997), 246.
5. Burchell, *Costs of Sprawl—Revisited*, 23–24.

6. Olga Bonfiglio, "Addressing Urban Sprawl," in *Urban Planning*, ed. Andrew I. Cavin (New York: H. W. Wilson Company, 2003), 20, 23.

7. William S. Saunders, "Will Sprawl Produce Its Own Demise?" in *Sprawl and Suburbia*, ed. William S. Saunders (Minneapolis: University of Minnesota Press, 2005), vii.

8. Dolores Hayden, *A Field Guide to Sprawl* (New York: W. W. Norton, 2004).

9. Robert W. Burchell, Anthony Downs, Barbara McCann, and Sahan Mukherji, *Sprawl Costs: Economic Impacts of Unchecked Development* (Washington, DC: Island Press, 2005), 3.

10. Robert W. Burchell et al., *Costs of Sprawl—2000* (Washington, DC: National Academy Press, 2002), 10–11.

11. Burchell et al., *Sprawl Costs*, 6.

12. *American Farmland: The Magazine of American Farmland Trust*, Special Issue, Sprawl (1997), 3, 8.

13. "Farmland Protection Issues," American Farmland Trust website, http://www.farmland.org/programs/protection/default.asp (accessed 27 June 2006).

14. "Stopping Sprawl Main Page," Sierra Club website, http://www.sierraclub.org/sprawl/ (accessed 27 June 2006).

15. Burchell et al., *Costs of Sprawl—2000*, 9.

16. "Wetlands Protect Us All," Sierra Club website, http://www.sierraclub.org/wetlands/factsheets/protect.asp (accessed 28 June 2006).

17. Reid Ewing, John Kostyack, Don Chen, Bruce Stein, and Michelle Ernst, *Endangered by Sprawl: How Runaway Development Threatens America's Wildlife* (Washington, DC: National Wildlife Federation, Smart Growth America, and NatureServe, 2005), vi.

18. Bruce Babbitt, *Cities in the Wilderness: A New Vision of Land Use in America* (Washington, DC: Island Press, 2005), 4, 78–84.

19. Burchell et al., *Sprawl Costs*, 109.

20. Dom Nozzi, *Road to Ruin: An Introduction to Sprawl and How to Cure It* (Westport, CT: Praeger, 2003), 3.

21. Paul Goldberger, "It Takes a Village," *New Yorker*, 27 March 2000, 133.

22. Moe and Wilkie, *Changing Places*, 24.

23. Marc Leepson, "Holding Their Ground," *Preservation* 57 (July/August 2005): 25.

24. Douglas E. Morris, *It's a Sprawl World after All* (Gabriola Island, British Columbia, Canada: New Society Publishers, 2005), 91.

25. Burchell et al., *Sprawl Costs*, 108. See also Reid Ewing, Tom Schmid, Richard Killingsworth, Amy Zlot, and Stephen Raudenbush, "Relationship between Urban Sprawl and Physical Activity, Obesity, and Morbidity," *American Journal of Health Promotion* 18 (September/October 2003): 47–57.
26. Morris, *It's a Sprawl World after All*, 4.
27. Nozzi, *Road to Ruin*, xix.
28. For a collection of essays by free-market, libertarian foes of the antisprawl campaign, see Randall G. Holcombe and Samuel R. Staley, eds., *Smarter Growth: Market-Based Strategies for Land-Use Planning in the 21st Century* (Westport, CT: Greenwood Press, 2001).
29. Robert Bruegmann, *Sprawl: A Compact History* (Chicago, IL: University of Chicago Press, 2005), 59, 61, 68, 151, 223.
30. Raymond J. Keating, "'Sprawl' Should Not Be a Dirty Word, Most Long Islanders Have Benefited from Suburbs' Development," *Newsday*, 9 January 2006, A33.
31. Jim Wooten, "Contempt for Sprawl Unwarranted," *Atlanta Journal-Constitution*, 29 November 2005, 15A.
32. Kevin Nance, "Learning to Sprawl," *Chicago Sun-Times*, 27 December 2005, Features Section, 39.
33. *Livability 101* (Washington, DC: American Institute of Architects, 2005), 4.
34. Kevin Kasowski, "Oregon: Fifteen Years of Land Use Planning," in *Balance Growth: A Planning Guide for Local Government*, ed. John Melvin DeGrove (Washington, DC: International City Management Association, 1991), 125–126, quoted in Eric Damian Kelly, *Managing Community Growth*, 2d ed. (Westport, CT: Praeger, 2004), 120–121.
35. Carl Abbott, *Greater Portland: Urban Life and Landscape in the Pacific Northwest* (Philadelphia: University of Pennsylvania Press, 2001), 169–170.
36. "A Conversation with Parris Glendening," in *Suburban Sprawl: Culture, Theory, and Politics*, ed. Matthew J. Lindstrom and Hugh Bartling (Lanham, MD: Rowman and Littlefield, 2003), 86–87.
37. Christopher Swope, "McGreevey's Magic Map," *Governing* 16 (May 2003): 46, 48.
38. "Greetings from Governor McGreevey and Commissioner Levin," *SmartGrowth, NJ* 1 (fall 2003): 1.

39. Swope, "McGreevey's Magic Map," 48.

40. Michael Jonas, "The Sprawl Doctor," *CommonWealth* 8 (spring 2003), http://www.massinc.org/index.php?id=361&pub_id=1312 (accessed 4 August 2006).

41. Michael Jonas, "House Rules," *CommonWealth* 11 (Growth and Development Extra, 2006): 45.

42. *Shelby County Comprehensive Plan* (Pelham, AL: Shelby County Department of Development Services, 2004), II-1–II-2, II-25, II-31, http://www.shelbycountyalabama.com/comprehensiveplan.shtm (accessed 5 August 2006).

43. Patrick Crotty, "Strategy Formed for Future Growth," *Shelby County Reporter*, 18 May 2004, http://www.shelbycountyreporter. com/articles/2004/05/19/news/news05.txt (accessed 14 July 2006).

44. Andres Duany, Elizabeth Plater-Zyberk, and Jeff Speck, *Suburban Nation: The Rise of Sprawl and the Decline of the American Dream* (New York: North Point Press, 2000), 260–261.

45. Ibid., 259.

46. Anthony Flint, *This Land: The Battle Over Sprawl and the Future of America* (Baltimore, MD: Johns Hopkins University Press, 2006), 62.

47. Dana Hedgpeth, "New Urbanism's Staying Power," *Washington Post*, 28 August 2003, Montgomery Extra, 14.

48. Flint, *This Land*, 64.

49. "New Urban Projects on a Neighborhood Scale in the United States, December 2003," http://newurbannews.com/ProjectsPage. html (accessed 31 May 2006).

50. Bill Ruthhart, "Village's Old-School Style Finds New Momentum," *Indianapolis Star*, 20 February 2005, B1–B2.

51. Evan West, "Brave New Mayor," *Indianapolis Monthly*, April 2006, 220.

52. "City Center Groundbreaking," City of Carmel news release, http://www.ci.carmel.in.us/government/newsrelease/03-23-06.htm (accessed 4 August 2006).

53. "Mega-suburb Takes Shape in Utah," CNN.com, 7 April 2006, http://www.cnn.com/2006/US/04/07/new.town.ap/index.html (accessed 9 April 2006).

54. Hank Dittmar and Shelley Poticha, "Defining Transit-Oriented Development: The New Regional Building Block," in *The New Transit Town: Best Practices in Transit-Oriented Development*, ed. Hank Dittmar and Gloria Ohland (Washington, DC: Island Press, 2004), 20.
55. Scott Bernstein, "The New Transit Town: Great Places and Great Nodes That Work for Everyone," in *The New Transit Town*, 243.
56. Dennis Leach, "The Arlington County Case Study: Rosslyn-Ballston Corridor," in *The New Transit Town*, 132, 135, 143.
57. Peter Whoriskey, "Planners' Brains vs. Public's Brawn," *Washington Post*, 10 August 2004, A12.
58. Ibid.
59. Swope, "McGreevey's Magic Map," 50.
60. Dorie Clark, "Growth Smarts," *CommonWealth* 8 (winter 2003), http://www.massinc.org/index.php?id=360&pub_id=1272 (accessed 4 August 2006).
61. Jim O'Sullivan, "Chapter 40R; Officials Have Hopes for Housing Plan," *Quincy Patriot Ledger*, 15 May 2006, 16.
62. Karen Goulart, "Selectmen in Kingston Like Idea of 'Smart-Growth' Zoning District," *Quincy Patriot Ledger*, 15 June 2006, 19.
63. Kim Ring, "Residents Balk at Condominium Project," *Worcester Telegram and Gazette*, 11 July 2006, B1.
64. Christopher Swope, "Rendezvous With Density," *Governing* 14 (March 2001): 36.
65. Michael Laris, "Nearly 200 Lawsuits Challenge Loudoun Slow-Growth Plan," *Washington Post*, 6 February 2003, A7.
66. Michael Laris, "Loudoun Landowners Battle Building Curbs," *Washington Post*, 17 August 2003, A10.
67. Michael Laris, "Showdown over Loudoun," *Washington Post*, 29 October 2003, A6.
68. "Voters Guide 2003," *Washington Post*, 30 October 2003, Loudoun Extra, 19.
69. Michael Laris, "Loudoun's Slow Growth Façade Splits," *Washington Post*, 6 November 2003, A18.
70. Peter Whoriskey, "Washington's Road to outward Growth," *Washington Post*, 9 August 2004, A9.

71. Candace Parker, "Citizens Protest Zoning Approval—Commission Ratifies Overwhelming Vote," *Shelby County Reporter*, 25 January 2005, http://www.shelbycountyreporter.com/articles/2005/01/25/news/news01.txt (accessed 14 July 2006).

72. "Controlled Growth a Necessity," *Shelby County Reporter*, 19 January 2006, http://www.shelbycountyreporter.com/articles/2006/01/19/opinion/opin01.txt (accessed 14 July 2006).

73. George Homsy, "Sons of Measure 37," *Planning* 72 (June 2006): 14.

74. Bob Stacey, "Law Lends Itself to Abuse," *Salem Statesman Journal*, 26 February 2006, http://159.54.226.83/apps/pbcs.dll/article?AID=/20060226/OPINION/602260314/1049 (accessed 5 August 2006).

75. Gwenda Richards Oshiro, "Measure 37," *Oregonian* (Portland), 2 March 2006, Metro Southwest Lake Oswego Section, 14.

76. Dana Tims and Steve Mayes, "Growth Could Ultimately Affect Farms," *Oregonian* (Portland), 10 November 2005, Metro West Neighbors Section, 1.

77. Jennifer Langston and Chris McGann, "Property Measure Likely on Ballot," *Seattle Post-Intelligencer*, 7 July 2006, B1.

78. Eric Pryne, "Property-Rights Initiative Likely to Spark Fierce Fight," *Seattle Times*, 9 February 2006, B1.

79. J. David Breemer, "The Wisdom of Growth," *Sacramento Bee*, 12 December 2004, E1.

INDEX

Romney, Mitt, 201, 210
Rosemead, Calif., 68
Roswell, Ga., 134
Roxbury, Mass., 15
Rusk, David, 141-142, 148, 152

S

Sandy, Utah, 115-116
Sandy Springs, Ga., 133-134, 139
San Gabriel, Calif., 68
San Gabriel Valley Council of
   Governments, 156
San Marino, Calif., 69
San Ramon, Calif., 112-113
Santa Ana, Calif., 83, 91
Santa Monica, Calif., 12, 29
Scarsdale, N.Y., 25-27, 30, 33
Schaumburg, Ill., 96-97, 100
Scituate, Mass., 178
Scottsdale, Ariz., 85
Self-built suburbs, 21-22
Senior citizens
   affordable housing, 173,185
   communities, 73-76
Shaker Heights, Ohio, 29-30, 63
   African American population, 61
   elite suburb, 26-27
Shelby County, Ala., 202, 212-213
Shorewood, Wis., 27, 29
Signal Hill, Calif., 20
Simmons, Patrick, 79
Skokie, Ill., 69
Smart growth
   definition, 197
   Loudoun County, Va., 210-212
   Maryland, 199, 208-209
   Massachusetts, 201, 209-210
   New Jersey, 199-200, 209
   Oregon, 198-199, 214-215
   proponents, 197
   Shelby County, Ala., 202, 212-213

Washington state, 215
Smithfield, R.I., 119
Somerville, Mass., 4
South Bay Cities Council of
   Governments, 156
South Brooklyn, Ohio, 15
Southfield, Mich., 35, 38-40
South Gate, Calif.
   Hispanics, 51, 66
   housing prices, 166
   race restrictions, 22
   working-class suburb, 21, 27, 30,
      220
South Hills Area Council of
   Governments, 154-155
South Omaha, Neb., 8-9, 11
South Pasadena, Calif., 14
South St. Paul, Minn., 9
South San Francisco, Calif., 9, 11
Southwest Ranches, Fla., 77-79, 135
Special districts, 28, 125-126
Spencer, Mass., 210
Sprawl
   alienation, 194
   central cities, effect on, 191
   costs, 189-190
   critics, 188-190
   defenders, 194-196
   definition, 188
   environment, 191-193
   farmland, 191
   historic preservation, 193
   obesity, 193-194
Springfield, Va., 96
Staten Island, N.Y., 3
Stearns, Gene, 130
Stoughton, Mass., 120
Subregional cooperation, 153-157
Sun City, Ariz., 73-75
Sunny Isles Beach, Fla., 130
Surprise, Ariz., 81, 85

DATE DUE
